Dirty Harry's America

University Press of Florida

Florida A&M University, Tallahassee

Florida Atlantic University, Boca Raton

Florida Gulf Coast University, Ft. Myers

Florida International University, Miami

Florida State University, Tallahassee

New College of Florida, Sarasota

University of Central Florida, Orlando

University of Florida, Gainesville

University of North Florida, Jacksonville

University of South Florida, Tampa

University of West Florida, Pensacola

Dirty Harry's America

Clint Eastwood, Harry Callahan, and the Conservative Backlash

Joe Street

University Press of Florida

Gainesville · Tallahassee · Tampa

Boca Raton · Pensacola · Orlando · Miami

Jacksonville · Ft. Myers · Sarasota

This book may be available in an electronic edition.

First cloth printing, 2016
First paperback printing, 2018

23 22 21 20 19 18   6 5 4 3 2 1

Library of Congress Cataloging-in-Publication Data

Names: Street, Joe, author.
Title: Dirty Harry's America : Clint Eastwood, Harry Callahan, and the conservative
backlash / Joe Street.
Description: Gainesville : University Press of Florida, [2016] | Includes
bibliographical references and index.
Identifiers: LCCN 2015035905 | ISBN 9780813061672 (cloth)
ISBN 9780813064710 (pbk.)
Subjects: LCSH: Dirty Harry films—History and criticism. | Motion pictures—
Political aspects—United States. | Conservatism—United States.
Classification: LCC PN1995.9.D54 S87 2016 | DDC 791.43/75—dc23
LC record available at http://lccn.loc.gov/2015035905

The University Press of Florida is the scholarly publishing agency for the State
University System of Florida, comprising Florida A&M University, Florida Atlantic
University, Florida Gulf Coast University, Florida International University, Florida
State University, New College of Florida, University of Central Florida, University
of Florida, University of North Florida, University of South Florida, and University
of West Florida.

University Press of Florida
15 Northwest 15th Street
Gainesville, FL 32611-2079
http://upress.ufl.edu

grant made by
Figure Foundation

make day

For Dad, who likes Clint Eastwood movies

Contents

Illustrations

Acknowledgments

In 1982, my father declared his intention to smuggle me into a Cardiff cinema to watch a new Cold War thriller called *Firefox*. Little did he know that some thirty years later I'd write a book about its star, Clint Eastwood. It would probably take a psychologist to work out the relationship between these two events.

The other seeds for this book were sown in a class at the University of Kent. My "America in the 1960s" module featured a session on the conservative resurgence and was normally accompanied by a class viewing of *Dirty Harry*, designed to illustrate how conservative ideas could be read into aspects of popular culture at the turn of the decade. One class was particularly frustrated that they couldn't find secondary reading about the film. One student, and shamefully I've forgotten who it was, told me that I should write something on it. So I did. This became an article published by *The Sixties: A Journal of History, Politics, and Culture*, which explores the same territory as chapter 3 here. Many of the ideas expressed in this article—and hence this book—first took flight in that session. They were refined in later iterations of "America in the 1960s," and I wish to thank the students in these classes for indulging, challenging, and helping to think through my ideas about Harry Callahan. I also wish to thank the editorial team at *The Sixties* for their assistance in transforming my early draft of "*Dirty Harry*'s San Francisco" into something publishable.

This book found its home at the University Press of Florida, and I want to thank Meredith Morris-Babb and especially Sian Hunter for their encouraging and soothing words throughout the publishing process. I'm very grateful for the press's continuing support for my work and could not wish for a better publisher. I also wish to thank the external readers for their highly supportive comments on the manuscript. Karen Jones and Ian Scott offered very encouraging comments along the way; Ian's support was particularly helpful in convincing me that I could write a book-length study. As ever, my good friends Simon Hall and Kev Watson have been great sounding boards; Malcolm McLaughlin offered typically sound advice; Ben Houston and my many friends from the British Association for American Studies kept my spirits high. Finally, I wish to thank this book's unsung hero, copy editor Jonathan Lawrence, who made sure that what you are about to read is readable.

My colleagues, firstly at Kent, and latterly at Northumbria University, have been supremely patient when listening to me drone on about Callahan. My thanks to Mike Brown, Karen Jones, and John Wills at Kent for their encouragement. At Northumbria, my colleagues have been as supportive, collegiate, and professional a group as I could have imagined. Thank you to the Americanists Mike Cullinane, Sylvia Ellis, David Gleeson, Henry Knight, Randall Stephens, and Brian Ward. My non-Americanist colleagues have also uncomplainingly suffered my inability to keep Callahan to myself, and I thank them all, especially Charlotte Alston, Joe Hardwick, Daniel Laqua, James McConnel, and Colin Reid. I am very lucky to be working among such an inspiring, intellectual, kind, and collegiate group of people. I thank those mentioned here most of all for the gift of their friendship.

Thankfully, this project was not as reliant on my family's largesse as my previous book. Their support, however, has been priceless. Thank you Mum, Dad, Anna, Tes, Jen, and Col, and the rest of the Streets, Mynotts, McGroarys, and Wottons for always being there. I also wish to thank my friends Matt Garlick, Pete Manning, John Brewin, my chums on that there social media, and my fellow long-suffering Albion fans (you know who you are) for enduring my company with patience and most of all good humor.

Finally, and most important, to my two best girls, Ruth and Carys: you make my day, every day. I love you both more than you could ever imagine.

Introduction

Why *Dirty Harry* Matters

Bring me men to match my mountains

Inscription on the facade of the Jesse M. Unruh State
Office Building, Capitol Mall, Sacramento, California

Hopefully, I always shot in a good cause. . . . I think audiences
were pleased to see me play a detective who was concerned
for the victim, a man he has never seen. People are sick and
tired of seeing the criminal glorified and made into an object
of sympathy. . . . Basic men and women who work hard,
bring up families, these people want order. They don't want
mayhem in their lives. They're concerned about the law, and
if a guy is let out on a technicality, the law was wrong.

Clint Eastwood, 1977

In January 1972 the film critic for *New York* magazine, Judith Crist, dismissed Don Siegel's recent movie *Dirty Harry* (1971) by concluding that
"it doesn't bear retrospection—or merit it."[1] She was not alone. Gary
Arnold claimed in the *Washington Post* that the film was quite simply
"laughable."[2] At first glance *Dirty Harry* does appear to be a simplistic
genre exercise which traces the cat-and-mouse chase between a police
inspector and a mass murderer—a "rough, ugly . . . melodrama" according to Crist.[3] It appeared in American cinemas at a time when genre films
returned as a major force in American film. As the film historians Michael Ryan and Douglas Kellner argue, the early 1970s saw "the ironic
and critical social realist styles of the late sixties give way to a mixture of

grandiose, bombastic and mannerist styles. . . . The resolution-oriented narrative of the classic Hollywood cinema return[ed] in full force, and the crest of reflexivity and experimentation in narration, image, and character that one finds in the more radical films of the late sixties recede[d]."[4] *Dirty Harry* was fully enmeshed in what might be termed a conservative backlash against the experimentation of late 1960s cinema. It is not as formally significant as *Bonnie and Clyde* (Penn, 1967); it does not challenge the genre of the cop thriller as stylishly as *Point Blank* (Boorman, 1967); it is not as experimental as *M*A*S*H* (Altman, 1970); nor is it as challenging in its social criticism as *Midnight Cowboy* (Schlesinger, 1969) or *Medium Cool* (Wexler, 1969). Its plot and structure are decidedly traditional, conservative even.

Yet time has proved Judith Crist to be wrong. *Dirty Harry* became one of the key films of the 1970s and offered the actor Clint Eastwood his defining role, rendering him an American icon. In 2001 Inspector "Dirty" Harry Callahan was listed as the seventeenth-greatest cinema hero in the American Film Institute's centenary lists, with the film itself ranked forty-seventh in the "Most Thrilling Films" list.[5] Callahan's most iconic moment—his instantly recognizable "You've got to ask yourself one question: 'Do I feel lucky?' Well, do ya, punk?" declamation—featured on the AFI's iconic quotes list and opens Paul Smith's acclaimed book-length study of Eastwood's significance in American culture.[6] Callahan's centrality to Eastwood's screen persona also seeped into his 1986 entry into electoral politics. Reporters covering his campaign for mayor of the small Californian town of Carmel-by-the-Sea could not resist the temptation to comment on the incongruity of "Dirty" Harry discussing the issue of public bathrooms.[7] The film even created an icon of Callahan's signature weapon. The president of Magnum Research Inc., which manufactured the gun, boasted many years later that "the Magnum .44 was nowhere as a caliber until Eastwood did the *Dirty Harry* movies. Now .44s account for maybe half the sales of all Magnums."[8] One of the models used by Eastwood in the first film is on display at the National Rifle Association's National Firearms Museum, and the gun's iconic status was confirmed in 2008 when a Twentieth Century Fox survey voted it the second most memorable cinema weapon, behind the *Star Wars* lightsaber.[9]

Dirty Harry, though, is more than simply a star vehicle for one man and his gun. It is a powerfully ideological film, both reflecting ideas that were percolating through American society in the late 1960s and offering its own refraction of recent American history. It is one of the first films to explore how intelligent criminals exploited legislation designed to protect their rights as American citizens. Through both its formal terms and its political subtext, *Dirty Harry* derides liberal bureaucracy and critiques the social licentiousness that conservatives considered a consequence of liberal government. Through his rejection of liberalism and reassertion of frontier justice, "Dirty" Harry Callahan becomes the film's only person or institution who cares about the victims of crime.[10] The film even hints at the illegal methods used by the Nixon administration to crush (rather than simply apprehend or defeat) its foes. Perhaps most important, it challenges its viewers to reconsider their stances on violence, the law, and illegality and to question many of the tenets of 1960s liberalism. Its presentation of what might be considered a commonsense response to crime is not only an articulation of the escalating tensions between 1960s liberalism and the new conservatism but also fuel for these very tensions. In this sense, Callahan offers the simplest and least-conflicted answer to a question that the film scholar Sara Anson Vaux argues is central to Eastwood's cinema: "How do we define the 'good'?"[11] The film prophesies the continued breakdown of civil society as a consequence of the failures of 1960s liberalism and anticipates an era in which criminals would be one step ahead of their pursuers in fact as well as in fiction. The "good" is the person who stands against this tide of criminality using whatever means are necessary to ensure the recovery of law and order. *Dirty Harry* is thus both a commentary on and an agent of change in this key period in American history.

John T. (Terry) Dolan, a founder of the National Conservative Political Action Committee, once told the journalist Alan Crawford that one of the key aims of the New Right in the 1980s was "to take control of the culture."[12] *Dirty Harry* might not have intentionally positioned itself within the New Right—that the film's director, Don Siegel, was a liberal and protested that he did not personally approve of Callahan's methods is evidence enough of his directorial intent.[13] Yet as Crawford observes, "the New Right admires such rugged individualists [as Harry Callahan], all of them 'tough,' 'gutsy,' 'mean,' 'no-nonsense,' '*macho*' loners who stand against Establishment authority, adhering to an internal code of honor in a world gone soft."[14] Richard Wirthlin, one of Ronald Reagan's pollsters, argued in 1980 that the American electorate wanted to "follow some authority figure" who could "return a sense of discipline to our government; manifest the willpower needed to get this country back on track."[15] Wirthlin might have been discussing his candidate's qualities, but his notion that the country had taken a wrong turn and needed a form of authoritarianism is central to the message and appeal of *Dirty Harry* and its sequels. Callahan's actions struck a chord with conservatives who were appalled at the excesses of the 1960s and the implicit and explicit threat of anti-authoritarianism to traditional American values. As the film historian Martin Rubin argues, police thrillers like *Dirty Harry* became increasingly popular in the late 1960s and early 1970s in part as a consequence of the "growing sense of urban crisis, a foregrounding of law-and-order issues in the 1968 and 1972 presidential campaigns, and a general (though still transitional and deeply conflicted) swing to the right in American politics."[16] The decline in influence of American cinema's Production Code, which had informed the depiction of sex, violence, and amoral behavior prior to the late 1960s, enabled a more bloody and perhaps more accurate on-screen vision of crime in the city, which itself boosted the sense that the nation's cities were declining into a hellish morass of debasement and depravity. As Rubin acknowledges, *Dirty Harry*'s almost sarcastic representation of the circumstances that produced the bank robbers, sex criminals, and murderers who were prowling the streets provided audiences with a wholly appropriate scapegoat on which to hang blame for the urban crisis: liberal bureaucrats.[17] That a lone hero with a clear and rigid sense of justice and a healthy cynicism toward liberal legal policy tidies up the mess is crucial to the conservatism of *Dirty Harry*. Thus if the goal of the political right is, as conservative politician Howard Philips claimed, to "organize discontent," then *Dirty Harry* was particularly useful evidence, because it highlighted to the discontented that the flaws in the modern metropolis were entirely the fault of the liberals.[18] In this sense, *Dirty Harry* helped to create a new American mood even as it emerged from an older mood. This mood was further explored in *Dirty Harry*'s four sequels, which appeared at regular intervals through the 1970s and 1980s. None were critical successes, although all except the final movie were box-office hits, demonstrating Eastwood's star power and perhaps a general sense that

Callahan was more of a hero to American cinemagoers than Siegel had originally intended.

The location of the *Dirty Harry* films is also pertinent in any discussion of their significance. San Francisco holds a particular geographic, historical, cultural, and symbolic meaning for the films. The mayor's office was keen to attract Hollywood filmmakers to San Francisco, establishing a Film Production Office to facilitate this, and *Dirty Harry* benefited significantly from the cooperation of the city's authorities.[19] Few scenes in *Dirty Harry* do not reference San Francisco either through location or through less obvious methods, and with the exception of *Sudden Impact* (Eastwood, 1983), which is based in a fictional Bay Area town, all of the subsequent films are set in the city. *Dirty Harry* makes use of a number of iconic locations, including the Golden Gate Bridge, Mount Davidson Park, Kezar Stadium (home of the San Francisco Forty-Niners until 1971), and city hall. These sites unmistakably locate *Dirty Harry* and its sequels within San Francisco's geographic boundaries. The preponderance of scenes set in San Francisco—only one sequence in the first film was shot outside the city, and location shots predominate in the sequels—cements Callahan's relationship with the city.[20]

Siegel later claimed that *Dirty Harry* was set in San Francisco because of the city's aesthetic qualities and its proximity to Eastwood's home in Pebble Beach, California. While his explanation might not emphasize the film's relationship with its surroundings, the film's semiotics place the city's culture center stage.[21] The sequels continued Callahan's relationship with San Francisco even though they make fewer explicit references to the city's recent political history. Yet they are unmistakably set in the same location, often featuring recurring characters, mentioning Callahan's previous escapades or simply using real San Francisco locations. In short, *Dirty Harry* and its sequels are San Francisco films, and to understand them fully we must view the films through the prism of this particular city. Precisely because San Francisco's geographic space is so important to *Dirty Harry* and to a slightly lesser extent its sequels, the location adds numerous layers of meaning to the films, the social and political context in which they were made, and their long-term significance. Scholars seeking to understand the political, social, and cultural themes that underpin the films' narrative must therefore interrogate the specificity of their location and acknowledge the corresponding role of

San Francisco's history in the films. As the film scholar Colin McArthur notes, "Hollywood cinema consistently takes 'real' American cities ... and reinscribes them into discourse."[22] In the case of the *Dirty Harry* series, this discourse is grounded in and should be considered as a refraction of San Francisco's history. It might, therefore, be appropriate to reverse Jean Baudrillard's observation: the movies seem to have stepped right out of the American city. To grasp their secret, you should begin with the city and move outward to the screen.[23] The encoding of San Francisco in *Dirty Harry*—irrespective of Siegel's directorial intent—and the series' continued use of the city invites a reading that interrogates this relationship.

Harry Callahan's beat is the most liberal major city in the United States. Callahan's battles with the liberal bureaucrats who run the city's police department are as important to the first film as his pursuit of the Scorpio Killer, a crazed murderer who is terrorizing the city. These battles also inform Callahan's quest against police death squads, terrorists, murderers, and the numerous other lowlifes who populate the films. Callahan is as disgusted by the bureaucrats as he is by the criminals— albeit for slightly different reasons—and his stance renders him an archetypal lone hero, standing up for and representing truth, justice, and the American way. As important, he becomes a prototypical conservative struggling against the overweening liberals who are determined to engineer society through large welfare programs, soft criminal policies, and a blasé attitude toward the pathologies that cause criminal behavior. As Crawford notes, the New Right was in part a manifestation of a "revolt of the New Old West against the East, a region that feels deeply alienated from the federal government, which seems at best a meddlesome absentee landlord."[24] This hostility was central to the insurgent political campaigns of George Wallace and the anti-Washington rhetoric of Republican candidates from the West such as Barry Goldwater and Ronald Reagan. Little surprise, then, that *Dirty Harry* was awarded an Honorable Mention by Nile Gardiner, a former aide to Margaret Thatcher and *Fox News* commentator, in his 2012 "Top Ten Conservative Movies of the Modern Era" list.[25] And no wonder that Eastwood himself featured on campaign posters offering his support for Richard Nixon's re-election in 1972 before being one of the movie stars lauded by the candidate for producing films that were "typically American."[26] An Eastwood panegyric in the noted right-wing magazine *Commentary* which stressed his appeal to the "real" America—the non-urban, non-university sector of the population—was merely the icing on the cake.[27]

This suggests a certain conflation of "Dirty" Harry and Clint Eastwood. David Thompson highlighted this in a 1984 interview with the actor. "I think the public understands that you're playing different characters," observed Thompson. "But there is a fantasy in this era of bureaucracy, of complicated life, income tax and politicizing everything, that there's a guy who can do certain things by himself. There'll always be that fantasy. I think there's an admiration for it."[28] "It's absurd," Eastwood retorted. "A person comes up and tells you how many bullets he might have fired and do you feel lucky? Everybody would like to be that cool at some point. How many times has someone said something smart to you and half an hour later you've thought of the perfect answer?"[29] Yet the fantasy remained, as Eastwood himself acknowledged. When David Letterman told Eastwood many years later that "you're always going to be Dirty Harry," Eastwood took the quip in good humor, although he pointed out that any future *Dirty Harry* films would feature the cop pursuing criminals with the aid of a walker.[30] Meanwhile, the London *Guardian* declared its astonishment in 2014 that Eastwood practiced transcendental meditation thus: "Clint Eastwood does it, for crying out loud. Clint Eastwood, the opposite of a hippy, a man who shoots hippies[!]" The accompanying photo montage included a classic shot of Eastwood as Callahan, aiming his Magnum at the viewer, to remind readers that Eastwood is "Dirty" Harry.[31]

This conflation of Eastwood and Callahan was not simply a product of Callahan's iconic status and box-office success. That Eastwood periodically returned to Callahan is evidence enough that he considered the character important to his career, if only in terms of leverage with Warner Brothers. The large profits of the first four *Dirty Harry* movies gave Eastwood enough credit with the studio to be given latitude to pursue less commercial but more creative and personal projects such as *Honky-tonk Man* (Eastwood, 1982). Callahan thus helped Eastwood to shape his directorial career, which supplanted acting as the focus of his cinematic work in the 1990s and 2000s. Yet Callahan is also central to Eastwood's screen persona, which is that of a cynical and occasionally brutal yet also moral, loyal, and dependable outsider. Callahan not only confirmed

Eastwood's box-office appeal but also decisively shifted Eastwood's persona from the cowboy of *Rawhide* and Sergio Leone's Westerns to a modern, urban hero. While Eastwood continued his career-long interest in the Western, his screen roles were increasingly set in modern urban contexts. Films such as *The Gauntlet* (Eastwood, 1977), *Tightrope* (Tuggle, 1984), and *The Rookie* (Eastwood, 1990) feature Eastwood fighting crime and often corruption in various American cities. The many different characters played by Eastwood frequently cite Callahan implicitly and explicitly, from their cynical attitude toward the American system of law enforcement, their solitary nature, and their sadistic sense of humor to their willingness to use violence. It is therefore no stretch of the imagination to state that Callahan is fundamental to Eastwood's screen career.

While happy to play along with the merging of his public identity with that of his screen persona, Eastwood protested at other times that he had no idea why anyone would wish to seek out "political ramifications in any film" of his.[32] "I start out on an animalistic level" when thinking about a film, he told Patrick McGilligan in 1976. "After I've got the script totally in mind, then I can move to it on almost any kind of level. But I prefer to be drawn to it on that emotional level; if you start out on an intellectual level, I think you're starting without the nucleus. . . . [T]he vast majority of the audience doesn't want to intellectualise it, they want to emotionalise along with it. They may want to intellectualise afterwards, particularly if they are film buffs."[33] Eastwood is, of course, entitled to his opinion, but as Ryan and Kellner indicate, cultural representations such as film "play an important role in determining how social reality will be constructed, that is, what figures and boundaries will prevail in the shaping of social life and social institutions. They determine whether capitalism will be conceived (felt, experienced, lived) as a predatory jungle or as a utopia of freedom."[34]

Popular film is not merely a static entertainment medium but one that is engaged in a constant process of what might be termed "memory creation." It encourages us to see the world through its own prism, creating a shared representation or simulacrum of the reality around us. The film historian Robert Brent Toplin observes that "historical films help to shape the thinking of millions. Often the depictions seen on the screen influence the public's view of historical subjects much more than books do."[35] Whether such films appeal to gut feelings or intellectual rationalization is immaterial. Moreover, as historians such as Steve Anderson indicate, in the popular cultural sphere such fictional constructions are as likely as purely factual productions to inform the public's understanding of history and indeed the world around them, in part because of their mimetic relationship with the "real" world.[36] For example, as numerous writers have argued, *Forrest Gump* (Zemeckis, 1994) reimagined American history between the 1950s and the 1990s in part through a clever use of computer-generated images that inserted its fictional hero into key moments in the nation's recent history, such as the discovery of the break-in at the Watergate hotel and George Wallace's attempt to prevent African American students from entering the University of Alabama. *Gump* offers a decidedly conservative representation of the 1960s, from the troubles experienced by Forrest Gump's true love, who leaves her abusive father only to end up a failed radical activist, drug addict, single mother, and AIDS victim, to the film's wholly unrepresentative depiction of African American protest in the decade. Its widespread popularity coupled with its thinly veiled political sensibilities suggests that we should approach such films with an eye to the ways in which they reimagine our history and create popular memories.[37]

This memory-creation process is not limited to films based on actual historical events, however. The film historians Leonard Quart and Albert Auster assert that most popular films "reveal something of the dreams, desires, displacements, and, in some cases, social and political issues confronting" their audiences.[38] In certain respects, popular films present a world that the audience might wish to see, or a version of the real world that is more akin to their ideal vision of the reality around them. The film theorist Jean-Louis Baudry identifies the similarities between the conditions of film-watching (silence and stillness in a darkened room) and the state of dream sleep. According to Baudry, film watchers thus enter a "regime of belief" in which they are more susceptible to collapse their previous separation of the events depicted on-screen and the reality of the rest of the world around them.[39] If this makes viewers seem too supine to resist the messages in the films they watch, the cultural theorist Stuart Hall offers a reminder that audiences are at liberty to embrace or reject any aspect of a particular cultural production and that the meaning of any production is itself socially produced rather than fixed by the producer.[40] *Dirty Harry*'s continued popularity some forty years after its first release suggests that it struck a chord with its audience that resonates through the decades. Callahan, as Nat Hentoff argued in 1988, has a broad appeal because he is an individual struggling to cope with both crime and the encroaching dominance of bureaucracy on his life, which itself is a major theme in the working lives of billions in the late twentieth and early twenty-first centuries.[41] That audiences continue to respond positively to the series' representation of law and order in the American city is an indication both of the films' success as entertainment and of the resonance of their underlying political sensibilities. This is in part because of the realism of the film and its sequels. *Dirty Harry*'s San Francisco might be a simulacrum, but audiences are discouraged from distinguishing this San Francisco from the reality, not least because of the regular appearance of real landmarks in the fictional city. The audience is thus encouraged to place themselves metaphorically in this filmic San Francisco and then translate the lessons they draw from the film into their own world. So, despite Callahan operating as a dream figure, taking actions that his audience might never contemplate, his experiences resonate with the reality experienced by his audience. Consequently, the diegetic world of Harry Callahan and the films' refraction of the "real" San Francisco cannot be dismissed as mere fantasy and must be subjected to rigorous analysis.[42] Moreover, the ideological construction of the films' politics is central to their appeal and deserves thorough evaluation. That Callahan's ideology is presented in such a way that audiences are prompted to consider it "common sense" (itself a highly ideological and contingent set of beliefs) again begs further investigation to unpack the series' many codes and hidden messages.[43]

*   *   *

Dirty Harry's America begins with a thorough assessment of the background to the first film. Chapter 1 places the dominant creative individual of the films in context, tracing Eastwood's rise through his work on Westerns and his partnership with Don Siegel, which exerted great influence on Eastwood's later career. It examines the development of his screen persona through the Man with No Name in Sergio Leone's "Dollars" trilogy before discussing the directorial career of Siegel, the director of *Dirty Harry*. The chapter offers an in-depth assessment of the Siegel-Eastwood partnership, focusing on the three films on which they collaborated before *Dirty Harry*: *Coogan's Bluff* (Siegel, 1968), *Two Mules for Sister Sara* (Siegel, 1970), and *The Beguiled* (Siegel, 1971). Together, these films help to establish some of the key themes of the *Dirty Harry* series. Through this analysis the chapter reveals Siegel's influence on Eastwood's career, from his working methods to his subject matter. It concludes with a brief discussion of the genesis of the *Dirty Harry* project and the process by which Eastwood became its star and Siegel its director.

Chapter 2 broadens this backstory, placing *Dirty Harry* in its wider cultural, political, and social context. One strand explores the development of American detective films, from the hard-boiled private eyes of the 1920s and 1930s through the films noir of the 1940s and 1950s to the development of the renegade or vigilante cop in the 1960s. The second thread develops logically from the discussion of the detective genre: screen violence. This section demonstrates the importance of violence in the films of the late 1960s and early 1970s, placing Siegel's work in the context of those directed by peers such as Sam Peckinpah and revealing how American cinema gradually opened itself to a more realistic and graphic representation of violence. This firmly locates *Dirty Harry* in its cinematic context, enabling a deeper understanding of its contribution to the ongoing discussion of screen representations of crime and policing. A third strand probes the concurrent debates in American society over crime and the so-called urban crisis, to which *Dirty Harry* and its sequels made an important contribution. Even though it was not explicitly designed as such, *Dirty Harry* offers numerous insights into late 1960s and early 1970s attitudes toward law and order. The chapter continues by examining San Francisco's position in American culture (as the "home" of West Coast radicalism, hippies, and the emerging gay-rights movement). San Francisco's liberalism caused Californian conservatives such as Governor Ronald Reagan and Richard Nixon great consternation, and their frustration with liberalism is echoed in the *Dirty Harry* series. Finally, the chapter will discuss events surrounding the Zodiac Killer in the late 1960s. The character of Scorpio (the villain in *Dirty Harry*) was loosely based on the Zodiac; the chapter will demonstrate how the *Dirty Harry* screenplay played on the fears in San Francisco and the wider culture that emerged from real events.

The first film is crucial in establishing the series' tone, themes, and subtexts, including its political position. It was conceived as a stand-alone production rather than as the opening chapter in an ongoing series, and as such it demands evaluation in isolation. Chapter 3 therefore offers an in-depth analysis of *Dirty Harry*, reinforcing the emphasis on the film's location and its social and political context. The chapter traces the film's plot while highlighting underlying ideological and thematic issues that casual viewers might miss. Acknowledging the film's relatively conservative formal structure, this chapter focuses on aesthetics and a "social construction" reading of its text and subtexts, arguing that the film presents a refraction of San Francisco's contemporary history. It pays particular attention to the film's relationship with San Francisco's geography; its representation of the counterculture, race, gender, and sexuality; and the relationship between the city's liberal elite, Callahan, and the film's villain. The chapter emphasizes *Dirty Harry*'s exploration of the methods used by criminals to manipulate legislation designed to protect their rights as American citizens before revealing how the film links this criminality to the failures of 1960s liberalism, thus echoing the political message of conservatives such as Reagan and Nixon. It also acknowledges the importance of ambiguous messages in the film, including its representation of the relationship between means and ends, and the film's conclusion, when Callahan casts aside his police badge in an echo of Will Kane (Gary Cooper) in *High Noon* (Zinnemann, 1952). Its overriding argument is that these ambiguities fail to destabilize the explicit and implicit conservatism of the film, which is only explicable if the film is firmly placed within its San Francisco context.

Dirty Harry's America then offers what might be termed a cultural history of the afterlife of Harry Callahan. Chapter 4 reveals the themes that unite *Dirty Harry*'s four sequels. Although each film is interesting in its own right, when taken as a whole the sequels demonstrate a continuity of tone and ideology that is best evaluated through combined analysis. The chapter acknowledges that the sequels attempt to denude Callahan's rough edges by having him accept partners of different ethnicities and gender while hoping to position him as a bulwark of moderation. All of the sequels are set in the San Francisco Bay Area, enabling an approach that emphasizes their representation and refraction of local politics, culture, and society. The chapter argues that the increasingly macho overtones of the series buttress the films' conservative credentials and highlights five key themes that are essential for understanding the series and its political sensibilities: race; gender and sexuality; the "outsider" status of many of the villains in the series; and Callahan's physical power and monolithic politics. So while the explicit political edge of the first film is blunted, for example, in Callahan's opposition to a police death squad in *Magnum Force* (Post, 1973) and through the increasing focus on his romantic side, many conservative undercurrents remain. Criticism of bureaucracy and certain conservative tenets remain hangovers from *Dirty Harry*, suggesting that we should approach the entire series as a conservative commentary on Californian and American politics of the 1970s and 1980s. Callahan is regularly derided for being out of touch with recent changes in San Francisco and the wider culture, thus presenting him as a solid, unbending representation of traditional American values—values that are central to conservative politics in the post-1960s era. The chapter therefore suggests that the sequels develop Callahan into a metaphor for modern American conservatism: unbending, moral, incorruptible, and most important, always right.

Lastly, chapters 5 and 6 apply a wide-angle lens to Harry Callahan's history and afterlife, exploring his resonance in the wider culture. Chapter 5 addresses Callahan's echoes in conservative political rhetoric and Eastwood's later film career, linking the two through an evaluation of Eastwood's tenure as mayor of Carmel-by-the-Sea. His brief political career echoed many of Callahan's character traits and led some commentators to suggest that Eastwood could become a serious political force in the United States. He did not, although Ronald Reagan's 1985 quotation of *Sudden Impact* reveals the close relationship between certain tributaries of conservative thought and Eastwood/Callahan's popular image. Callahan's films did not decisively influence conservative political debate but they most definitely tapped into similar reservoirs of fear and resentment while also advocating similar solutions, most obviously in proposing sterner application of law and order while promising to abandon the liberal attempt to understand the sociological causes of crime and misbehavior. As important, they should not be divorced from the larger cultural narrative of the modern conservative era in the United States, since they echoed and in some cases anticipated key themes in recent conservative thought and action. In order to demonstrate these parallels, this section of the book reveals the reverberations of Callahan's ideals in presidential rhetoric during the Reagan–George H. W. Bush–George W. Bush years. It proposes that Callahan be appreciated as a symbol of the conservative backlash of the post-1960s period, not least because his distaste for liberal bureaucrats, tough stance on crime, and rejection of the cosseting of the general public was also expressed by the most powerful politicians in the land. These traits also reappeared in many of Eastwood's other acting roles in which he often played a laconic outsider or law enforcement agent. Such roles built on the screen persona established by his early roles, and Harry Callahan in particular. *Unforgiven* (Eastwood, 1992) confirmed a new phase in Eastwood's career, one in which his screen persona gradually acknowledged and then interrogated the effect of advanced age on his body. This reached its apogee and climax in *Gran Torino* (Eastwood, 2008), in which Eastwood's Walt Kowalski gradually and then finally accepts that his outmoded beliefs can play no role in twenty-first-century America. Like Eastwood's Wes Block in *Tightrope*, Kowalski explicitly references Callahan. This final major acting role for Eastwood thus invites further consideration of the development of what might be termed the Callahan archetype in Eastwood's career.

Chapter 6 moves beyond politics to focus on other manifestations of Callahan in American popular culture, thus revealing the extent to which Callahan's influence continues to be felt long after Eastwood formally retired the character. It briefly touches on the vigilante cop genre, now a staple of recent American cinema, and suggests that Callahan's influence came to a logical conclusion in films such as *Robocop* (Verhoeven, 1987), which present killer robots as the final solution to urban crime. The chapter is more concerned with echoes of Callahan in less-celebrated media, however. It analyzes a series of pulp novels that appeared in the early 1980s and attempted to exploit Callahan's popularity while confirming his low-culture credentials. This theme continues in the chapter's assessment of references to Callahan in television, video games, graphic novels, and fan fiction. All focus on base elements of Callahan's character: his violence, laconism, simplistic moral viewpoint, and distaste for criminals. It suggests that, while these representations and refractions of Callahan are not as explicitly conservative as the expressions of Callahanian attitudes in conservative political rhetoric, they serve to confirm Callahan, and consequently *Dirty Harry*'s vision of America, as not merely a fictional construct but an articulation of a very real American political persuasion.

Before *Dirty Harry*
Making Clint Eastwood

I think I appeal to the escapism in people. . . . In other words, in the complications of society as we know it today, sometimes a person who can cut through the bureaucracy and the red tape—even if I'm playing in a modern film—a person who thinks on that level is a hero. A person who can do that, such as a "Dirty Harry" character, a man who thinks on a very simple level and has very simple moral values, appeals to a great many people. I think that's one of the great frustrations in the world. People see things becoming more complicated. . . . For major drama, for major conflicts like crime, they like to see a guy who can hack his way through all that. A very self-sufficient human being is almost becoming a mythical character in our day and age.

Certain things that come out of the collage of characters you play *are* you; certain elements of the person can't be withheld.

Clint Eastwood, 1976

"The World's Favorite Movie Star Is—No Kidding—Clint Eastwood," trumpeted *Life* magazine in July 1971.[1] Owner of his own production company and able to command fees upwards of a million dollars per movie, Eastwood was among the most bankable movie stars of the early 1970s.[2] His status as a superstar was cemented by the movie that was being filmed as he was interviewed by *Life*: *Dirty Harry* (Siegel, 1971). The film perfectly illustrates how far Eastwood had come from his first screen role as a lab technician in the forgettable B movie *Revenge of the*

Creature (Arnold, 1955). Yet it also establishes how close he remained to his roots: after all, it was shot in the city of his birth. "Dirty" Harry Callahan cemented Eastwood's cinematic persona as an insouciant, laconic outsider who has a frequently insubordinate relationship with the structures of law and order.[3] Eastwood's creative partnership with *Dirty Harry*'s director, Don Siegel, was similarly important in developing both Eastwood's career and his persona. The role also signified his transition from a star most closely associated with Westerns to one whose roles were more firmly entrenched in urban settings. This chapter examines the development of Eastwood's screen persona through "Rowdy" Yates in *Rawhide* before demonstrating how his role as the Man with No Name in Sergio Leone's "Dollars" trilogy potentially positioned him as the cinematic heir to John Wayne. This is a consequence not only of Eastwood's box-office success but also reflects elements of their shared on-screen persona: the tough, masculine, self-reliant, and occasionally brutal loner whose cynical streak conceals a moral core.

Born in May 1930 in San Francisco, Eastwood moved around the West Coast as a child due to his father's shifting employment. During his final year in high school, Eastwood's parents moved to Seattle. After graduating from Oakland Technical High School, where he seemed to have developed an outsider image, he relocated briefly to join his parents. His return to California was swift: during the Korean War he was stationed at Fort Ord near Monterey, where he spent considerable time watching films while working as a lifeguard. Eastwood seemed to be living an unremarkable life until his good looks were spotted and he signed a contract with Universal Studios in 1954.[4] There followed a series of disappointing auditions, minor bit parts and the lapsing of his Universal contract before he was cast in the CBS television series *Rawhide*, which began airing in January 1959. Set during the 1860s, the show was about the travails of a group of men driving cattle up the Sedalia Trail. Over the course of *Rawhide*'s first run, Eastwood's "Rowdy" Yates grew in stature to become the show's central character, his rough edges gradually softening as he became a more dependable and less reckless member of the cattle drive. Rarely as rowdy as his name would suggest, Yates began as eye candy to attract a female audience but assumed greater authority as the series progressed, eventually becoming the trail boss. Eastwood's official biographer, Richard Schickel indicates that despite this apparent promotion,

Eastwood remained frustrated at Yates's lack of depth and darkness; he was, according to Schickel, "trapped in low-key amiability."[5] Despite his dissatisfaction, according to another Eastwood biographer, Patrick McGilligan, *Rawhide* also gave Eastwood a "permanent feeling of ease in a Western."[6] This ease was apparent both on the set and on camera, helping to develop a key aspect of Eastwood's cinematic persona.

Eastwood's relaxed demeanor on-set and on-screen ensured first that he developed a reputation as a good worker and second that audiences found his characters agreeable and believable. His casting in an Italian film tentatively titled "The Magnificent Stranger," however, offered the opportunity to break out of the straitjacket that Yates increasingly represented.[7] "What I saw [in Eastwood], simply, was a block of marble," said the film's director, Sergio Leone.[8] This opaque, unyielding exterior would be put to good use in Leone's Westerns. "For the first time," McGilligan notes, "Clint would play a character who was cold, fierce, morally ambiguous."[9] In many respects, this character would prove to be a template for Eastwood's whole cinematic persona. Eastwood himself considered his character to be recapturing something that had been lost in recent Westerns. "The West was made by violent, uncomplicated men," he later mused, "and it is that strength and simplicity I want to recapture."[10] As Leone put it, "the law [of the West] belonged to the most hard, the most cruel, the most cynical."[11] The Man with No Name whom Eastwood portrayed in Leone's Westerns would exemplify these characteristics in three films that, according to the cultural critic Paul Smith, "effect[ed] a radical shift in the paradigms of the [W]estern" and paved the way for Eastwood's later role as Harry Callahan.[12]

"The Magnificent Stranger" was based on the plot of a 1961 film directed by Akira Kurosawa. *Yojimbo* told the story of a nineteenth-century masterless samurai who wreaks death and destruction upon a small village that was under the control of two competing crime syndicates. To avoid comparisons with *The Magnificent Seven* (Sturges, 1960), which was also based on the plot of a Kurosawa film, "The Magnificent Stranger" was retitled *A Fistful of Dollars* (Leone, 1964). The film's moral ambiguity is apparent from Eastwood's very first appearance. He comes across a pair of houses seemingly in the middle of nowhere. A young boy scampers from one to the other but is roughly expelled by two bandits and chased back to the arms of his father. The father is beaten as Eastwood's stranger impassively notices that the child's mother is a prisoner of the bandits. Whereas a traditional Western hero would likely have imposed a moral solution on this situation by killing the bandits, Eastwood's stranger remains indifferent, content to allow the family's predicament to come to its natural conclusion. Only later does he discover the history behind this scene and work to reunite the family. By this time, he has been drawn into a struggle between two gangs in the neighboring town. After attempting to play both sides against each other, he is savagely beaten for meddling in the town's fortunes and retreats to tend to his wounds. His return precipitates the movie's climactic shootout, during which he wears an improvised bulletproof vest. The metal vest helps to create an aura of invincibility, enabling him to defeat his enemies and restore order before handing the family the money he had swindled from the gangs. His final action is to ride his mule out of town.

A Fistful of Dollars was not released in the United States until 1967.[13] Its European success, however, meant that Eastwood returned to the part of the Man with No Name for two sequels. Meanwhile, in January 1966, Rawhide was abruptly canceled and Rowdy Yates made his way to the great wagon train in the sky.[14] Eastwood's anti-authoritarian bearing is reinforced in his first appearance in Fistful's sequel, For a Few Dollars More (Leone, 1965). After collecting his bounty for killing a wanted man, he faux-naïvely asks the local sheriff whether a sheriff shouldn't be "courageous, loyal, and above all honest?"[15] The sheriff concurs. Wordlessly, the Man plucks the sheriff's badge from his waistcoat and strolls outside, commenting to two nearby men, "You people need a new sheriff." He then casually and contemptuously tosses the badge at their feet. As this scene suggests, the cruel humor of the Man with No Name is amplified in For a Few Dollars More, as it is in the final film in the Leone-Eastwood collaboration, The Good, the Bad, and the Ugly (Leone, 1966). In the former, the Man sets up a duel with a rival bounty hunter, Mortimer, first by treading on and scuffing his boots and then by shooting repeatedly at Mortimer's hat, sending it spiraling down the street like tumbleweed. In the latter, he devises a brutally cynical scam with an infamous bandit named Tuco. The Man, now referred to as Blondie, rides into a town with Tuco lashed to a mule. Tuco is handed over to the authorities, and Blondie collects the ransom money before departing to a safe distance, knowing that Tuco will be hanged for crimes including murder, armed robbery, theft, kidnap, extortion, and perhaps most egregiously in the lawless West, gambling with marked cards. Tuco's noose is tied to a tree while he sits on a horse. The horse will bolt after being whipped, leaving Tuco to swing by his neck. Blondie's intervention is to shoot the rope, allowing Tuco to ride free, and then to distract the townsfolk before escaping himself. The film's conclusion sees this scenario cruelly reprised. Blondie (the Good), another bounty hunter (the Bad), and Tuco (the Ugly) have arrived at a desolate and isolated cemetery, where they are searching for $200,000 that is encased in a grave. They fight a three-way duel in which the Bad is killed. Blondie then strings up a noose while Tuco searches for the treasure. After Tuco uncovers the gold, Blondie forces him to stand on a cross that doubles as a gravestone, so that he might be hanged from the overhanging tree. "Well now, seems just like old times," drawls Blondie before dividing up the money and riding away into the distance. Tuco knows that he will die if he slips from the cross, and pleads to be freed. Blondie's final gestures before he disappears over the horizon are to shoot the rope and give Tuco one last cynical smirk, a gesture that encapsulates the cynical humor which defines many of Eastwood's screen roles. Tuco might have half of the treasure, but he is alone in the wilderness with no transport, food, or water and no longer partnered by his guardian angel. "You know what you are!" he roars to the unhearing and uncaring Blondie. "A damn son of a bitch!"

Maddened by Leone's laborious working methods, Eastwood was unwilling to continue to work with the Italian, although his next major role contained elements of Leone's interpretation of the Western. Jed Cooper, Eastwood's character in *Hang 'Em High* (Post, 1968), can be read as a transitional role.[16] Blending Rowdy Yates's way with cattle and the Man with No Name's single-mindedness, Cooper demonstrates Eastwood's growing centrality to the movies in which he starred. In many respects, Cooper is a traditional hero, standing up for justice in an amoral and corrupt world. He also shares the Man with No Name's invincibility, although in a slightly less realistic manner. Shot eight times toward the end of the film, and without a metal vest to protect him, he improbably survives to fight another day. In another Eastwood signature, Cooper casts aside his marshal's badge, although in tune with the film's more liberal sentiments, this gesture is one of frustration that the law is prepared to hang the only innocent member of a mob that attempted to lynch him at the start of the film. The major significance of *Hang 'Em High* lies in its box-office success, which according to Eastwood biographer Marc Eliot placed Eastwood and his recently established production company, Malpaso, in powerful positions within the industry.[17] According to McGilligan, Malpaso was initially established not only to give Eastwood the greatest possible control over his career but also to minimize his tax burden, a subtle indication of the actor's political considerations.[18]

Eastwood's Westerns positioned him as one of the premier Western actors of the age, and his characters added new layers to the classic Western hero established by a previous generation of actors. Chief among this generation, and arguably the singular essence of the Western masculine hero, was John Wayne. The film scholar Richard McGhee identifies Wayne's archetypal role as "the loner, the rugged individualist who serves the community without being completely a part of it."[19] To Andrew Sarris, Wayne personified "the survival of certain vestigial virtues—bravery, loyalty, stoicism in the face of pain, loss, and even death—in a world reduced to mealy-mouthed relativism."[20] His men were men of "action, not words."[21] He was, in the words of Garry Wills, "the most obvious recent embodiment of the American Adam—untrammeled, unspoiled, free to roam, breathing a larger air than the cramped men behind desks, the pygmy clerks and technicians. He is the avatar of the hero in that genre that best combines all these mythic ideas about American exceptionalism—contact with nature, distrust of government, dignity achieved by performance, skepticism toward the claims of experts."[22] As Tom Doniphon in the classic *The Man Who Shot Liberty Valance* (Ford, 1962), for example, Wayne was a "selfless bushwhacker whose conscience was not confused with conventional morality."[23] His ideology was frontier common sense where order emerged through physical dominance abetted by the gun. By the late 1960s, Wayne's career was headed toward its twilight. He was arguably now more than ever playing "John Wayne" on-screen, and his continued popularity was as much to do with his longevity and stature as his continuing performances. As McGhee thought, Wayne's persona became "larger than any single role in any single film."[24] *True Grit* (Hathaway, 1969) won him his Oscar, but few viewers would argue that it was a superior performance to his Ethan Edwards in *The Searchers* (Ford, 1956).[25] *True Grit*, however, enabled Wayne to develop his final persona, that of the "living anachronism," an aging figure who represented timeless American values and certitudes.[26] Eastwood's characters tapped into these very principles, and his impassive, almost monolithic on-screen appearance and minimalist acting style offered more echoes of The Duke, positioning him as Wayne's natural heir.[27]

Eastwood's Western collaborations were essentially preludes to the most important creative partnership of his career. While he argued that he learned a great deal from Vittorio De Sica's near-parsimony when it came to shooting scenes in *The Witches* (De Sica, 1967), and conversely from Leone's profligacy in ordering retake after retake, Eastwood's relationship with Don Siegel was the central influence on his career, in terms of both his screen presence and his development as a creative force behind the camera.[28] Siegel worked on six films with Eastwood, directing five and appearing briefly in Eastwood's directorial debut, *Play Misty for Me* (Eastwood, 1971). Their partnership, however, was defined by the four Siegel-directed films that starred Eastwood between 1968 and 1971: *Coogan's Bluff* (1968), *Two Mules for Sister Sara* (1970), *The Beguiled* (1971), and *Dirty Harry* (1971).[29] These are the true transitional films for Eastwood, marking his gradual withdrawal from Westerns and his first substantial entrance into the modern urban movie. They bookended Eastwood's late-1960s dalliance with big-budget studio films, an experiment that cemented his status as a cinematic superstar but proved to be less satisfactory on a creative level.[30] They also further molded his cinematic persona. Perhaps more importantly, Siegel allowed Eastwood to become a real creative partner, paving the way for the start of his directorial career.

Born in Chicago in 1912, Siegel was an archetypal studio director. Starting as a film librarian, he worked his way up to a second-unit director at Warner Brothers during World War II, where he developed a reputation for creating exciting montage sequences. As a director he achieved renown for efficient and spare genre pieces, with his films often placing antiheroes in heroic situations while exploring the tension between conformity and nonconformity and the individual's ability to operate within the constraints of a system (be it social, political, institutional, or even cultural). Siegel's films are also characterized by a certain moral or political ambiguity, particularly in terms of characters' motivations and often in the films' conclusions.[31] When the Siegel-Eastwood partnership began he was chiefly noted for his ability to work within strict budgetary constraints and for directing three classic genre pictures: *Riot in Cell Block 11* (1954); *Invasion of the Body Snatchers* (1956); and *The Killers* (1964). *Riot in Cell Block 11* is a quintessential prison movie in which a group of prisoners riot in an attempt to draw attention to their mistreatment and effect some change in government policy. Siegel considered the script to be "semi-documentary" and shot on location in Folsom Prison, northeast of Sacramento ("Actually Filmed behind Prison Walls!" blared the promotional posters). Its apparent simplicity is overcome by Siegel's skill in constructing the film and its deeply ironic and cynical ending.[32] *Invasion of the Body Snatchers* was Siegel's only cinematic foray into science fiction. One of the few alien invasion movies of the 1950s to transcend the genre, *Invasion* is now widely acknowledged as a classic, and in 1994 it was included in the United States National Film Registry.[33] The plot is simple: people in a small California town start behaving strangely, and the local doctor begins to suspect that something is amiss. As the film progresses he becomes aware that the townspeople have had their bodies snatched and replaced by aliens, and in this process—which occurs as they sleep—they have lost all emotion and individuality. Siegel suggested that these "pods" were reminiscent of numerous people he knew who "woke up in the morning, ate breakfast (but never read the newspaper), went to work, returned home to eat again and went to sleep" before repeating the process the next day.[34] This, however, underestimates the disturbing resonances of the metaphor of the pods. There has been considerable debate over the nature of the possible political allegory at the heart of the film, centered on whether the "pod" people represent the herd mentality of McCarthyite America or the collectivism and authoritarianism of Stalinist Russia. Yet such is the film's power and subtlety that other themes can be read into its central plot, including fears of nuclear annihilation, the loss of individuality or the breakdown of community in suburban America, the role of psychiatry in modern America, gender relations, the role of vigilance in the modern city, and plain old fear of "the other." The film's ending, with the alien invasion threatening to spread nationwide, was deemed so disturbing that the studio imposed a framing device that was intended to allay the audience's fears by indicating that the U.S. Army was in control of the situation.[35] *The Killers* was the second movie adaptation of Ernest Hemingway's short story of the same name. In Siegel's version, two hit men kill a man but are so puzzled by his fatalism when faced by death that they attempt to investigate his life. In doing so, they uncover the reason behind their target's resignation and become embroiled the dysfunctional relationship between a mob boss (played by Ronald Reagan in his last role before heading into a political career) and his duplicitous moll. A spare, violent movie in which all of the major characters die, *The Killers* cemented Siegel's reputation as a director of tough-minded, violent, and somewhat amoral thrillers.

Siegel brought his expertise and lean working methods to his Eastwood collaborations. Although *Coogan's Bluff* was the first to be released, *Two Mules for Sister Sara* and *The Beguiled* most immediately reinforced and extended Eastwood's existing screen persona. Both were scripted by Hollywood Ten blacklistee Albert Maltz and are, on the surface, Westerns.[36] In the first, set in Mexico during the 1860s, Eastwood plays a drifting mercenary, Hogan, who comes across the titular nun at the film's outset. After freeing her from kidnappers who are threatening to rape and kill her, he allows her to tag along with him. She is being pursued by French cavalrymen who have discovered that she is working with a group of Mexican revolutionaries. As is often the case in "buddy" or "odd couple" movies, such as *The Defiant Ones* (Kramer, 1958) or *The Odd Couple* (Saks, 1968), Hogan and Sara bicker and squabble but develop mutual respect. In essence, Sara represents civilization. She returns Hogan to a life of relative purpose and reintroduces him to the concept of community while gradually humanizing him. He declares his previous history of fighting for the Confederacy in the Civil War to be the actions of a sucker, but he is drawn into another rebellion and joins the revolutionaries' assault on a local French garrison, ostensibly to liberate some treasure. In the final twist, Sara reveals that her nun's habit was a disguise: she is in fact a prostitute. This does not stop Hogan's blossoming love for her, and they ride off into the sunset after successfully assisting the raid. Early on he claims that he will never marry on account of how women are: "They ask me to quit drinking, quit gambling, save my money, and they bitch about their aches and pains all day. No thanks." Yet by the conclusion he is happily allowing Sara to depart alongside him, indicating a certain softening of his attitude toward the other sex.

The Beguiled is an altogether stranger film. Based on a 1966 novel by Thomas P. Cullinan, it is an anomaly in Eastwood's career. Eastwood plays John McBurney, a New Yorker fighting for the Union deep in southern territory during the final months of the Civil War. He is mortally wounded at the start of the film but is discovered by a young girl who resides at a nearby boarding school for girls. Her fellow pupils, their headmistress, and the female slave who works the school fields nurse him back to health while debating whether they should turn him over to roaming Confederate troops. Flashbacks reveal to the audience that he is lying to them about his Quaker roots and his role in the Civil War; meanwhile, a number of the women become sexually attracted to him. When he spurns the advances of one, she pushes him down a flight of stairs, reopening a leg wound and enabling the headmistress to decide in an action of high symbolism that his leg ought to be amputated in order to prevent him from dying of gangrene. When he returns to consciousness he embarks on a drunken rampage which compels the women to decide that he is now a danger to them all and should be killed. At a final supper, they serve him poisonous mushrooms, causing him to die an agonizing death.

McBurney is a thoroughly dislikable character. He is short-tempered, amoral, selfish, priapic, duplicitous, and has no redeeming features. After discovering why his leg was amputated, his rage reaches its peak: "Why the hell didn't you just castrate me!" As his strength returns, he attempts to use his physical prowess and possession of the school's only gun to dominate and sexually exploit whichever of the women he wishes. McBurney thus becomes a representation of a hypermasculinity based on cynicism, physical power, and psychological control. Even his declaration of love at the film's conclusion seems cold and calculated, designed to enable his escape. And yet he is tricked by an even more devious character who has been manipulating the girls of the school for many years. His metaphorical castration comes at the conclusion of a series of scenes in which the women compete for his attentions; the headmistress's domination of them comes not through her sexuality but through her single-mindedness: none of the other women are prepared to amputate his leg in order to keep him at the school. Thus, whereas Sister Sara draws Hogan into a self-supporting community, the women of The Beguiled offer a community that is self-sufficient but riven with repressed resentments.

The Beguiled remains one of Siegel's most impressive films, characterized by Bruce Surtees's low-lit, moody photography and an eerie Lalo Schifrin soundtrack that combine to underscore the Gothic atmosphere of the plot and the location. It was, however, not successful at the box office. Advertised as another Eastwood Western, it failed to attract a suitable audience, something that irked Eastwood: "People who go in expecting to see a western are disappointed, and people who don't like westerns—but who might like *The Beguiled*—don't go because of the ad. The only way the film could do really well is if we could draw on those people don't ordinarily like 'Clint Eastwood' as well as those who do. People who like 'Clint Eastwood' won't like *Beguiled*. I get offed."[37] Even at this stage it is clear that Eastwood was aware of his cinematic persona. Although McBurney was not necessarily any more cynical, amoral, or antiheroic than the Man with No Name, his cowardliness and misogyny are perhaps the key to understanding why he did not appeal to those who were fans of "Clint Eastwood." Unlike the Man with No Name, he runs away from the Civil War rather than exploiting it for his own ends. Unlike Hogan, he fights not for the supposedly honorable and gentlemanly South but for the rapacious North, thus siding with the establishment rather than the rebels. He does not at any point work to aid the women he encounters, let alone pull them out of their predicament; instead, he seeks merely to exploit them. Unlike almost all of Eastwood's characters, he is deservedly killed as a result of his mendacity, and his grisly fate chimes with the film's Gothic sensibilities. The catharsis that results is one of relief for the girls of the school rather than one resulting from the normative dispensing of justice by Eastwood.

The two Siegel-Eastwood Westerns added new dimensions to Eastwood's Western persona. Hogan's humor is broader and less cynical than that of the Man with No Name. From his exclamation "What the hell's a nun doing out here!" when he first sets his eyes on Sister Sara's habit to his final dive into the hot tub with her, his wry sense of humor seems gentler and less ironic and alienating than the Man with No Name's. Part of this broadening is down to the script: Hogan says more in under two hours than the Man with No Name did in three entire movies. He also develops a form of enlightened self-interest in aligning his mercenary quest for money with the Mexican liberation struggle. The contrast with the Man with No Name's exploitation of San Miguel in *A Fistful of Dollars* demonstrates this development perfectly. Rather than playing the two sides against each other, Hogan takes the side of the revolutionaries even though his own selfish motives continue to drive him. The Man with No Name, by contrast, is blithely unconcerned with the fate of San Miguel after he has departed. Conversely, *The Beguiled* perhaps reveals the logical conclusion of the Man with No Name's amorality and cynicism. In attempting to humanize McBurney, the women merely unleash his misanthropy, and his death is a fitting conclusion to a life defined by the exploitation of others. These films also gelled neatly with Eastwood's personal image in the media. *Life* euphemistically called the real Eastwood "an old-fashioned man, basically, who holds to his own old-fashioned western ethic. . . . Eastwood feels most comfortable in the all-male world of beers, admiring women and uncomplicated language."[38]

The first movie in the Siegel-Eastwood partnership, however, is the singular transitional movie within Eastwood's career. In *Coogan's Bluff*—the title is a pun on a recurring plot feature and the upper Manhattan promontory that features as a location—Eastwood plays the libidinous Walt Coogan, an Arizonan deputy who specializes in tracking down offenders in the style of a wilderness tracker. This "modern-day primitive," in Siegel's words, is first seen outwitting and then humiliating an American Indian in the desert before heading to his married girlfriend's house for a spot of cuckolding.[39] The local sheriff spots the Indian handcuffed to a door frame outside the house, enters the house to discover Coogan bathing, and immediately sends him to New York City to extradite an escaped criminal. As soon as Coogan arrives in the metropolis he is educated in the bureaucratic necessities of modern urban policing and gets into trouble for chivalrously defending the honor of a female probation officer. The criminal has been admitted to a psychiatric unit following an LSD overdose, and Coogan is obliged to wait until the clinic agrees that the criminal is fit to travel. Impatient with the bureaucracy that is delaying his mission, Coogan decides to take matters into his own hands. After outwitting the New York Police Department, he frees the criminal from the psychiatric unit, but en route to the helicopter that will return them to Arizona, Coogan is ambushed by the criminal's associates. Insult is added to injury when the NYPD then removes him from the case for his insubordination. In an anticipation of Harry Callahan's attitude toward police work, Coogan pursues the criminal through New York City's countercultural underworld on his own time, seducing the criminal's girlfriend along the way before making a citizen's arrest and handing him over to the authorities. The film ends with Coogan and his quarry flying back to Arizona.

Coogan's Bluff is a classic urban Western. As the film scholar Martin Rubin points out, it "signifies the point at which the police thriller supplanted the western as the dominant form of American action movie."[40] From Coogan's refusal to remove his Stetson and cowboy boots to the barroom brawls and tension between the hero, his enemy, and the law, not to mention the stock characters, the film simply transposes many Western tropes to New York City, including a climactic chase scene (using motorcycles rather than horses) set in New York's Riverside Park.[41] Coogan ruefully notes how urbanization has destroyed something essential about the country. When gazing over the city from a vantage point on the bluff, he laments, "[I'm] trying to picture it the way it was. Just the trees and the river. Before people fouled it all up." Coogan's "Westernness" is reinforced by numerous comments from his major antagonist in the NYPD, Lieutenant McElroy. After Coogan recovers from the ambush, he is upbraided by McElroy: "You're in a whole another kind of ball game! You're out of your league!" "Well, it's gotten personal now," Coogan responds. Drawling sarcastically as if to impersonate John Wayne, McElroy retorts, "Yeah, and a man's gotta do what a man's gotta do. That it?" Later, the references become more obvious still. McElroy yells at Coogan, "This isn't the O.K. Corral around here! This is the city of New York; we've got a system. Not much, but we're fond of it. We don't like it when some two-for-a-nickel cowboy thinks he can bend it out of shape." In bringing the cowboy to the East Coast, *Coogan's Bluff* reversed the traditional geographic direction of the Western while also bringing the Western's genre characteristics into the mid-twentieth century.

Coogan's cowboy identity is also a running joke within the film. To his increasing exasperation, numerous people assume that he is from Texas, and the continued presence of his Stetson elicits an abundance of comments, often from women who declare their interest in bedding a cowboy. As a cowboy, he is obviously a representation of traditional morality, which puts him at odds with the ultra-modern and corrupt values of the city. His violent response to witnessing a man sexually harassing a female probation officer leads to him, rather than the lecher, receiving a dressing-down. "We don't treat people like that in New York," she scolds.

Although he is more respectful of women, his old-fashioned attitude toward gender roles is considered out of step with the modern city. On other occasions, Coogan's antiquatedness gives him the upper hand. His skill at tracking enables him to outwit a fraudulent taxi driver and more importantly offers insight into the escaped criminal's modus operandi: "You learn a lot about a person when you hunt him," he tells McElroy. While he often partakes in alcohol, he is contemptuous of those who overindulge. His straight edge ensures that he wins a battle of wits with a stoned drug user in a nightclub. After wandering through the scantily clad crowd at the Pigeon-Toed Orange Peel nightclub, Coogan spots the criminal's girlfriend, sitting with two men and sharing some marijuana. One of the men, played by Albert Popwell, threatens him with a flick knife. Coogan, clearly accustomed to this sort of provocation, grabs an empty wine bottle, smashes it against another drug user and brandishes it at his African American antagonist. Popwell inevitably backs down to the superior strength and speed of the white man.

Popwell, who later appeared in four Dirty Harry films, is not the only foreshadow of Harry Callahan in *Coogan's Bluff*. When the Arizona sheriff rebukes Coogan for his ill-treatment of his prisoner at the film's outset, Coogan snaps, "My shirt's in there on the bed. There's a badge on it that comes right off." Promised "every lousy one-man job that comes along," Coogan merely shrugs, as if he was expecting a truly dirty assignment. As important, his instinctive policing method, which was shaped in the West, stands in sharp contrast to the bureaucratic inertia practiced by his eastern, urban counterparts. McElroy is heard educating a subordinate officer about the Supreme Court: "Ever heard of it?" he yells. He repeatedly spells out exactly how Coogan may set about extraditing the criminal. First, Coogan must head to the district attorney, then the state supreme court, and then obtain a medical release. At first, Coogan replies in classic Callahanian style, "You can walk in and get him [instead]," but by the end he has realized that the bureaucracy is there for a reason and proffers his assent for due process. Coogan thus demonstrates that frontier justice has its limits. In maintaining equidistance between bureaucracy and savagery, then, Coogan positions himself as an archetypal Western hero, reaffirming the notion that western methods and western justice remain central to the American way while fully understanding that the rule of law must ultimately prevail.[42]

The Siegel-Eastwood films were punctuated by Eastwood's appearance in three high-budget productions that served to cement his box-office appeal. *Where Eagles Dare* (Hutton, 1968) and *Kelly's Heroes* (Hutton, 1970) placed Eastwood in World War II, and *Paint Your Wagon* (Logan, 1969) gave him the opportunity to perform as a singing cowboy. More important, Eastwood's directorial debut, *Play Misty for Me,* was released in November 1971 and displayed Siegel's clear influence. Eastwood plays Dave Garver, a radio DJ who lives and works in Carmel, California. He meets and sleeps with a fan who is a regular caller to his show. She turns out to be mentally unstable and begins terrorizing him and his ex-girlfriend, leading to a conclusion in which she is killed. The film does not side fully with Garver, suggesting that his libidinous behavior was as much at fault as his fan's illness. Garver is a decidedly ambiguous, antiheroic character who is adept at exploiting his celebrity and the late-1960s atmosphere of free love but who finds that this culture is more problematic than he expects. Like McBurney, he is drawn into a situation beyond his control by his sexual urges, but like Coogan, he is able to extricate himself at the end, thus avoiding the troublesome implications that McBurney's fate held for the Eastwood persona. While Siegel was present on the set and was rewarded with a bit part, Eastwood's regular collaborators Dean Reisner and Bruce Surtees also made important contributions. Reisner polished the script prior to the shoot, and Surtees was the film's director of photography, a role in which he significantly influenced the film's look, enabling Eastwood to shoot with low lighting and emphasizing the darkness that lay behind the apparently sunny atmosphere of Carmel. They also influenced Eastwood's working methods, including his preference for speedy shoots in order to bring the film in under budget. As important, *Misty* was a hit at the box office and opened the eyes of studio executives to Eastwood's potential as an important and commercially successful filmmaker. Eastwood claims that the studio was baffled at the film's success: "They'd say, 'well, I don't know [why it is doing well], it isn't a Western and you're not a cop.' Their eyes were really channeled" by the film, which gave him further leeway with the bureaucrats and opened the possibilities for a long-term directorial career.[43]

As important, the Siegel-Eastwood films laid the groundwork for *Dirty Harry*. The Clintus-Siegelini[44] partnership was mutually satisfying, with both individuals consulting each other on shot placement, dialogue, and scene construction. Siegel later said that he found East-wood unusually knowledgeable for an actor. "He started to come up with ideas for camera set-ups," Siegel recalled. "And even if I decided not to use them they invariably gave me another idea."[45] For his part, East-wood said, "Don . . . kind of breeds an atmosphere of participation."[46] The Siegel films further refined Eastwood's cinematic persona as a tough, laconic outsider with a contemptuous streak, an ambivalent attitude toward bureaucracy, and a cynical sense of humor. As suggested by the box-office response to *The Beguiled*, audiences were increasingly attending Eastwood's films in anticipation of a certain type of entertainment and a particular role for the male lead. Siegel added an element of sex appeal to Eastwood's cowboy persona but, just as important, undercut the Man with No Name's aura of ironic detachment. Indeed, Hogan, Coogan, and Garver rely on the audience's awareness of Eastwood's persona for their success. While Hogan and Coogan share a cynical attitude to those around them, they are aware of the need to engage with society rather than merely exploit it. Meanwhile, McBurney's refusal to do so leads to his downfall. The Siegel films thus solidified Eastwood's persona as a rugged loner prepared to adopt a heroic mantle when it suited him but who remained steadfastly critical of the organizational structures of modern life. They perhaps also confirmed to Eastwood that his career was best served by avoiding explicitly political films. As he pointed out to Judy Fayard of *Life*, "a lot of actors have gotten too involved with trying to make message pictures. And there's nobody in the theater to get the message. You have to give people good entertainment first."[47]

*   *   *

Eastwood agreed to star in *Dirty Harry* after the project was rejected by, among others, Frank Sinatra.[48] Having starred in the first and completed filming on the second of his Tony Rome movies, Sinatra had also recently played the lead in *The Detective* (Douglas, 1968), a film that became one of *Dirty Harry*'s most important precursors. Sinatra became frustrated with the progress of rewrites and pulled out, citing an injury. Paul Newman apparently also rejected the role, concerned at the political undertones of the film's title character, while John Wayne himself also rejected it, blaming his inability to find space in his schedule.[49] Callahan would have been perfect for Wayne, as he later acknowledged. "How did

I ever let that one slip through my fingers," he apparently lamented after watching *Dirty Harry*.[50] As Wayne's biographers Randy Roberts and James Oslen report, "Harry Callahan *was* John Wayne."[51] By the 1960s, his conservative politics were almost inseparable from the politics implicit (and sometimes explicit) in his films. The history of the Alamo, for example, was refashioned to reflect Wayne's patriotic instincts in his film of the same name (which perhaps foreshadowed *Dirty Harry*'s refraction of San Francisco's history). A staunch believer in a low-tax, low-regulation economy and a good friend of Barry Goldwater, Wayne, like Ronald Reagan, was prepared to blame California's student unrest on "immature professors" giving youngsters too much latitude. He even moved to the spiritual home of the new conservative movement during this decade, although his decision to take up residence in Newport Beach, Orange County, was more due to the effect that its bracing sea air might have on his ailing body than its political significance.[52]

There is another intriguing, if bizarre connection between The Duke and Harry Callahan. Wayne reportedly contracted cancer while shooting *The Conqueror* (Powell, 1956) in St. George, Utah. The location was about 140 miles downwind of the Yucca Flats, Nevada, where nuclear tests were conducted in the early 1950s. Between March 17 and June 4, 1953, a sequence of tests was conducted as part of Operation Upshot-Knothole. The ninth and southernmost detonation in the Flats was code-named "Harry," which dosed its observers with the third-highest level of gamma radiation of the Upshot-Knothole tests. Harry's radioactive cloud spread dozens of miles southward, and residents of St. George, some fifty miles east, were advised to stay indoors as the mushroom cloud from Harry's explosion had mingled with some thunderclouds that were headed in their direction. Hundreds of cattle in the vicinity suffered strange burns or died, with similar effects being reported by local human residents, including unrepresentatively high incidences of leukemia and other cancers. Of all of the mainland nuclear tests, Harry produced the most radioactive contamination for those who lived downwind, not least because a hot gray ash blanketed and then became mixed into the local sands, resulting in Geiger counters registering high levels of radioactivity from strontium 90 and cesium 137 even one year later.[53] In the immediate wake of Harry's detonation a "purple, putrid-smelling fog" enveloped Alamo, the nearest town to the bombsite, and nearby residents who were outside that morning reported their skin burning.[54] Later that summer, Wayne and the rest of the crew from *The Conqueror* began filming in the Escalante Valley, near St. George. Daily shoots frequently ended with the cast and crew covered in dust; a disproportionately high number of them later developed cancer, including Wayne himself. The test was known colloquially as "Dirty" Harry.[55]

Warner Brothers took the movie project to Eastwood who agreed to star, insisting on two provisos: first, that Siegel would direct, and second, that the film be relocated to San Francisco. The original script set the action in New York City, but San Francisco was attractive for simple reasons: Eastwood liked his place of birth, and Siegel felt comfortable filming there. The first draft of the script was written by Harry Julian Fink and Rita M. Fink. John Milius provided some rewrites in return for a $2,000 gun, and Dean Reisner produced the final shooting script with input from Siegel. Filming began in April 1971, with Bruce Surtees as cinematographer, whose interest in low lighting influenced the large number of scenes shot at night. As was traditional on a Siegel film, principal photography was completed rapidly, with minimal retakes, and postproduction was similarly swift, ensuring that *Dirty Harry* was released into theaters in time for the Christmas 1971 season.[56]

The Roots of *Dirty Harry*

I like the way heroes are now. I like them with strengths,
weaknesses, lack of virtue.... And a touch of cynicism at
times.... [I]f some guy is trying to kill the character I'm
playing, I shoot 'em in the back.

Clint Eastwood, 1978

An understanding of the political and social context from which *Dirty
Harry* emerged is crucial in order to comprehend the film's deepest
meanings. *Dirty Harry*'s prehistory exists within a number of different
historical structures. The foundations for the genre framework in which
Dirty Harry operates were laid by American detective films, from the
hard-boiled private eyes of the 1920s and 1930s through the films noir of
the 1940s and 1950s to the development of the renegade or vigilante cop
in the 1960s. *Dirty Harry* and its sequels also contributed to the ongoing
discussion in the public sphere over the role and importance of on-screen
violence. A small number of films that were released in the late 1960s and
early 1970s made particularly important contributions to this debate,
and evaluation of their impact helps to place Siegel's film within context.
Yet *Dirty Harry*'s context was not only cinematic. The film offers a scath-
ing critique of the liberal approach to crime and the law, even suggesting
that liberalism facilitates the killing spree of its main villain. It fed on
and contributed to contemporary debates in American society about law
and order, and to the breakdown of the liberal consensus which became
apparent as Lyndon Baines Johnson's presidency stumbled toward its
dissolution. The film's setting also played a role in these debates. The
liberalism of the Bay Area, the "home" of West Coast radicalism, hippies,
and the emerging gay-rights movement, caused California conservatives

such as Governor Ronald Reagan and Richard Nixon great consternation. In 1969, Nixon insisted that street protesters in San Francisco were
a "vocal minority" who in their attempt to "prevail . . . over reason and
the will of the majority" constituted a danger to the very concept of a free
society.[1] Reagan articulated his ambition more pithily, promising during
his 1966 campaign to "clean up the mess in Berkeley."[2] The frustration
of such conservatives with West Coast liberalism is reflected throughout
the *Dirty Harry* series. Finally, and perhaps most disturbingly, the film
commented obliquely on actual events surrounding a serial murderer
who operated in the Bay Area during the late 1960s who became known
as the Zodiac Killer. The character of Scorpio (the villain in *Dirty Harry*)
was loosely based on the Zodiac Killer, and the *Dirty Harry* screenplay
played on the fears in San Francisco and the wider culture that emerged
from real events related to the killer's activities.

Violence and Censorship

Until the 1960s Hollywood existed in a state of constant self-monitoring.
Fearing federal regulation, the capricious actions of state and municipal
authorities which might take unilateral action to censor film, and the
threat of protest from religious groups, Hollywood created its own be-
havioral code. In 1922, amid increased public clamor that motion pictures
avoid explicit depiction of immoral acts, the industry established its own
censorship organization, often known as the Hays Office (after its head,
Will Hays). The Hays Office codified all the objections that various states
and municipalities submitted and advised the film companies on what it
might want to avoid depicting. In 1929, Martin Quigley, devout Catholic and owner of the important trade paper *Motion Picture Herald*, and
Daniel Lord, a Jesuit priest, drew up a stricter set of censorship rules for
closer enforcement of the so-called Production Code. Films that broke
the code were punished with $25,000 fines. The major studios largely
ignored this move, which is evidenced in the realistic violence of such
films as *The Public Enemy* (Wellman, 1931) and *Scarface* (Hawks, 1932).

Matters came to a head in 1934 when the Roman Catholic Church
in America threatened to call a boycott of the cinema. The industry
finally took note, and in mid-1934 Hays agreed to strengthen the Production Code and its mechanism, and persuaded the industry that its

best interests were to accept. Hays oversaw the appointment of Joseph Breen, a conservative Catholic journalist, to head the revamped Production Code Administration (PCA). From 1934 to the 1950s the industry agreed to work within his narrow interpretation of the rules, which included such diktats as "correct entertainment raises the whole standard of a nation. Wrong entertainment lowers the whole living conditions and moral ideals of a race."[3] Under Breen, the PCA recommended that on-screen murders should not inspire imitators and that revenge in modern times should not be justified; depictions of illegal drug traffic were prohibited because of the "evil consequences" of the drug trade; and the use of liquor "when not required by the plot . . . will not be shown." "Pictures shall not infer that low forms of sex relationship are the accepted or common thing." "Excessive and lustful kissing, lustful embraces, suggestive postures and gestures are not to be shown . . . passion should . . . not stimulate the lower and baser element." "Dances which suggest or represent sexual actions, whether performed solo or with two or more; dances intended to excite the emotional reaction of an audience; dances with movement of the breasts, excessive body movements while the feet are stationary, violate decency and are wrong." As important, the code dictated that criminal acts should not be presented in such a way that they could inspire or facilitate imitation. In particular, "brutal killings" were not to be shown "in detail."

There was a brief relaxation of the limits on violence during World War II, but the rise of film noir, with its focus on crime in the city, further pushed the boundaries of screen violence. Meanwhile, the 1948 U.S. Supreme Court decision in *United States v. Paramount Pictures Inc.* separated the major film studios from their own cinemas, allowing additional independent companies to distribute their films. The impact was not only felt in terms of the vertical integration of the movie business, for these smaller companies had not necessarily signed up for the Production Code, meaning that their films could be presented by cinemas without the approval of the PCA. A further Supreme Court decision in 1952 in *Joseph Burstyn, Inc. v. Wilson* decreed that cinema was an artistic medium and was thus protected by the First Amendment right to freedom of speech. In 1956 the Production Code was relaxed further, with the guidelines on sex and violence becoming vaguer and more akin to suggestions than rules, although according to the film writer David Cook, by this time filmmakers' decisions on what to include in their movies and audience demand rendered the code "nearly irrelevant."[4]

Splendor in the Grass (Kazan, 1961) placed further pressure on the code. The film's plot implied that its two young lovers suffered emotional problems for ignoring rather than satisfying their sexuality, a development that constituted a radical reversal of cinematic sexual norms. *Splendor* echoed a number of contemporaneous European films in treating sex and sexuality with a maturity and honesty that seemed at odds with the chastity desired by the code. A series of imports like *Room at the Top* (Clayton, 1959), *A Bout de Souffle* (Godard, 1960), and *La Dolce Vita* (Fellini, 1960) rendered the cinematic representation of sex more complex and sophisticated than anything permitted under the code. American cinema soon followed suit. Female nudity briefly featured in *The Pawnbroker* (Lumet, 1964), which received approval from the Production Code's masters after a minor debate. Pubic hair was spotted in *Blow-Up* (Antonioni, 1966). That this potential outrage did not affect the film's box-office receipts effectively destroyed the Hollywood Production Code, leading to the creation of Motion Picture Association of America's ratings system. This system barred persons under seventeen from watching particularly violent or sexual films and provided guidance on the suitability of every film for an American audience.[5] According to Stephen Prince, the revisions to the code were "designed to move cinema closer to the mores characteristic of . . . a more permissive era and to expand the creative freedom of filmmakers."[6] Language was also liberalized: *Who's Afraid of Virginia Woolf?* (Nichols, 1966) was not censored, despite featuring "eleven 'goddamns,' seven 'bastards,' one 'screw you,' an 'up yours,' one 'hump the hostess,' and a reference to 'monkey nipples.'"[7] Jack Valenti, who became president of the MPAA in 1966, commented on the absurdity of MPAA meetings debating offensive language in the wake of *Who's Afraid*: "I'm not going to spend my life sitting in . . . offices and saying, 'I gotta take out one "shit" and one "screw." This is crazy.'"[8]

On-screen violence was another contentious issue, related in particular to two films of the late 1960s: *Bonnie and Clyde* (Penn, 1967) and *The Wild Bunch* (Peckinpah, 1969). The liberalization of the Production Code ensured that cinema could comment effectively on the changes that were then being wrought on American society. A 1966 revision of the Production Code offered filmmakers further leeway in their decisions on how to present violence and sex. As Stephen Prince notes, Arthur Penn took advantage "to make a film that audaciously mixed slapstick humor with graphic violence."[9] While Penn was preparing *Bonnie and Clyde* for release, Sergio Leone's "Dollars" trilogy appeared on American screens. The number of deaths from gunshots in Leone's Westerns was unprecedented but did not harm their commercial success. *Bonnie and Clyde* opened one month after *The Dirty Dozen* (Aldrich, 1967), another film that was noted at the time for its violence.[10] There was something different about Penn's film, however. At the end of a botched bank robbery, Clyde shoots a bank manager in the face as his victim attempts to apprehend the criminals. Penn depicted the incident in a close-up shot that spared little detail of the bullet's impact. Meanwhile, the Barrow Gang's escapades were often backed by a frantic banjo soundtrack and the action was repeatedly sped up, thus making it seem as absurd as exciting. This link between violence and humor was profoundly depressing for critics such as Bosley Crowther of the *New York Times*, who sneered, "It is a cheap piece of bald-faced slapstick comedy that treats the hideous depredations of that sleazy, moronic pair as though they were as full of fun and frolic as the Jazz Age cutups in *Thoroughly Modern Millie*."[11] More shockingly, the end of the film consisted of a bloody, slow-motion, almost balletic scene of Bonnie and Clyde's death at the hands of the authorities. Intercutting slow-motion and real-time footage with over fifty cuts in less than a minute, Penn and his editor, Dede Allen, created a scene that at once shocked, appalled, and fascinated. According to Stephen Prince, the death of Bonnie and Clyde was a "seminal moment in American cinema," one which helped create a new language of cinematic violence.[12] The gangsters' bodies were riddled with bullet holes, and copious quantities of fake blood spurted from the entry wounds. This was unprecedentedly gruesome and cemented *Bonnie and Clyde*'s position in film history as solidly as Bonnie and Clyde's death cemented the real characters in American folklore.[13]

If anything, Sam Peckinpah went further in *The Wild Bunch*. As David Cook notes, the film would not have passed even the 1966 revised code and only the creation of the new Code and Rating Administration in 1968 ensured that it could be presented in American cinemas. Like Penn, Peckinpah shot gunfights with multiple cameras running at different speeds and, alongside his editor Lou Lombardo, intercut between the different footage. Like Penn, he used "squibs" containing a viscous red liquid that would be punctured to show blood spurting from bullet wounds. But unlike that in *Bonnie and Clyde*, the violence Peckinpah depicted was relentless and occurred throughout the film.[14] Whereas *Bonnie and Clyde*'s shock value lay in part with the brutality and finality of its wordless ending, *The Wild Bunch* shocked through the regularity and scale of bloodletting. "The point of the film," said Peckinpah, "is to take this façade of movie violence and open it up, get people involved in it . . . and then twist it so that it's not fun anymore, just a wave of sickness in the gut. . . . It's ugly, brutalizing, and bloody fucking awful. It's not fun and games and Cowboys and Indians. It's a terrible, ugly thing."[15] Yet the violence was also fascinating, and such was Peckinpah's skill as a filmmaker that audiences felt compelled to lament the deaths of the Wild Bunch, despite the fact that this was a group of vicious, amoral, and self-serving men. This and the deaths in *Bonnie and Clyde* also served to comment on the increasing visibility of violence in American life, whether in the news reports of the Vietnam War, political assassinations, or the urban rebellions that seemed to be sweeping the nation's cities in the later years of the 1960s.[16] Peckinpah himself made this link explicit, commenting in 1972 that the media's coverage of the Vietnam War "anesthetized" the population, creating a simulacrum in which the American public "see men die, really die, every day on television, but it doesn't seem real. We don't believe those are real people."[17] Through heightened reality and skillful characterization, *The Wild Bunch* reminded cinemagoers of the real impact of death in war, confronting them with its brutality, its arbitrariness, and its beauty.

Crime Films

The issue of screen violence accompanied the release of crime films almost since the appearance of the first major film that had a gangster as its protagonist: *Underworld* (von Sternberg, 1927). By the early 1930s, the gangster was a central figure in American film. The first wave of gangster movies rendered the gangster a glamorous character, although he almost always received a thoroughly moral comeuppance at the film's conclusion. The values that gangsters held—their amoral standpoint, their lust for money and power, and their association with loose women—were indicted as well in their grisly deaths. The Production Code led to a greater focus on morality, as suggested by *Angels with Dirty Faces* (Curtiz, 1938), in which James Cagney's gangster is convinced by his childhood friend to "turn yellow" on his way to the gas chamber. This, it was hoped, would convince a group of boys who hero-worshipped him not to emulate his life of crime.

The forces of law and order were also made to seem more glamorous in *G Men* (Keighley, 1935), in which Cagney was cast against type as a law enforcer. Superficially this represented a reversal of his normal gangster role, but his methods were not far removed from those of the gangsters themselves, suggesting that gangster tendencies were never far from the surface of even the FBI's finest, and placing the film alongside *M* (Lang, 1931) in exploring the often fine line that separated criminals from lawmen.[18] One of the most celebrated crime films of the 1930s, *M* explores themes that are also present in *Dirty Harry*. It follows the pursuit of a serial killer in Berlin. Tormented by pedophilic urges, the killer draws both the police and the city's criminal underworld into a chase. The criminals are able to capture the killer, but before they are able to mete out justice, the police arrive to bring him to a fair trial. The film's director, Fritz Lang, deliberately drew parallels in the film between the police and the criminals as a comment on the two types of order that they imposed on the city. This duality featured prominently in *Dirty Harry*'s theatrical trailer, which opens with a narrator announcing that the film is about "a couple of killers: Harry Callahan and a homicidal maniac. The one with the badge is Harry."[19]

In part as a response to Lang's mastery of film techniques, American crime films went through a major stylistic shift in the 1940s. Film historians Leonard Quart and Albert Auster identified a number of distinct features of crime films from this period: "deliberately disquieting editing, low-key lighting, night-for-night shooting, subjective view shots, voice-over and flashback and oblique camera setups. . . . images of rainswept, foggy-night streets, shadowy figures, seedy bars, flickering street lamps, isolated coast roads, and rooms dominated by mirrors."[20] These films noir offered paranoid visions of decaying cities populated by glamorous yet duplicitous women, morally compromised or pessimistic male protagonists, criminals who often shared characteristics with the heroes, and ambiguous victories for the forces of good. Visually influenced by German expressionism, Val Lewton's work with RKO, and *Citizen Kane* (Welles, 1940), notably the latter's deep-focus compositions, film noir was characterized by chiaroscuro lighting, oblique camera angles, and unsettling cinematography. Fog and mist frequently added a layer of mystery to the action, which made San Francisco a particularly apt location for the classic noir *The Maltese Falcon* (Huston, 1941). The fog in this film both increased the suspense and served as a dual metaphor for the shadowy figures that populated the film and the murk of the mystery that the film's protagonist, Sam Spade, investigated. Similarly, San Francisco's high-rise buildings enabled noir filmmakers such as John Huston to add a claustrophobic aura to the action, where skyscrapers formed gigantic corridors that loomed over the action and entrapped the film's characters. As suggested by Huston's adaptation of Dashiell Hammett's novel, noir also had a close relationship with hard-boiled crime fiction. Works by writers such as Hammett, James M. Cain, and Raymond Chandler transplanted British detective fiction to the United States.[21] The literature scholar Megan Abbott identifies a focus on "the solitary white man, hard-bitten, street-savvy, but very much alone amid the chaotic din of the modern city," as a central feature of hard-boiled fiction.[22] Because their protagonists usually roomed in dingy apartments or at their offices, films noir rarely pictured the private spaces of their heroes. These men were often working class or lower middle class, had few ties to family or friends, and were firmly enmeshed in corrupt, crime-ridden, mysterious, and dangerous cities. In the "mean streets," to quote Chandler, opportunity and excitement often ran hand-in-hand with hopelessness and ennui, prosperity with poverty, and life with death.[23]

As Andrew Spicer notes, by the 1950s, noir focused more heavily on documentary-style exposés of organized crime in the city. Essentially, the focus shifted from small-time criminals to a corporate world in which wide-scale corruption is concealed by apparently legitimate and respectable bosses.[24] In *Touch of Evil* (Welles, 1958), which remains the exemplar of so-called late noir, the corrupt activities of a racist police captain, Hank Quinlan, are gradually uncovered during an investigation of a bomb plot. Evil is also ever-present in *Kiss Me Deadly* (Aldrich, 1955), whose protagonist, Mike Hammer, is a fascistic, borderline psychotic detective whose emotions have been repressed under his tough-guy exterior. He becomes caught up in a plot so sinister and fantastic that it ends with apocalypse. Far away from the traditional noir image of the private eye, Quinlan and Hammer point to key features of Harry Callahan's psyche.

Bullitt and *The Detective*

Frank Sinatra's *The Detective* (Douglas, 1968) and Steve McQueen's *Bullitt* (Yates, 1968) opened a new era for police films, and are particularly important in any consideration of *Dirty Harry*. Frank Bullitt, played by McQueen, is the archetypal police officer who goes rogue in single-minded pursuit of his case, arguably preparing the ground for Harry Callahan. Like Bullitt, Joe Leland, played by Sinatra, is not only fighting crime but also struggling with the moral failings of his colleagues. Both films exude a cynical attitude toward politicians and the failings of the political system.

Leland is the star detective of an overwhelmed Manhattan Police Department, and after solving a particularly gruesome murder of a gay socialite he is promoted to lieutenant. Yet he gradually realizes that he was complicit in the railroading of an innocent man with a personality disorder and that his department is intimately linked to a corrupt property scam. His decision to come clean is the plot's fulcrum. It ultimately costs him his job, and in his final speech he reveals his motives: "I was a good cop. I saw things that terrified me. And I thought I was above it all. But I wasn't. No, I want out. Because there are things to fight for, and I can't fight for them while I'm here." A seemingly nondescript San Francisco police lieutenant, Bullitt is assigned to protect Johnny Ross, the brother of a Chicago Mafia boss, over the weekend before a Senate subcommittee hearing at which Ross will testify against the mob. Ross is killed by hit men, and a local politician who hoped to use the hearing to boost his own career puts pressure on Bullitt to admit culpability and negligence. Over the course of a weekend, Bullitt discovers that the man who was killed is not Ross, but a patsy who has been set up by the mob in an elaborate scheme to fool the politician and enable Ross's escape from the United States. During the investigation, Bullitt keeps vital information from his superiors, and by the end of the weekend he is being pursued by the mob and the politician's cronies in the San Francisco Police Department (SFPD). Eventually he tracks down the real Ross at San Francisco airport, precipitating the film's final showdown.

Both Leland and Bullitt become painfully aware of the failure of modern urban policing. They represent perhaps the last bastion of morality amid the crime wave fostered by the urban crisis of the 1960s. Both films imply that the American public's ambivalence toward or even disrespect for the law was justified in the late 1960s, a time when violent crime seemed to be increasing exponentially each year.[25] The slightly hysterical response of the *Washington Post*'s reviewer to *The Detective* was perhaps an indication of popular feeling about the decline of law and order: the film's vicious and cynical presentation of police corruption would, according to the reviewer, likely "increase the shocking disrespect the law presently commands."[26] The *New York Times* later reflected on *The Detective*, stating that it "radiates a kind of liberal authoritarianism right out of the Johnson administration," rendering the film "a bitter-sweet last hurrah for the Great Society, just as it was yielding its place to the Silent Majority."[27] In this sense, *The Detective* anticipates a key element of *Dirty Harry* even as it attempts to hold back the conservative tide. Its suggestion that the Silent Majority was in the process of rejecting Great Society liberalism was amplified in Siegel's film; crucially, Siegel's protagonist was at the forefront of the backlash. Leland is conflicted about his relationship with his department. Increasingly aware that its corruption is morally wrong, he knows that it nevertheless is the last line of protection against the crime wave. The resolution of Leland's moral quandary firmly sides with liberalism, suggesting that honorable, decent, and righteous men remained central within the nation's police force. Yet in its presentation of corruption *The Detective* feeds the sense that the thin blue line between order and chaos was becoming ever more blurred and that the police were firmly enmeshed in the decline of American society. *Bullitt*, meanwhile, reveals that individual policemen might need to operate outside the law if they are to compete with the criminals they pursue. Bullitt's final act against Ross seems particularly coldhearted and perhaps even reckless, an impression that is reinforced in the film's final scene when Bullitt returns home to contemplate his actions while staring silently at the bathroom mirror. Significantly, the politician, Bullitt's major antagonist, departs the scene of Ross's death in a car sporting a "Support Your Local Police" bumper sticker. Both films, then, suggested that only the actions of brave and upstanding individuals prevented crime, complacency, and corruption from overwhelming American cities.

McQueen was adamant that *Bullitt* be as realistic as possible, from his research work with the SFPD prior to principal shooting, through the use of numerous street locations, and in the attempt to maintain the fidelity to San Francisco's geography of the film's legendary car chase. Consequently, *Bullitt* demands consideration as a San Francisco film.[28] Significantly, the major villains come from Chicago rather than San Francisco itself, suggesting that large-scale criminal operations were not an indigenous threat to San Franciscans. Aside from Bullitt's cramped and scruffy apartment, San Francisco itself appears as a sparklingly clean, modern city. In stark contrast to the miasma that enveloped *The Maltese Falcon*'s city, *Bullitt*'s San Francisco is bathed in northern California sunshine. *Bullitt* is thus a major departure from film noir, an almost self-consciously modern film, and one that inaugurated a new era for police films. It was released in October 1968, months after the assassinations of Dr. Martin Luther King Jr. in Memphis and of Robert F. Kennedy in Los Angeles. More than one hundred American cities experienced civil disorder in the wake of Dr. King's death. The mass protests and accompanying violence at the August 1968 Democratic National Convention in Chicago prompted further anguish over a crisis in law and order that seemed to be overwhelming the nation. While *Bullitt* does not explicitly touch on these issues, its presentation of a police officer who frequently clashes with judges, politicians, and fellow police officers suggested, as did *The Detective*, that tensions were rising within the police and the legal service over how to respond to the urban crisis.

Law and Order and the Urban Crisis

This so-called urban crisis manifested all of the fears of American liberals in the 1960s. Welfare costs and the numbers of welfare recipients were booming, and violent crime was on the rise even as Lyndon Johnson's Great Society programs were attempting to bring all down. In August 1965 an urban revolt consumed the Watts neighborhood of Los Angeles, causing more than thirty deaths and $40 million of damage to property.

One of the central events of the 1960s, the Watts rebellion suggested that the Great Society was little more than a Band-Aid attempting to staunch a gaping wound. Racial tension erupted again the following year when civil rights demonstrations in Chicago provided the novel and tragic sight of African American marchers being protected from white mobs by local police.[29] That year's gubernatorial campaign in California provided further evidence of widespread disenchantment with the Democratic Party's liberal social policy. Ronald Reagan, the Republican nominee, had previously campaigned for both FDR and Truman, but he drifted rightward during the McCarthyite era. The transformations in American society during the 1960s "baffled" him, according to his son, Ron.[30] His first major retort was a campaign speech at the 1964 Republican nominating convention, which also formed the basis of a television broadcast on October 27. This speech fundamentally transformed his image, firmly establishing his political credentials and rendering him a credible figurehead for the Republican Party. Known as "A Time for Choosing" and in some quarters simply as "The Speech," it was an apocalyptic assault on big government, socialism, and communism that transformed Reagan from a former actor to a potential future president.[31] The Speech assailed liberals for spending beyond their means and for failing to prevent the erosion of natural liberties that true Americans held dearly while raising taxes and constructing a bloated federal bureaucracy. "So they're going to solve all the problems of human misery through government and government planning," Reagan acidly commented. "Actually, a government bureau is the nearest thing to eternal life we'll ever see on this earth. . . . Somewhere a perversion has taken place. Our natural, unalienable rights are now considered to be a dispensation of government, and freedom has never been so fragile, so close to slipping from our grasp as it is at this moment."[32] So, just as Harry Callahan was to be an authority figure who hated bureaucratic authority, Reagan presented himself as a politician who hated government. He also offered his support for staunch conservative and opponent of big government Barry Goldwater in a campaign ad that unequivocally outlined Reagan's belief that Goldwater was a dependable anticommunist who was doing more than anyone else to ensure that the complacent politicians in Washington were constantly reminded of the threat to freedom posed by godless communism. "Let's get a real leader, and not a power politician in the White House," he concluded.[33] Goldwater's defeat by LBJ later that year did little to dispel Reagan's belief that only conservatism offered the solution to the country's problems. As he told the California Republican Assembly in March 1965, "Nothing has changed. What was true before the [presidential] campaign started is still true. And what was false then is still false. Even if the vote was unanimous."[34] This notion of eternal truths and the certainty with which conservatives held such beliefs would be echoed in Harry Callahan's supreme self-righteousness.

The Speech cleared the path for a run at the governor's mansion in California at a propitious moment for a conservative, particularly one with such a marketable personality as Reagan. Even though the state had three registered Democrats for every two Republicans, it also housed a large right-wing community, centered in southern California. Such people were incensed that Governor Edmund "Pat" Brown had embarked on what the historian Jonathan Bell calls "one of the biggest spending sprees in the history of any single state" in the wake of his 1962 election victory.[35] Brown's enlargement of the welfare state, bolstered on a national scale by Johnson's Great Society program, rested on an ideal that welfare was a right to all.[36] It massively increased welfare spending and threatened to end the relationship between welfare and moral standards. In bringing marginalized groups into the body politic, Brown hoped to nurture a natural Democratic majority in the state. His mistake was to underemphasize the level of resentment this policy wrought among voters who, prior to his election in 1959, had returned Republican governors to the state capital in every twentieth-century election bar 1938. The Republican opposition to big government and high taxes found receptive ears in the 1960s. The California Taxpayers Association was not alone in complaining that it was "downright dishonest and immoral to take money to pay it out to support indolence, idleness, illegitimacy and welfare cheats and chiselers."[37] And it was precisely these supposedly indolent, illegitimate chiselers who provided one of the mortal blows to Pat Brown prior to the 1966 gubernatorial election. The Watts rebellion had major implications for California politics. It suggested that the Brown administration's generous spending plan had failed to alleviate poverty and indicated that California's African American population resented the police presence in their neighborhoods. Predictably, the well-funded and well-organized Reagan campaign took advantage, making law and order one of its central themes. The candidate regularly expressed his outrage at Watts and the rising crime rate in the state, throwing in regular swipes at campus radicalism at the University of California–Berkeley campus for good measure. This was all part of Reagan's desire to create clear distinctions between him and California's liberals, in order to win the white electorate's vote. At the outset of his campaign in January 1966, he suggestively linked race with law and order, asserting that the streets of the nation's cities streets had become "jungle paths" at night. Although this was not an explicitly racist statement, the inclusion of a key racial signifier—the jungle—indicated exactly where Reagan's racial sympathies lay. It had the added advantage of being subtle enough to retain plausible deniability, as Reagan could say that he was merely citing the danger of walking through urban areas at night. Either way, the statement and the political morass from which it emerged contributed to his overwhelming victory in the gubernatorial election.[38]

Reagan's victory demonstrated that California's Democrats completely misread the political runes. The Democratic State Chairman Spencer Coate might have declared Reagan to be "radically wrong . . . wrong on welfare, wrong on industrial growth, wrong on unemployment, wrong on taxes, wrong on tidelands, wrong on crime, wrong on education, wrong on water," but the voters disagreed by a considerable margin, with white working-class Democrats proving to be a key group who swung to the Republicans. The California electorate then followed Reagan's victory by electing a Republican state assembly and senate in 1968.[39] These victories relied on Reagan's southern California voter base, as evidenced by the 1964 primary victory of Barry Goldwater over moderate Republican Nelson Rockefeller. Political analysts spotted similar trends in Reagan's victory over George Christopher in the 1966 gubernatorial primaries, and some suggested that Reagan's success was a portent of the end of the New Deal Order. Russell Kirk, one of the nation's prominent conservative voices, argued that the nation was shifting rightward at such a rate that President Johnson ought to be worried. Louis Harris predicted that 1966 could herald a new era in the American political system and was as significant an event as Al Smith's 1928 campaign had been for the Democrats. For the Republicans, as Garry Wills observes, Reagan was the major "light of hope for the future" thanks to his stern conservative message that was enveloped by a professional, sunny, and natural demeanor.[40]

These election victories, however, were not a harbinger of a period of far-right rule. Reagan was relatively centrist as California's governor, particularly prior to the 1968 state elections. In 1967 he signed the Therapeutic Abortion Act, which liberalized abortion law in the state, and with the support of Assembly Speaker and Democrat Jesse Unruh, launched a raft of tax increases. While he limited the number of people who were able to claim state benefits, he raised the level of support for those who qualified and in 1968 threw his support behind the Rumford Fair Housing Act, which had previously been the target of a concerted conservative campaign for its repeal. Amid a sequence of environmental protection measures, he approved various clean-air acts and expanded the state park system. Significantly, and despite earlier promises to cut $250 million in his first budget, he doubled state spending. There was to be no shrinking of California's public bureaucracy under Reagan's watch. He also signed into law the Mulford Act, which would penalize with a $1,000 fine or a year's imprisonment anyone who was caught on a public highway with a loaded gun in his or her possession.[41] This brought him into conflict with one of the San Francisco Bay Area's most notorious political groups, the Black Panther Party (BPP). Formed in Oakland in October 1966 and with a strong presence in the black communities on both sides of the Bay, the BPP considered the Mulford Act a direct provocation. BPP members were expected to be prepared to use firearms at any time and frequently monitored the activities of police offers while openly carrying their weapons, in full accordance with California law. On May 2, 1967, incensed at the impending passage of the bill, a group of around thirty Panthers headed for the capitol building in Sacramento, intending to deliver a statement outlining their opposition to the bill. After piling out of their cars in front of the capitol, the Panthers began loading their guns, attracting the attention of a television news crew that was filming Reagan giving a presentation to a group of schoolchildren (Reagan allegedly scuttled off at great speed when he caught sight of the guns). Upon entering the building, the BPP group became hopelessly lost before eventually locating and barging into the Assembly Room. They were then unceremoniously removed to a small room elsewhere in the building to deliver their statement, which they reprised on the capitol's steps soon afterward for the benefit of the media. The event catapulted the BPP into the national spotlight and prompted Reagan to comment on their display: "This is a ridiculous way to solve problems that have to be solved among people of goodwill. There's no reason why a citizen should be carrying loaded weapons on the street today."[42] It is not difficult to imagine Harry Callahan's response to the BPP's display of defiance.

Although based in Oakland, the BPP had a visible presence at the University of California campus in nearby Berkeley, which lay at the northern end of Telegraph Avenue, the thoroughfare that linked the two Bay Area cities. Berkeley was by then the heart of the Bay Area's radical community. It had been the epicenter of the Free Speech Movement that erupted in 1964 in opposition to the university's restrictions on freedom of speech. Within two years the university was a hotbed of political activism and cultural ferment, which led to Reagan's campaign guarantee to clean up Berkeley's mess, a promise that did his campaign no harm at all. Indeed, he later claimed that Berkeley excited his campaign audiences throughout the state like no other issue.[43] Among his other campaign pledges were the promise to form a commission, headed by John McCone, a former CIA chief who led the federal inquiry into the Watts rebellion, that would investigate the links between the campuses, communism, and promiscuity. As the historian Gerard De Groot observes, Reagan's promises often exceeded the powers granted to the governor but hit a nerve with the electorate, who "simply wanted a governor who would address their fears."[44] These fears Reagan sparked and stoked in his successful attempt to present Berkeley as the nation in microcosm. He argued that a group of cossetted, ungrateful, and worst of all, hirsute students had been given too much latitude for protest by a cabal of timid, liberal bureaucrats, thus reducing a formerly upstanding institution to the brink of anarchy. Moreover, the rabble's actions had been facilitated by the tax dollars of the working majority, just as the War on Poverty was supposedly rewarding inner-city rioters with job programs and state aid. This was an alluring, if simplistic, vision of the nation's present problems, posing the electorate a simple question: How far are you prepared to allow this permissiveness to spread? Reagan's correspondingly simple response was as attractive to California's voters. Soon after his election, Reagan effectively declared war on Berkeley, announcing his intention

to hike tuition fees while cutting state funding for the university, pro-
posals that opened up further schisms between him and the University
Regents, including University of California president Clark Kerr. Meanwhile, student groups responded by burning Reagan in effigy.[45] Within
three weeks of Reagan's inauguration, Kerr, a prominent Democrat, had
been removed from office, an event that made the front pages across the
nation and was interpreted by some as payback for Kerr's failure to deal
with campus dissent more robustly.[46] Reagan used his position on the
University of California Board of Regents to overthrow Kerr, a tactic that
seemed at odds with his campaign criticism of Pat Brown's supposed
willingness to use the Regents as a political tool. Yet Reagan's attitude
toward Berkeley was perhaps best summed up in a small but significant
action alleged to have taken place in January 1969. A group of students
had noticed that Reagan was present in University Hall and began chant-
ing "Fuck Reagan." The governor's response was brief, unmistakable, and
pointed: an upright middle finger.[47]

Although Kerr might have been sidelined, political dissent continued
to dominate Berkeley. Ron V. Dellums was elected to the city council
in 1967 in part because he was the only Democrat deemed acceptable
by both the radical and liberal wings of the local Democratic coalition.
Meanwhile, the city's liberals and conservatives agreed that a truce was
in needed to prevent the radical groups from overwhelming them.[48] In
April 1969, Berkeley activists annexed a dilapidated two-acre lot near the
campus. They set about beautifying what they dubbed "People's Park,"
but Reagan saw no public spirit in their actions. He was quoted asserting that the activists, just like the Soviets, could not and should not be
appeased. "If there has to be a bloodbath, then let's get it over with,"
he ominously declared, words that likely excited the more trigger-happy
members of the local police and armed forces.[49] Continued public protests about the seizure of the park compelled Reagan to order in the
National Guard to challenge demonstrators. Thirty people were shot and
one killed in the subsequent battle before Reagan declared martial law.
He even stooped to engage in heated personal debates with university
staff after claiming that a "noisy dissident minority" had brought the
university to its knees.[50] In his 1966 gubernatorial campaign, Reagan
asked the California electorate whether it would stand for these dissi-
dents bringing the university into disrepute and meet these "neurotic

vulgarities with vacillation and weakness."[51] After guardsmen had run amok spraying tear gas around the campus, he was unrepentant in his response to this very question: "There was no alternative. Whether that was a tactical mistake or not, once the dogs of war are unleashed, you must expect that things will happen and that people, being human, will make mistakes."[52] Yet these mistakes were not regrettable. Soon after the situation calmed, Reagan blamed the victims of police violence in terms that anticipated the attitude of Harry Callahan: "those relative few who are seeking to destroy us . . . must be dealt with firmly, swiftly, and with the justice they deserve."[53] In front of Orange County Republicans he was even tougher. James Rector, the student killed by police buckshot during the Berkeley disturbances, was actually killed "by the first college administrator who said some time ago it was all right to break the laws in the name of dissent," he said.[54] Clearly, the bureaucrats were as bad as the rebels, and both got what they deserved.

During the 1966 campaign Reagan had called on student protesters to "observe the rules or get out"—a threat he later repeated to their professors—and won national acclaim for his tough response to uprisings in the inner cities. His populist appeals to the "voice of those who built the University" were designed to isolate students and intellectuals while appealing to the average voter, painting the masses (and Reagan) as the outsiders determined to cleanse an Augean stable.[55] The mostly left-wing academics, he told the *Sacramento Bee*, treated California's nonacademic citizenry with contempt while indoctrinating their youthful charges with values inimical to American society. A leadership, morality, and decency gap had opened up as a consequence of their actions, and they needed to be brought to heel.[56] Such barely concealed anti-intellectualism proved popular with voters and constituted one of the first salvos in the culture wars that later erupted on the campuses and in popular politics. This popularity, the *San Diego Union* argued, was because Reagan offered a commonsense approach to politics: "Common sense may be 'simplistic,' as the liberals like to call it. But the people understand it."[57] Californians responded more positively to Reagan's simple primary campaign promise to slash the state budget by 10 percent than to his Republican rival George Christopher's nuanced appreciation of eliminating duplication and the natural wastage of employees. This was backed up by the appearance of a privately published campaign leaflet titled "America

Can Use the Good Common Sense of Ronald Reagan." In simple terms, as Pat Brown's adviser Fred Dutton suggested, Reagan presented issues in stark black and white.[58] Moreover, Reagan's actions in ordering confrontations with the radicals were proof that the governor did not make empty threats and that physical enforcement of law and order was at the top of the political agenda, even in the liberal Bay Area's stronghold. Simple answers were available, provided you had the guts, and perhaps the guns, needed to carry them out.

The historian Michelle Reeves argues that, for Reagan, "a simple morality overrode all of the inconsistencies in his ideas and policies."[59] Thus he could mesh his distaste for big government with his stern law-and-order policies, which relied on tough state action. He could continue to censure Berkeley's politically active students while promoting the "Creative Society," which encouraged civic activism and political engagement across the state and which Reeves defines as a philosophy that involved protecting the "sanctity of individual rights [alongside] an abhorrence of entrenched bureaucracy."[60] This latter facet of the campaign message gelled neatly with Reagan's image as a citizen-politician who, untarnished by involvement in California's political infighting, would restore decency, morality, and common sense to the state's politics. These would also become central character traits of Harry Callahan. Like Reagan, Callahan fashioned an outsider identity, had a strong moral code, and had a distaste for bureaucracy that bordered on the visceral. This attitude also aligned him with evangelical conservatives, who saw in liberal bureaucracy an amoral attempt to create change that should come from within the individual. To this important conservative constituency, state control infantilized individuals, robbing them of their sense of self, their individual purpose, and their agency. In September 1969 Billy Graham told his southern California flock that the United States had "built such a bureaucratic machine in this country and a monster, nobody can control it. It's feeding upon itself . . . [and] become like an octopus reaching into every home and life in America." Notably, he had been introduced to the Anaheim crowd by Governor Reagan.[61]

For conservatives like Reagan, events outside California offered further evidence of the collapse of law and order, decency, and morality. More than one hundred U.S. cities experienced violent unrest in the summer of 1967, leading many Americans to conclude that LBJ's Great Society, with its barrage of false promises leading to dashed hopes, unfulfilled dreams, and brooding resentment in the inner cities, was at the core of the problem rather than its solution. This was compounded by the conclusions of Johnson's Commission on Law Enforcement and Administration of Justice, which argued that social justice was a key solution to the crime problem and advocated shifting the focus of prison from punishment to the rehabilitation of offenders, notions that were anathema to genuine conservatives. The assassination of Martin Luther King in April 1968 fomented outrage, unrest, and rebellion in dozens of American cities and prompted the National Advisory Commission on Civil Disorders, established in response to the urban rebellions of the previous summer, to broaden its remit to investigate the causes and prevention of violence in a broader sense.[62] Robert Kennedy's assassination swiftly followed in June, which led to further questions from the American public about the value of the Great Society. That month, William F. Buckley's *National Review* fulminated that "liberal ideologues" had whipped up "orgiastic frenzies" in promoting "the permissive, responsibility-destroying, criminal-coddling, police-hounding, law-eroding ideology that has been a primary stimulus to law-breaking and violence." The United States, concluded the journal, was no longer a civilized nation.[63]

Buckley was doubtless appalled at events surrounding the Democratic National Convention in Chicago during August 1968. The presence of large numbers of protesters, police, and National Guardsmen rendered the city center more reminiscent of a Vietnam warzone than the Midwest. The National Mobilization Committee, an umbrella group of antiwar activists, planned to march on the convention center. The Yippies, a group of countercultural tricksters influenced by situationism and anarchism, hoped to actualize the "politics of ecstasy" while nominating a pig named Pigasus for president and distributing cigarettes doused in distilled cannabis oil. One of their founders, Abbie Hoffman, was arrested for breaking obscenity laws on account of having written "fuck" on his forehead.[64] Student leader Tom Hayden announced that the protesters were in Chicago "to vomit on the politics of joy."[65] Chants of "fuck you LBJ," "fuck the pigs," and "Ho, Ho, Ho Chi Minh" revealed exactly where the protesters' sympathies lay. Twelve thousand police, approximately six thousand National Guardsmen and seventy-five hundred army troops were called up to keep the convention from descending into the kind of violence that had plagued the nation's cities over the summer. It came as no surprise to see the media focusing on the result: demonstrators, many of whom chanted "the whole world is watching," were beaten and tear-gassed while protesters rampaged around the area, much of which was broadcast on national television. Mayor Richard J. Daley denounced the protesters as "a lawless, violent group of terrorists" who deserved to be shot. He was not alone in considering the demonstrators a threat to the very fabric of the American political system: polls revealed that the vast majority of Americans agreed with his repression of the protesters.[66] Viewing such terror on their television screens with such frequency rendered this a perfectly sensible and logical, if extreme, response, opening the way for police like Harry Callahan to shoot first and ask questions later.

As the historian Jonathan Schoenwald observes, the opening salvos of the 1968 election campaign revealed to the Republican Party that the political pendulum was decisively swinging rightward, facilitated by "each dollar spent on the Great Society, each student protest, and each publicized Black Power struggle."[67] Moreover, as the historian Michael Flamm argues, conservatives articulated a more cogent "moral voice" on the law-and-order issue than the liberals, appealing to many Americans' visceral response to public disorder.[68] In many respects, the election campaign revealed that the Democrats had become divorced from and failed to understand the fears and frustrations that animated many Americans. The Johnson administration's support for the civil rights movement had led many voters to associate the Democrats with increased levels of violence in the inner cities and threw white southern voters into the embrace of the Republican Party. George Wallace's presidential campaigns revealed that large numbers of white voters were incensed at the Democrats' liberal attitude toward black Americans and welfare, and the Johnson Democrats' failure to heed the warning of the 1964 Wallace campaign was a factor in their ousting. The conservative commentator Russell Kirk argued vehemently that liberal politicians simply had no answer to the problems of crime and urban violence.[69] Meanwhile, libertarian conservatives in southern California offered a further critique of centralized government and the liberal elite. This group wrested control of the state Republican Party in the 1960s and propelled Reagan into the governor's mansion before aiding Richard M. Nixon's run for the presidency. Their form of conservatism was staunchly in favor of law and order, advocated a policy of "benign neglect" toward African Americans, and was largely fearful of the chaos that appeared to reign in the inner cities.[70] During the early stages of the 1968 presidential campaign, Curt Furr, a white family man from North Carolina, wrote to his senator, Democrat Sam J. Ervin. This letter has become emblematic of the resentment of the so-called silent majority at the excesses of the 1960s and helps to explain why law and order and the urban crisis became major battlegrounds in the campaign. It also anticipates Harry Callahan's attitude toward the San Francisco that he policed:

> I'm sick of crime everywhere. I'm sick of riots. I'm sick of "poor" people demonstrations (black, white, red yellow, purple, green or any other color!). . . . I'm sick of the US Supreme Court ruling for the good of the very small part rather than the whole of our society. . . . I'm sick of hippies, LSD, drugs, and all the promotion the news media give them. . . . But most of all, I'm sick of constantly being kicked in the teeth for staying home, minding my own business, working steadily, paying my bills and taxes . . . and footing the bill for all the minuses mentioned herein.[71]

The Republican Party played on these sentiments and exploited the footage from the Democrats' Chicago convention in a series of campaign advertisements that juxtaposed stills of the Democratic candidate Hubert Humphrey with violence, disorder, and mayhem on the streets. In one titled "Failure," a voice-over positioned law and order at the core of the election campaign by asking rhetorically, "How can a Party that can't keep order in its own backyard hope to keep order in our fifty states?"[72] A further ad, titled "Woman," highlighted urban crime as its central issue. As a middle-aged woman walks a street at night, a male voice-over intones violent crime statistics: a robbery every two and a half minutes, a mugging every six minutes, a murder every forty-three minutes—"and it will get worse unless we take the offensive," it promised. Like the other ads, it concluded in ominous fashion: "Vote like your whole world depended on it."[73] In September, Nixon informed the nation's radio listeners that "something has gone terribly wrong in America" and reminded them that he had issued a "program for freedom from fear."[74] For Wallace, running as an independent, the solution to all this was simple: allow the police to run the country without interference. There would be no riots in Wallace's police state, not least because he promised to bring Alabama law to the nation: "First one of 'em [rioters] to pick up a brick gets a bullet in the brain," he promised. "And then you walk over to the next one and say, 'All right, pick up a brick. We just want to see you pick up one of them bricks, now!'"[75]

Nixon's election, however, did not end the turmoil. The National Commission on the Causes and Prevention of Violence published its findings in June 1969, reporting that "today's civil commotion" was "so disturbing" that it threatened to destabilize all of the "old certitudes" of the nation.[76] In August 1969, news of brutal murders in Los Angeles spread around the nation. Charles Manson and his self-styled "family" were rounded up by the end of the year, but the terror and shock that followed in their wake lingered. Campus disturbances remained frequent occurrences, reaching their nadir in May 1970 when police killed two students at Jackson State University and National Guardsmen shot four students dead at Kent State University. All of the dead had been protesting the war in Vietnam. Construction workers in New York City exacted their own retribution on antiwar protesters on May 8 in the so-called Hard Hat Riot, injuring some seventy people in the process. Meanwhile, violent crime continued to rise. On February 16, 1970, a bomb exploded in a city police department station in the Upper Haight neighborhood of San Francisco. Rumored to be the work of the Weather Underground, a splinter group from Students for a Democratic Society, the bomb killed police Sergeant Brian McDonnell and injured eight other officers. Less than a month later, a nail bomb exploded prematurely in Greenwich Village, New York City, killing three Weather Underground activists. The Weathermen, as they were colloquially known, had previously achieved notoriety for their self-styled "Days of Rage" in October 1969, when over fifty police officers were hospitalized by an organized mob. Their threat to foment revolution in "Amerika" was largely rhetorical, but even so, to many Americans it seemed as though the hordes were on the verge of storming the battlements and letting violent anarchy loose on the streets.[77] As Vice President Spiro Agnew claimed, this "criminal left is interested [only] in power. It is not interested in promoting the renewal and reforms that make democracy work; it is interested in promoting those collisions and conflicts that tear democracy apart."[78]

This historical context is vital for an understanding of the relationship between *Dirty Harry* and the United States of the late 1960s and early 1970s. It is not difficult to imagine Callahan's withering response to the many instances of urban unrest that occurred in the late 1960s. He was a symbol of the silent majority who were too busy working on the country's problems to be out protesting on the streets. He was the ideal protector of the vulnerable perambulators in Reagan's jungle paths and would have ensured the subduing of the Black Panther Party and the Berkeley radicals. He provided the perfect physical manifestation of Curt Furr's frustration and would have reassured the Republican Party's "Woman" that the streets would be safe. Moreover, his mere existence would have prevented the need for George Wallace's promise to let loose the dogs of war on the rioters. Ultimately, as screenwriter John Milius later pointed out, for credulous voters watching this mayhem on television screens and in their city centers, "society *needs* Dirty Harry."[79]

The Bay Area Context

On a different historical-geographical level, *Dirty Harry*'s San Francisco setting is crucial for an understanding of the film and encourages us to reconsider the city as a key location in the political struggle between liberals and conservatives in the late 1960s and early 1970s. Callahan's relationship with the city's law-enforcement hierarchy impedes his pursuit of the Scorpio Killer. *Dirty Harry* thus indicts San Francisco's liberal administration for its failure to deal with the countercultural figure of Scorpio and the world from which he emerges. Through this, the film cites the recent political history of San Francisco, and particularly the corporate liberalism of the John Shelley and Joseph Alioto mayoral administrations (respectively, 1964–68 and 1968–76). San Francisco consequently becomes a scene of confrontation between liberals (the local power structure), conservatives (Callahan), and the counterculture (Scorpio). *Dirty Harry* cites and references the city's politics and culture in such a way as to render the city another character in the film, one that Callahan is set on reconstructing in his own image.[80]

The links between *Dirty Harry* and San Francisco's history are stronger than even the filmmakers might have been aware. As many writers acknowledge, Callahan's vigilantism is a key element of the film, yet only

J. Hoberman's discussion of *Dirty Harry* makes even fleeting reference to San Francisco's long tradition of vigilante action.[81] A short-lived Committee of Vigilance was established by local residents in 1851 and revived in 1856. This was the largest vigilante movement in American history, and in defiance of the local authorities it sought to police the city itself. In its attempt to control crime in the city it executed eight men and precipitated the death of another, who committed suicide while in custody. For the historian Philip Ethington, the Committee expressed San Franciscans' bitterness at the seeming erosion of their liberties by "an organized despotism" that corrupted local justice and local elections, threatened their rights to property, and usurped local elected offices.[82] Faint echoes of their republicanism are evinced in Callahan's disgust with the stifling bureaucracy of the San Francisco liberal administration. He shares with the vigilantes a reliance on Old West codes such as the power of the individual and the doctrine of "no duty to retreat," in which an individual retains the right to stand her or his ground and kill in self-defense when faced by a potentially violent assailant. Vigilantism's deep roots in the nineteenth-century American West demand that we position *Dirty Harry* within the Western cinematic tradition, albeit in an urbanized form. Yet whereas a John Fordian hero such as Rance Stoddard in *The Man Who Shot Liberty Valance* (Ford, 1962) would likely have represented and maybe even accepted the values of the bureaucracy in his quest to bring civilization to the frontier, Callahan rejects both the city authorities and the lawless individual they pursue, in true vigilante style. As a lone hero, Callahan abides by the notion that the individual holds ultimate power over his surroundings. His respect for victims' specific rights overrides the law's protection of the general rights of all individuals.[83]

While nineteenth-century vigilantism is a general reference point for the film, *Dirty Harry* is most clearly rooted in San Francisco's recent history, especially its position as the spiritual home of the 1960s counterculture. From Municipal Judge Clayton Horn's 1957 declaration that Allen Ginsberg's *Howl* was not obscene to the January 14, 1967, Human Be-In at Golden Gate Park, San Francisco seemed to be at or near major events in the coalescing of one of the most important youth movements of the era. Horn's decision enabled the San Francisco–based publisher City Lights Press to continue to distribute the printed version of

Ginsberg's poem, to the outrage of many conservative commentators.[84] A few years later the Free Speech Movement flared in nearby Berkeley when University of California authorities banned students from distributing political literature on campus. One of the participating students, Mario Savio, perceptively highlighted the common enemy that united left- and right-wing groups at Berkeley—"depersonalized, unresponsive bureaucracy."[85]

The Human Be-In brought the hippie subculture to the attention of the nation.[86] Hoping to initiate a "new epoch" in human history, the organizers promised "flags, [Allen] Ginsberg, flutes, [Dick] Gregory, heads, [Timothy] Leary, families, lovers, [Gary] Snyder, children, heroes, animals, [and] cymbals" at a gathering that would "shower the country with waves of ecstasy and purification."[87] Resplendent in white pajamas, flowers, and beads, Ginsberg purified the ground from demons alongside Snyder before a crowd of roughly twenty thousand gathered to listen to the speakers and music performed by local bands including Jefferson Airplane and the Grateful Dead. Unafraid of any police reprisals, the members of the gathering generally expressed themselves in any way they saw fit. Adults and children wandered around the park in blissful states, imbibing the heady brew of peace, love, and the sense that they were creating an alternative society. The Diggers, an anarchist group, who like the Yippies found inspiration in situationism, handed out free food to anyone who requested. The congregation even cleared up the litter at the event's conclusion.[88]

The widespread publicity that followed such shenanigans compelled thousands of young people to flock to San Francisco mid-decade to partake in the city's libertarian atmosphere, despite the attempts by the city's chief of police, Tom Cahill, to warn off newcomers. Yet the libertarian atmosphere that pulsated from the Haight attracted more than just idealistic and peaceful hippies. The presence of thousands of young people who were perhaps more interested in taking drugs than finding jobs was almost inevitably going to attract less-principled sorts. By mid-1967 a reported two hundred runaways were being picked up by the authorities every month. The *San Francisco Chronicle* was moved enough by this development to begin a regular series titled "Runaway Girls: Life with the Hippies," which told the story of a fifteen-year-old girl who had abandoned suburbia for San Francisco's bohemia. Fueled in part by the drug culture, violence and criminality rose, putting extra strain on the city's authorities. Haight-Ashbury became colonized by starving drug addicts and riven by murders related to the drug trade.[89] This was accompanied by a flagrant disregard for traditional morality among some hippies. As the *Berkeley Barb*, the infamous countercultural magazine from across the bay declared, "We defy law and order with our bricks bottles garbage long hair filth obscenity drugs games guns bikes fire fun & fucking—the future of our struggle is the future of crime in the streets."[90] Ordinary San Franciscans did not find these words comforting, and increasingly considered this orgy of long hair, sex, drugs, anger, violence, rock and roll, and general misbehavior to be an apocalyptic threat that was fully enmeshed in the urban crisis. Cahill, meanwhile, threatened the new-comers with arrest and even injury, declaring with a drop of snide humor that "law, order, and health regulations must prevail." Cahill's vision of policing was firmly rooted in San Francisco's frontier past, and he re-garded the city's youth culture as a potential threat to law, order, sanita-tion, and the police's traditional dominance over the city. "The swift kick in the buttocks by the old Irish policeman in the old days immediately becomes a violation of civil rights today," he lamented.[91] Cahill demon-strates that the city was far from united in its embrace of the hippie sub-culture. More importantly, however, he reveals that the SFPD strained at the leash of liberal law enforcement policy, suggesting that a renegade cop like Harry Callahan was a character with deep roots in the police department's history.

The rock festival organized by the Rolling Stones at the nearby Al-tamont Speedway on December 6, 1969, was the nadir of the Bay Area counterculture. According to the writer Stanley Booth, the Rolling Stones faced severe criticism during their 1969 tour that ticket prices were too high. Their response was to organize a free festival at which the band would perform.[92] Conceived as a West Coast rejoinder to Wood-stock, the festival was to take place in San Francisco's Golden Gate Park. As Stanley Goldstein, an observer working on a documentary film of the event, noted, "In the aftermath of Woodstock, there was a general euphoria—more than a feeling—the sure knowledge that we, the rock & roll, be-in, wear a flower in your hair community had triumphed and could, in anarchy, find peace, and overcome with love any who had an in-terest in violence."[93] Organizational failures led to the show being moved to Altamont, roughly fifty miles east of San Francisco, twenty-four hours before it was due to begin. Local chapters of the Hells Angels motorcycle club were given a $500 case of beer in return for providing an "Honor Guard" at the track. A motley crew of volunteers also provided assistance, some of whom were clearly suffering the effects of overindulgence in various illicit substances. Meanwhile, a vast crowd clamored to get close to the music, which at various points resulted in clashes between audience members and the Hells Angels, who had a space reserved for them close to the stage. Various observers noted that drugs were freely available. Violence regularly interrupted the procession of support acts for the Rolling Stones, events that escalated as the day wore on, culminating in the death of Meredith Hunter, who was killed by a Hells Angel during the Stones' performance of "Under My Thumb."[94] The whole event, according to Rolling Stones guitarist Mick Taylor was, "just completely barbaric."[95] Altamont demonstrated that talk of a peace-and-love generation was merely hyperbolic and that the counterculture's promise of individual freedom, joy, and transcendence attracted not just nonviolent dreamers but others who were less inclined toward beatitudes.

By 1970, San Francisco was more closely associated with the counterculture than any other American city. It was also among the most ethnically diverse in the country.[96] While hippies congregated in Haight-Ashbury, other areas of the city also experienced demographic shifts. A large African American population filled the Fillmore, Hunters Point, and Oceanview districts, and young homosexual men were gradually cementing their place in the previously Irish working-class Castro district. In 1964 the Society for Individual Rights was founded by gay activists in San Francisco who wished to develop a more active form of agitation and support for and by the gay community which included becoming publicly involved in city electoral campaigns. As Jonathan Bell notes, by the mid-1960s "it was clear that gay rights activists [in San Francisco] were developing into an increasingly organized interest group that could . . . push for political recognition in city politics."[97] The huge demographic changes in the city during the 1960s contributed to the contemporaneous transformation of its political culture. By 1964 the city's politics were firmly located on the left of the American and Californian political spectrum. The election of John Shelley as mayor in November 1963 signaled the end of more than fifty years of Republican mayors and ushered in a period of Democratic control of the mayor's office.[98] The regularity with which the city elected Democrats during the 1960s rendered it a perfect representation of everything opposed by the American right: "militant workers, race-mixing, beatniks, hippies, free love, drugs, homosexuals, and bleeding-heart liberals."[99] Areas such as Hunters Point, Chinatown, the Western Addition, and the Mission District attracted Great Society programs, in part because of the assumed link between poverty and race in American cities; meanwhile, activists were pushing for Great Society funds to be awarded to the Tenderloin, which had a large gay population.[100] Shelley's successor, the nonpartisan Democrat Joseph Alioto, was able to work alongside moderate Republicans in the city, although he maintained policies that were friendly to San Francisco's African American population. San Francisco historian David Talbot identifies April 5, 1968, as one of Alioto's greatest moments. In the wake of the assassination of Martin Luther King, Alioto immediately announced that a memorial service would be held outside city hall. With police snipers observing, Alioto sat alongside religious leaders, local activists, and a group of four armed students who may have been moved more by Dr. King's death than by his commitment to nonviolence. The service ended with a mass rendition of the civil rights anthem "We Shall Overcome." San Francisco was one of the few major cities in the United States not to suffer another round of urban violence that evening, which is perhaps testament to Alioto's sensitivity. As demonstrated by the presence of the snipers, however, Alioto was no soft touch. He was quite prepared to allow the SFPD tactical squad to use violent tactics to quell disturbances during the 1968–69 student strike at San Francisco State College and on the occasional incursion into the Haight.[101]

The Alioto administration presided over a period of unprecedented growth for the city, during which construction began on the Transamerica Pyramid and the Embarcadero Center.[102] During the 1950s Alioto had been chair of the San Francisco Redevelopment Agency, which planned to regenerate downtown San Francisco through land acquisition and other deals that would allow developers to expand the city's corporate and commercial zone. He made his backing for further regeneration clear during his election campaign, and found support among numerous local businesspeople who stood to benefit from the removal of downtown's poorer residents and the rebuilding of key areas in the city center, including the Market District, Chinatown, and the Tender-loin. This policy enabled Alioto to attract the labor vote through pledging to create construction jobs as part of this regeneration program. Urban regeneration was a central theme of his mayoral administration, with of-fice blocks, skyscrapers, and civic centers gradually replacing older build-ings as San Francisco's center was modernized and downtown's poorer residents removed to other areas. Although the public was not united behind this policy, Alioto's form of bureaucratic liberalism paved the way for San Francisco's transformation in the 1970s, particularly in terms of the city's built environment.[103]

As John H. Mollenkopf highlights, the 1960s was characterized by a "class-based struggle over the nature of urban development." The quest of modernizing mayors such as Alioto had a near-paradoxical outcome. "By doing its part to reinforce the command and control functions of the central city," Mollenkopf argues, "the pro-growth coalition imposed tremendous costs on central city residents. Growth generally and state intervention specifically displaced stable communities, exacerbated ra-cial tensions, imposed heavy tax on those least able to pay, and prolifer-ated burdens like commuting time, congestion, and pollution."[104] Conse-quently, even regeneration contributed to the sense that an urban crisis was in process. By 1970, San Francisco's urban population was over 20 percent African American, which rose to 25 percent in the subsequent decade. Although white flight was not as widespread as in many other American cities, some thirteen thousand white students were removed from urban schools in San Francisco between 1968 and 1972, illustrating that the fears exploited by Reagan in the 1966 election and the increas-ing tax burden exerted an influence on the city's demography. So even though San Francisco, as Richard Walker notes, had an idiosyncratic class identity, with a large middle class and average wages higher than the national norm, it was not wholly insulated from the problems that many American cities faced as their white populations fled to the sub-urbs and took their tax dollars with them.[105]

The final and arguably most disturbing thread of San Francisco history touched on by *Dirty Harry* involves events surrounding the Zodiac Killer. Robert Graysmith, the *San Francisco Chronicle* cartoonist who ended up devoting more than a decade of his life to solving the Zodiac case, called *Dirty Harry* the best of the movies based on or related to the case.[106]

Between 1968 and the time of *Dirty Harry*'s release, the serial killer killed five people in the San Francisco area, crimes that remained unsolved more than forty years later. That the murders were committed in Vallejo, Lake Berryessa near Napa, and San Francisco meant that each came under the jurisdiction of a different police department. Each wished to solve its own case, and interdepartmental competition resulted in a lack of coordination over information, sources, and manpower. The bureaucratic gymnastics that the SFPD investigating officers Dave Toschi and Bill Anderson were forced to perform did little to aid their investigation; that Callahan dispensed with the Scorpio Killer through other means must have rankled with the real cops. The *Dirty Harry* screenplay played on the fears that emerged from the reality of living in a city that was threatened by a serial killer. The film director and Marin County native David Fincher recalls his father blithely informing him that the Zodiac Killer intended "to take a high-powered rifle and shoot out the tires of a school bus, and then shoot the children as they come off the bus," a somewhat terrifying thought for a seven-year-old to comprehend and one that is eerily reminiscent of Scorpio's final atrocity in *Dirty Harry*.[107] The Zodiac Killer himself informed the characterization of Scorpio, *Dirty Harry*'s major villain. In the film, the tensions between San Francisco's counterculture, its liberal establishment, and the emerging national conservative consensus erupt through this figure. Most obviously, Scorpio's very name references the Zodiac, but the similarities run deeper. Both killers seemed to select random victims, including schoolchildren. Both seemed to delight in sending messages to the police boasting of their crimes, and even more unsettlingly, appeared to relish their criminality, as evidenced in the Zodiac Killer's letters and Scorpio's manic laughter at various points in the film.[108] Robert Graysmith notes that Scorpio's letters to the city authorities are "exact cop[ies]" of the Zodiac's printing in the letters that the real killer sent to the *San Francisco Chronicle*.[109] These letters reveal the Zodiac's adept use of the local media. By insisting that further murders would be committed unless the letters were published, the Zodiac ensured maximum publicity for and public concern about his crimes. Scorpio similarly uses the media to vilify Harry Callahan and mock the city's authorities to a television news reporter, and he communicates with the police via advertisements in the *San Francisco Chronicle*.[110] Scorpio is thus not merely a fictional construct but a reflection of the SFPD's failure to apprehend a serial murderer and an articulation of very real fears about criminals in the San Francisco region. This refraction of San Francisco's history adds to the film's verisimilitude, heightening its tension and intensifying the power of its political message.

*   *   *

This was the context in which *Dirty Harry* was filmed. Like Nixon, Reagan, and the Republicans, the film cast a critical eye over the previous decade's missteps and mistakes, both from a national and a local perspective. Siegel generally rejected any insistence that he had made a conservative film, encouraging observers to focus on his well-known liberalism and the lack of ideological discussions between him and Eastwood on-set as evidence.[111] Yet he also commented that he was upset that popular films of the time failed to "give credit" to the police for protecting ordinary citizens.[112] As he pointed out in his autobiography: "When you're in trouble, possibly being mugged, raped, robbed, threatened . . . who do you call for help? . . . Without hesitation, all members of the police department will risk their lives trying to save yours."[113] These words are as close to an ideological interpretation of the film that Siegel ever offered. While he claimed that Callahan was merely rejecting "the stupidity of a system of administration, marked by officialdom and red tape," he clearly sympathized with Callahan's position vis-à-vis crime and policing.[114]

Irrespective of such slightly confused protestations, it remains entirely possible that this liberal filmmaker could make a film with conservative political under- (or over-)tones. Moreover, authorial intention is not necessarily the most important factor when assessing ideological messages contained within cultural productions. Siegel and the film's scriptwriters might not have intended the film to be such a conservative commentary on the failures of liberalism and the collapse of the 1960s dream, but knowledge of the many historical, political, and social currents that swirled around *Dirty Harry* during its gestation renders it almost impossible to isolate the film from this environment. Far from merely reflecting important contemporary issues, *Dirty Harry* made an important contribution to the law-and-order debate by presenting liberal policies as a major cause of urban unrest and in proposing tough policing and reduced bureaucracy (both of which are central conservative tenets) as the solution. Furthermore, its frustration with San Francisco's liberals echoed the anti-liberal rhetoric of both California conservatives like Reagan and national figures like Nixon. While Harry Callahan himself is a thoroughly San Francisco character, as revealed for example by his echoing of the city's Committee of Vigilance, the methods through which the film touched on national debates, including law-and-order policies, the rise of bureaucracy, and urban change, indicates that *Dirty Harry* is much more than simply a film based in San Francisco.

Dirty Harry

San Francisco in the Nixon Era

> There are people who line themselves up with the political
> overtones of the film [*Dirty Harry*]. But there are none really.
> Those people are crazy.
>
> **Clint Eastwood, 1976**

> The people who call it a fascist film don't know what they're
> talking about. . . . [T]here's nothing like that in there. The
> guy was just a man who fought bureaucracy and a certain
> established kind of thing. Just because he did things a little
> unorthodox—that's the only way he knew how to handle
> it. He had so many hours to solve the case and as far as he
> was concerned, he was more interested in the victim than
> the law.
>
> **Clint Eastwood, 1976**

> I can't understand why, when a film is made purely for enter-
> tainment, it should be criticized on a political basis.
>
> **Don Siegel on *Dirty Harry*, 1993**

Dirty Harry is entrenched in urban San Francisco. The film opens with
a close-up of a memorial to dead San Francisco police officers that is
embedded in the walls of the city's Hall of Justice, a shot that serves
to confirm numerous aspects of the film's meaning. Most obviously, it
sets the film's location. It also suggests that *Dirty Harry* holds a verisimilitude which sets it apart from many typical detective films. Viewers

are therefore encouraged to overlook the fictionality of the film and instead approach it as a realistic representation of San Francisco policing. As important, the appearance of the memorial during the introduction establishes the film's ideological stance. By reverently citing a tribute to fallen policemen, the opening shot indicates an acceptance that these public servants died as heroes, protecting the city from crime. It thus suggests that the film is dedicated to and thus a supporter of these same police officers, irrespective of their behavior.[1] The film's exposure of the violent, extralegal, and occasionally unconstitutional actions of a police officer must consequently be approached within this framing concept— the police officer is always right, even if he is wrong.

This chapter pays particular attention to the film's representation of numerous key themes. It focuses on aesthetics and a "social construction" reading of its text and subtexts. The film's impressionistic use of San Francisco's geography firmly locates the film in the city and begs consideration of the meaning of San Francisco within the context of the film's diegetic world. Its representation of the counterculture, race, gender, and sexuality must be approached within the context of recent San Francisco and national history, as outlined in chapter 2. The "real" San Francisco also intrudes on the film's depiction of the relationship between the city's liberal elite, Harry Callahan, and the villain, Scorpio. In particular, the film's suggestion that criminality is a consequence of the failures of 1960s liberalism, which becomes explicit in its exploration of the methods used by criminals to manipulate legislation designed to protect their rights as American citizens, demands serious consideration within the San Francisco context. Although much of this discussion points to the political conservatism of the film, its numerous ambiguous messages—including its representation of the relationship between means and ends, and the film's final image of Callahan tossing his police badge in an echo of Will Kane (Gary Cooper) in *High Noon* (Zinnemann, 1952)—suggest that *Dirty Harry* is far more complex than simple right-wing propaganda.

Following its opening tribute, *Dirty Harry* cuts to a close-up of Scorpio peering through the rangefinder of a silenced rifle. It is a clear blue day, and the wind ruffles Scorpio's long hair. He sits on the roof of the Bank of America Center, San Francisco's tallest skyscraper, methodically tracking a woman swimming in the rooftop pool of the nearby Holiday Inn. His single shot hits its target in the back. This killing is only made possible by the city's Alioto-led regeneration: Scorpio's vantage point was completed in 1969 and was an opulent display of the Bank of America's power in the city and beyond; the slightly more modest Holiday Inn was completed soon after.[2] Immediately, then, the viewer's attention is drawn to the role of the city's architecture in facilitating criminality.

Harry Callahan first appears investigating the woman's death. After inspecting the body, he instinctively heads for the Bank of America rooftop. The camera tracks Callahan as he moves through the bowels of the skyscraper to reach the roof, the first of the film's ambiguous visual metaphors. The scene signals Callahan's willingness to enter the depths of a case, to engage with the inner workings of its underbelly in order to get the job done. It also suggests that Callahan is at once part of the city's architecture and subjected to its structures, rendering San Francisco an active agent in the film. This latter metaphor is continued as Callahan reaches the roof. Rather than heading straight for the point at which the Holiday Inn may be seen, Callahan prowls around the edge, surveying his domain. As the camera pans around the roof, San Francisco's urban sprawl is laid out below, from its southern tip toward San Francisco International Airport through the predominantly African American neighborhood of Hunters Point and the Central Waterfront on the eastern side of the city, the Bay Bridge, and finally the Kearney Street Holiday Inn in the city's financial district on San Francisco's northeast shoulder (see fig. 1). In direct contrast to the film's tightly framed first image of the murderer Scorpio, the camera places Callahan in the center of the city, suggesting by his height that he is the master of this territory, but also indicating by the geographic spread of the city that much of it escapes his control. This method also establishes Callahan's feeling of responsibility as he watches over "his" city, a recurring theme of the film, and introduces the city itself as a character in the film. The Golden Gate Bridge, arguably San Francisco's most iconic location, becomes visible only in the far distance, at the very end of Callahan's perambulation, encouraging the audience to move beyond the clichéd popular image of the city to appreciate the reality that Callahan faces. Until this point in the film, not a word has been spoken. Callahan's discovery of a ransom note attached to a television aerial on the roof breaks this verbal silence when the detective utters the single word: "Jesus."[3] Callahan's appeal to a higher authority reveals another of the film's themes: the role of religion in the modern city.

Dirty Harry's political stance is made clearest in Callahan's interaction with the local power structure. Callahan is forced to contend with an increasingly bureaucratized police force and a cowardly liberal elite. More concerned with protecting their own image and upholding liberal shibboleths such as nonviolence, good sportsmanship, trust, and reasonableness, the power brokers serve only to enable Scorpio to continue his murderous spree while frustrating and imprisoning Callahan at every turn. Yet when faced with the realities of policing on the street, the liberals are forced to defer to the logic of Callahan's stance. In many respects, Callahan echoes Ronald Reagan in working hard in service of the public while maintaining a highly skeptical public attitude toward, and often working to undermine, the public institutions that he represents. He meets with the mayor in the latter's salubrious wood-paneled office. Shot in the actual San Francisco mayor's office, this space stands in vivid contrast to the grimy streets Callahan patrols and the shabby offices that he and his colleagues occupy.[4] Scorpio's ransom note has been copied and projected onto a screen, from which the mayor reads. Upon discovering that Scorpio threatens to kill a "nigger," the mayor blanches and refuses to utter the racist epithet before requesting a written report from Callahan: a needlessly bureaucratic imposition on Callahan's policing methods and limited time. Callahan's withering retort serves to encourage audience sympathy with his position while providing a glimpse into the film's underlying political sensibilities. That Callahan has spent the last forty-five minutes "sitting on [his] ass in [the] outer office" rather than compiling a suitable report reveals the gulf between him and the bureaucracy. After mildly chastising Callahan, his superior officers then play to the mayor's technocratic impulses by revealing that they are using computer files to target possible suspects born under the zodiac sign of Scorpio and have set up rooftop surveillance with the city's police helicopter unit, dismissing Callahan's traditional methods of analyzing ballistics and investigating known criminals (see fig. 2).

The mayor is convinced by the discussion that Scorpio's ransom should be paid, in order to obtain some breathing space for the city. Demonstrating his identity as a man of action, Callahan rejects this plan and offers instead to meet with the "son-of-a-bitch," but he is rebuffed by a superior officer who argues that the last thing the police need in this situation is a "bloodbath." As Callahan leaves, the mayor warns him that he does not want a repeat of the trouble witnessed in the Fillmore district during the previous year. "Well, when an adult male is chasing a female with intent to commit rape, I shoot the bastard," replies Callahan. When asked how he established intent, he comments, "When a naked man is chasing a woman through an alley with a butcher's knife and a hard-on, I figure he isn't out collecting for the Red Cross." The mayor ponders this for a moment before conceding that approaching the world in such Manichaean terms is no bad thing, muttering to himself, "I think he's got a point." Here, viewers see *Dirty Harry's* articulation of a "commonsense" approach to crime receive its first and potentially most subtle indication. Callahan's instinct is correct, despite the likelihood that he shot the adult male in the back without first announcing his presence in less deadly terms. Its location—the Fillmore, which was one of the local counterculture's hangouts—is also significant, denoting Callahan's rejection of the sexual politics of the hippies and their friends. The sequence suggests that, had Callahan not shot first and asked questions later, a rape would have occurred. Moreover, the mayor's short consideration of Callahan's explanation suggests that his own instincts are similar, that his bureaucratic mind would have come to the wrong conclusion and allowed the crime to take place. In many ways this reflects the campaign slogan of 1964 Republican presidential nominee Barry Goldwater—"In your heart you know he's right"—while also playing on Eastwood's persona as the Man with No Name, who rarely uses words when a gunshot will suffice.[5]

Perhaps the film's most famous scene follows. Callahan is taking his regular lunch at his regular diner, on the same block as a cinema that is showing *Play Misty for Me*, Eastwood's own directorial debut. After asking the owner to call the police department to inform them of an impending bank robbery across the street, he settles back to enjoy his hot dog and wait for the "cavalry" to arrive. Unfortunately, Callahan's intention to enjoy a front-seat view of a live-action modern-day Western is thwarted by the bank's alarm. A brief shootout follows in which Callahan is wounded in the leg, two criminals are killed, and a third is wounded. Faced by a triumphant Callahan, the robber attempts to reach for his shotgun, an action that prompts Callahan to aim his Magnum and utter the film's most indelible line: "I know what you're thinking: 'Did he fire six shots or only five?' Well, to tell you the truth, in all this excitement I kind of lost track myself. But being as this is a .44 Magnum, the most powerful handgun in the world, and would blow your head clean off, you've got to ask yourself one question: 'Do I feel lucky?' Well, do ya, punk?" The robber backs down, but after Callahan turns to leave, he pleads "I gots to know," prompting Callahan to point his gun, cock the hammer, and pull the trigger on the increasingly traumatized robber. As the robber realizes that the gun is empty, Callahan smirks to indicate his enjoyment of this short scene of mental torture—"playful interaction" in Eastwood's later words—that foreshadows both the film's concluding scene and Scorpio's torture.[6] Here Callahan presents the audience with a vicarious thrill. As Richard Slotkin suggests, hero-leaders are delegated the responsibility to act "on our behalf, to achieve things that are beyond us."[7] They represent an idealized version of ourselves, unfettered by our commitments to home, family, mortgage, job, and social niceties. Callahan appears to be the quintessence of cool, responding to mayhem calmly and nonchalantly, even concluding the incident with style. The film does not reveal what happens following this shootout, leaving viewers to assume that Callahan's actions are an appropriate and proportionate response to the robbery. Moreover, it sets up Callahan as a true antihero who does what we dare not do, while offering a sly link to Alabama governor George Wallace's threat to rioters: "We just want to see you pick up one of them bricks, now!"[8]

Siegel argued that Callahan behaved this way because the man was a bank robber, not because he was black.[9] Yet the casting of African Americans as the robbers—rather than as other incidental characters—suggests otherwise. For Siegel, Callahan's lack of racism is clarified by the subsequent scene, in which Callahan's wound is treated by an African American intern. The intern tells Callahan that "we Potrero Hill boys" have to stick together, indicating that they grew up in the same neighborhood. Potrero Hill traditionally attracted immigrants, and most pertinently for *Dirty Harry*, a wave of African Americans in the 1940s; Callahan's upbringing here suggests that he has lived among San Francisco's African American population for some time, the implication being that his background is evidence that he is no racist.[10] Whether this is enough to absolve him is another matter. Placed side-by-side, these scenes suggest that a subtle form of racism pervades the film. Callahan's interactions with whites, such as his relationship with the mayor and the diner owner, imply that he has an affinity with working-class males and a relatively hostile attitude toward middle-class men and figures of authority, a position that is reinforced as the film progresses. Yet his interactions with African Americans reveal a reverse polarity. His relationship with the doctor is mediated by the doctor's status as a middle-class professional. The doctor's roots in Potrero Hill, an integrated area of the city that did not become an African American ghetto as did the Western Addition or Hunters Point, must be juxtaposed with the presumed roots of the robbers, whose dress and criminality suggest that they hail from one of San Francisco's ghettos. As a "good Negro," the doctor has proved his ability to fit in with white expectations, to advance in the system rather than challenge it, and (crucially) to serve white people. Thus by tending to Callahan, his acceptability is juxtaposed with the "bad Negroes" who commit robbery and antagonize him while also supposedly benefiting from the munificence of the Great Society.[11] Callahan deals with the first in friendly terms, but with the second through brute force, demonstrating that African American–led urban unrest deserves only violent suppression.

The film then returns to plot development, although its underlying ideological stance remains detectable. Back at the office, a patched-up Callahan is upbraided by a lieutenant, not for his reckless endangering of human life, but for having long hair. Callahan responds by declaring that he'll get a haircut when he next gets some free time. The suggestion that he put in for overtime to cover the extra hours that he puts into police work is given short shrift. In the hospital, Callahan suggests that he has little disposable income: when the intern offers to cut his trousers, Callahan declines: "at $29.50, let it hurt." In the office, however, he refuses to countenance filing for overtime, thus confirming his dedication to his job. Police work, the film therefore suggests, is Callahan's calling, and the sacrifices he makes are in stark contrast to the lethargy, cynicism, and incompetence that surrounds him. The lieutenant then announces that Callahan is to be paired with a new partner, Chico Gonzales. Callahan's ire at being assigned an unwanted partner is intensified both by his awareness that this "boy" lacks suitable experience and by the lieutenant's refusal to back down. This distaste is perhaps as much xenophobic as it is professional: Callahan's first question to Gonzales is, "You from around here?" Gonzales is indeed local to San Francisco, although he studied sociology at San Jose State University. His anti-intellectual partner sneers, "Just what I need is another college boy." Even though Gonzales proved his physical prowess by boxing at the university, his status as an intellectual prompts the sarcastic response, "You'll go far . . . if you live. Don't let your college degree get you killed." So, just as Wallace denounced liberal intellectuals for elitism and hypocrisy for developing theoretical solutions to the real problems of the inner cities, Callahan is highly suspicious of the increasing numbers of university graduates in the police force: those who were more likely to analyze than act. Like Reagan, whose gubernatorial campaigns Eastwood supported, Callahan considers the California campuses breeding grounds of radicalism that produced thinkers rather than doers.[12] Like Wallace, Callahan wears cheap suits, does not eat at fancy restaurants, and considers himself a "real American." Designed to render him the "embodiment of 'square' values," Callahan's wardrobe becomes another manifestation of his ordinary values, dedication to his work, and lack of egotism.[13] It also serves as a template for Gonzales and other police officers, who look up to him in more ways than one.

These subtle indicators position Harry Callahan as a middle-aged Californian who felt embittered by many of the changes wrought on American society by the 1960s. Like many working-class voters, Callahan would have been targeted by Reagan's 1966 gubernatorial campaign managers. Reagan appealed to people who resented the cost of welfare as represented in their tax dollars and who were terrified that the Watts rebellion was a portent of more urban violence. Many of these same voters were appalled by the California Supreme Court's nullification of Proposition 14 in May 1966. Prop 14 had been approved by voters in the 1964 elections. It nullified the Rumford Fair Housing Act, which had been passed the previous year and which outlawed racial discrimination in the sale or rent of property. Governor Pat Brown denounced Prop 14 as "legalized bigotry" and was one of a number of California political leaders who publicly supported the supreme court's action.[14] That so many politicians were prepared to reject the will of the California electorate reinforced a sense of alienation from mainstream politics among many voters. Callahan's outsider status emerges from a similar position:

he holds a "commonsense" attitude toward crime that is often at odds with the highly intellectual, even elitist attitude of his supposed leaders, who rarely engage with quotidian life on the streets. At once, then, Callahan is a representation of ordinary Americans and a vicarious release through which these same Americans could metaphorically strike back at the forces of elitist liberalism that were threatening to bring California to its knees.

Gonzales's ethnicity highlights the centrality of racial politics to *Dirty Harry*'s worldview. It is vital to place this within the film's immediate geographical context. The San Francisco Police Department had been particularly slow to integrate in the 1960s, and no significant attempts were made at diversifying the force until the mid-1970s. In 1973, African American officers filed a civil rights case alleging racially discriminatory practices in the SFPD. By 1975 only 80 of a total 1,937 sworn personnel were of Latino origin. Furthermore, police brutality against racial minorities was a causal factor in the rising racial tension in the city during the late 1960s.[15] *Dirty Harry*'s next scene, one of the film's most famous, directly references this issue. Although intended to remind viewers of Callahan's race-neutral position, it reveals how the overwhelming white majority within the SFPD ranks helped to create an atmosphere of casual racism. Soon after his appointment, Gonzales is enlightened as to Callahan's philosophy by a phlegmatic colleague, Di Giorgio: "Harry hates everybody: limeys, micks, hebes, fat dagos, niggers, honkies, chinks. You name it." With a wink, Callahan adds the rider, "especially spics." Thus the film contrasts Callahan's willingness to talk straight with the mayor's lily-livered inability to utter a racist epithet even when faced by its stark appearance on a ransom demand. The mayor's race-neutral position is presented as cowardice, Callahan's as a humorous form of equal opportunities.

With Callahan's character fully established, two humorous interludes follow that play on his relationship with the city. These scenes further establish the contours of Callahan's character—a man who, in Gonzales's words, "gets the shit end of the stick every time"—and firmly enmesh him in the city. In the first, Callahan spots a suspect while on patrol with Gonzales. They pursue through backstreets and alleyways until the suspect reaches his destination. Unaware that this is the home of the suspect's girlfriend, "Hot" Mary, Callahan inadvertently becomes a

Peeping Tom, peering through a window as Mary disrobes to try on her paramour's gift. A gang of local men spot him and defend Mary's honor by beating Callahan, reminding him that the law of the streets can trump the law of the land. Their impromptu Committee of Vigilance clearly impresses Callahan and reflects his own understanding of the law, since he declines Gonzales's suggestion that the men be arrested for assaulting a police officer. In the second interlude, Callahan rescues a man who is threatening to commit suicide by jumping off a skyscraper. Echoing the film's first scene, Callahan is raised above street level in a fire-truck basket crane to accost and rescue the man (unlike another San Francisco detective, "Scottie" Ferguson, Callahan does not suffer from *Vertigo*). Once again, he becomes the city's higher authority. Nauseated and enraged by Callahan's graphic description of the bodies of successful "jumpers," the man attempts to fight him. Callahan punches him in the face and then grabs the unconscious man while the basket descends, thus saving his life. There is a corollary benefit to this heroism: Callahan will now avoid the extra paperwork that the suicide would have produced and that the detective is always determined to avoid.

The film is also brought back down to Earth in the next scene, where Callahan and Gonzales investigate the shooting of a ten-year-old boy in Potrero Hill. This is where *Dirty Harry*'s racial politics are at their most subtle and perhaps pernicious. Callahan and Gonzales treat the death of an African American boy seriously and sympathetically. The SFPD, on the other hand, had decided that the helicopter which was searching for Scorpio would not patrol to this area of the city, and the boy thus becomes a victim of the liberal system's willful inattention to the African American areas of San Francisco. This brings the mayor's concern about pronouncing racial epithets into stark focus, confirming that he is more concerned with *appearing* to be opposed to racism while doing nothing tangible to protect the lives of San Francisco's African American population. Yet that Callahan hails from Potrero Hill adds another layer of significance to his treatment of the murder. While on the one hand, Callahan is righting the wrong of the liberal administration, he is also indicted in the SFPD's failure to protect the boy, since at no point does he call for greater police presence in the area, despite himself being native. His actions in dealing with the case, however, reflect his sensitivity to the potential for racial tension in the area. As the historian Keith

Miller notes, police brutality contributed to the rising racial tension in San Francisco's African American population in the late 1960s, a fact that was perhaps exploited by the Oakland-based Black Panther Party, which held a rally in Potrero Hill during June 1967. The Black Panther Party must have considered the area a prime recruiting ground for young, disaffected African American people.[16] Callahan consequently must be seen to be doing his job here, if only to keep the lid on simmering racial tensions and prevent the outbreak of disorder similar to that experienced in nearby Hunters Point in September 1966. The violence there erupted in the wake of the death of Matthew Johnson. The sixteen-year-old boy had been shot in the back by a police officer, an event that outraged the entire local community. Sensitized by Watts, Mayor Shelley called in the National Guard, a decision that resulted in six days of violence, events that contributed to the downfall of Governor Brown in that November's gubernatorial election.[17]

Meanwhile, Callahan's police department announces that Scorpio is being lured toward North Beach in an attempt to flush him out. Callahan and Gonzales encourage the priest of Saint Peter and Paul Church to agree to act as bait for Scorpio while they prepare to shoot the serial killer with a high-powered rifle. They take up a position on the roof of a nearby building beneath a neon sign that reads "Jesus Saves." Using powerful binoculars, Callahan observes the area. While scanning the windows of an apartment block, his eyes rest on a naked woman. Enjoying the privacy of her own home, she wanders to her front door, welcoming two friends, who enter and are presumably about to join her in an evening of sexual frolics. Callahan and the cinema audience gaze on. "You owe it to yourself to live a little, Harry," he smirks before his revelry is interrupted by Scorpio's appearance on the rooftop. After Callahan uncharacteristically misses with his first shot, Scorpio turns his submachine gun on the police before escaping. Scorpio's behavior powerfully reinforces the earlier suggestion that he sees the church as a location for mayhem. His gleeful destruction of the "Jesus Saves" sign with a machine gun (in direct contrast to his calm, methodical use of a silenced rifle in his first killing) is a reflection of his general attitude toward Christianity. In his preparedness to kill a man of the cloth, he acts out one of the accusations that American conservatives leveled at the counterculture, namely, its lack of respect for religious authority.[18] This positions Scorpio as a prototypical countercultural figure, juxtaposing his maniacal indulgence in wanton destruction with Callahan's respect for law and order even as the film suggests that they share a similar distaste for authority.

The film then turns to its central plot with Callahan searching for a young white girl named Mary Ann Deacon whom Scorpio has kidnapped. Even though Callahan believes the girl is dead, he agrees to transport a ransom to the criminal. Upon receiving the money, Callahan again witnesses the indolence of his superiors when he discovers that the lieutenant has not bothered to check the amount. Conversely, the lieutenant is hugely animated by the discovery that Callahan intends to conceal a flick knife under his trousers. Aware that the police will not wish to hand over the ransom money without surveillance, Scorpio has planned a wild-goose chase for Callahan, in order to ensure that Callahan's movements are not being tailed by other policemen. The ensuing hunt cements Callahan's relationship with San Francisco's geography. It begins with Callahan being sent to answer a public telephone on the South Side Marina (located on the city's northern edge, near Fisherman's Wharf). There he is told to answer a series of further telephone calls at various locations. Callahan runs about six miles to the south to the Forest Hills train station, where he is directed to catch the K car to Church and Twentieth Streets in the Castro District. He then runs a further four miles north to a hamburger stand at Aquatic Park before heading to Mount Davidson Park (six miles to the south).[19] Callahan's dominance of the urban setting once again comes into play—despite having run roughly sixteen miles, he still has the breath to dismiss "Alice," a young gay man who propositions him in the park, with a pithy one-liner. After being rejected, "Alice" laments, "if you're vice I'll kill myself." "Well, do it at home," comes the response. Like his colleagues, who were bringing nearly 250 public sex charges against the city's gay men each month, Callahan would prefer homosexuality back where it can be controlled: in the closet.[20]

Surtees and Siegel present Callahan's chase as a dirty job for Dirty Harry, designed to push him to his physical limit. He meets Scorpio at the base of the Mount Davidson Park cross. Built in 1934, the cross was designed to provide a focal point for the "contemplative and spiritual peace" that visitors were encouraged to experience in the park.[21] Scorpio tells Callahan to discard his Magnum and lasciviously comments, "My, that's a big one," when he sees the size of the gun barrel. In light of Callahan's meeting with "Alice," Scorpio's comment seems to suggest that he is sexually deviant, thus reinforcing the heteronormativity of Callahan. The implicit link here between homosexuality, criminality, and mental illness is among the most distasteful aspects of the film. Next, Scorpio reminds us of his outright rejection of spirituality and the notion that the church is a place of sanctuary by choosing this location to beat Callahan and taunt him with the knowledge that Mary Ann Deacon will die. Callahan is saved from certain death by Gonzales, who distracts Scorpio and is shot and wounded; taking advantage of the chaos, Callahan stabs Scorpio in the left thigh. Scorpio escapes as Callahan finally succumbs to pain and exhaustion.

Upon his return to work, Callahan is encouraged to take some time off to recuperate. Naturally, he refuses. He also defends Gonzales's actions, stating that Gonzales was acting on Callahan's initiative and was unaware that they contravened an order to refrain from involvement in the battle with Scorpio. It is at this point that the audience is prompted to conclude that Gonzales has proved himself in Callahan's eyes, first by becoming a man of action (rather than the man of thought), and particularly in disobeying orders not to intervene in the confrontation: in essence, he adopts Callahan's attitude to higher authority. Callahan, meanwhile, has tracked Scorpio to a groundskeeper's room at the scruffy home of the San Francisco Forty-Niners, Kezar Stadium. According to Fuensanta Plaza, this location was used because Eastwood and Siegel felt that it was reminiscent of a Greek amphitheater. It would therefore conjure up thoughts of a titanic struggle between the forces of good and evil.[22] Although warned by his new partner, Di Giorgio (in contrast to Gonzales, older and fatter than Callahan), that without a search warrant his actions are illegal, Callahan breaks into the stadium and pursues Scorpio to the center of the field. When Scorpio raises his hands in surrender, Callahan shoots him. The ensuing confrontation as Callahan approaches Scorpio is shot using a handheld camera, heightening the sense of dislocation, disorientation, and vulnerability. Scorpio pleads with Callahan: "Please get me a doctor! Don't kill me! . . . I want a lawyer . . . I have the right to a lawyer . . . I have rights!" His self-serving prayers have no impact on an indomitable Callahan, who aggravates Scorpio's leg wound by stomping on it. Eastwood claims that he suggested to Siegel that this would be an appropriate action for Callahan to take.[23]

The torture of Scorpio prompts the film's most impressive single shot and perhaps its most ambiguous moment. As the discordant soundtrack reaches a peak that is eerily reminiscent of Bernard Herrman's *Psycho* strings, the camera zooms out to a helicopter shot of the stadium enveloped in fog, a frequent cinematic metaphor for mystery and ambiguity (see fig. 3). This is arguably the only point at which the film seriously questions Callahan's methods and even his sanity. By turning away from the scene of torture, Siegel challenges the audience to question Callahan's methods and even indicts the audience for failing to question Callahan beforehand.[24] Until this moment, the audience has been encouraged to support Callahan's methods since they are the most efficient and effective. Yet at Kezar Stadium the audience observes the (il)logical outcome of supporting these methods. As fog enshrouds the stadium, viewers are given enough time and space in which to begin querying their prior approval of Callahan. This ambiguity continues in the following scene, where the outcome of Scorpio's torture is revealed: the girl is already dead. While she is exhumed from her grave in Marin County, Callahan watches over his city, once again leaving the audience to ponder the justification of Callahan's earlier behavior (see fig. 4).

Although Scorpio's appearance is suggestive of San Francisco's hippie counterculture, there are clues that point to other motivations beyond a simple causal relationship between the character's pathology and his hippie identity. Callahan's search of Kezar Stadium reveals that Scorpio has been living in the tiny groundskeeper's room. Decorated with pornography and dirt, the room is no place for long-term habitation. The suggestion is that Scorpio is of no fixed abode, which raises an important issue related to San Francisco's regeneration. Part of the Alioto administration's urban-renewal plan was to remove nearly five thousand people from houses in the South of Market area, a section of the city that had attracted large numbers of poor, white, single men. Eighty percent of those to be displaced were single white men. They proved to be a singularly controversial group of the many more thousands of San Franciscans who were threatened with relocation. Their resistance brought Mayor Alioto and eventually former governor Pat Brown into the fray in an attempt to push the plans ahead. By the time of *Dirty Harry*'s filming, this campaign had been rumbling for over a year.[25] Scorpio fits the profile of these displaced people. His lack of backstory in the film might position him as one of the indigent poor who were forced elsewhere by the threatened destruction of their homes: hence his distinctly insalubrious short-term living space. This presents him as another victim of corporate liberalism amid the post-industrial transformation of the American city.[26] It also perhaps explains his nihilism, for he has nothing to lose. Much as Callahan has been shunted aside by the bureaucrats, Scorpio finds himself on the wrong side of his city's modernization. So, even as it presents Scorpio as wholly unsympathetic, *Dirty Harry* hints at the circumstances that produced such a character, while again suggesting that 1960s liberalism caused more problems than it solved.

The discovery of Mary Ann Deacon's body leads to the film's pivotal scene, which cements Callahan's alienation from the power structure and all but erases the previous scene's moral ambiguity. Callahan receives an unequivocal dressing down from the district attorney. The scene starkly contrasts Callahan's reliance on a commonsense approach to policing—Scorpio needed to be tortured to reveal the whereabouts of the kidnapped girl, even though Callahan clearly suspected that she was already dead—with the bureaucratized approach of the D.A. It even hints that Callahan held a similar attitude toward public policy as the conservative organization Americans for Effective Law Enforcement (AELE). Founded in 1966, AELE took a "firm position . . . that policemen should not be punished for their good faith efforts to carry out their primary function of protecting the public."[27] According to the American Civil Liberties Union, AELE had a clear bias toward police officers: "If the police are doing it, it must be right and legal. And if it isn't legal, then certainly right."[28] This is certainly Callahan's interpretation of events at the stadium. The D.A. demurs: "What I'm saying is, that man had rights." In Callahan's world, however, Scorpio forfeited his own rights by depriving others of theirs, which naturally absolves the detective of any accusations of torture. The D.A. then points out that, thanks to Callahan's willful disregard for due process, any trial for the death of the girl could not be won. His view is backed up by a fellow lawyer who is present in the D.A.'s office. Judge Bannerman sits on the appellate court and also holds classes in constitutional law at the University of California–Berkeley. Bannerman confirms that the lack of a search warrant rendered any evidence gathered from the stadium inadmissible and that Callahan's actions amounted to police torture (see fig. 5). This prompts an outburst from the D.A. "Where have you been?" he cries to Callahan. "Does *Escobedo* ring a bell? *Miranda*? I mean, you must have heard of the Fourth Amendment?" As suggested by the D.A.'s exclamation, Callahan's frustration is as much with 1960s liberalism as it is with bureaucracy. *Escobedo v. Illinois* (1964) and *Miranda v. Arizona* (1966) were key decisions of the liberal U.S. Supreme Court led by Justice Earl Warren, whose crowning glory was the *Brown v. Board of Education* (1954) decision, which declared racially segregated schooling to be unconstitutional. Both *Escobedo* and *Miranda* affirmed certain rights for criminal suspects: *Escobedo* the right to counsel during interrogations, and *Miranda* the right to be told of this right to counsel and the right to remain silent prior to interrogation. Significantly, both were fiercely criticized by Richard Nixon during his 1968 presidential campaign.[29]

The conservative bias of this scene is compounded by the presence of Bannerman. Although seemingly an innocuous detail, the professor's identity as a representation of Berkeley reinforces Callahan's alienation from and disgust with the liberal elite.[30] That Bannerman is an expert on constitutional law links him to the stance of the California Supreme Court, which overturned Prop 14. The outpouring of rage at this decision was a clear indication that experts and political leaders were out of touch with the emotions and opinions of ordinary Californians.[31] His elevation of suspects' rights over victims echoed U.S. Supreme Court justice Abe Fortas's silence on the issue of the 1957 *Mallory* decision. *Mallory* freed its petitioner, who confessed to raping a woman after a prolonged interrogation during which he was not informed of his rights or that any statements he gave could be used against him. When Fortas was nominated for chief justice in 1968, Strom Thurmond asked whether Fortas believed in a kind of justice that let an admitted rapist free on a technicality. Fortas's mute response was protracted and only broken when he stated that his position on the bench meant that he ought not answer. As the historian Michael Flamm observes, this was a highly symbolic silence, reflective of the inability of liberals to articulate their feelings on the law-and-order issue.[32] It also suggested a bias toward criminals and away from their unfortunate victims, a stance that anticipated Bannerman's position on the Kezar Stadium incident.

Bannerman also reinforces Callahan's alliance with politicians such as Reagan and Nixon, who were intensely suspicious of the liberal tendencies of campus academics. Much to Callahan's annoyance, the balding "pointy-headed intellectual" (to quote George Wallace) concludes that Callahan should have requested a search permit: yet another inane bureaucratic diversion for the detective.[33] Again, however, the scene's conclusion allows Callahan a minor victory. When asked how he knows that Scorpio will commit further crimes, he responds, "Because he likes it." The pause before he says this suggests that Callahan intuitively knows because he and Scorpio are one and the same. It also elevates him above the bureaucrats: after all, he has an instinct for crime-fighting, while they rely on thought rather than action. The audience is thus reminded that, even when he is wrong on legal grounds, Callahan's common sense is morally, logically, and instinctively right.

Meanwhile, Scorpio has been freed on the technicalities outlined by the D.A. and is able to taunt Callahan by reveling in his liberty. He fashions a belt buckle to mimic and thus appropriate the internationally recognized symbol for peace and heads for a children's playground where he affects a friendly demeanor. Here, the film reinforces Scorpio's countercultural credentials and suggests that a psychopath could easily hide himself among the freaks of the hippie community: after all, he looks much like many of them, and they like him. Naturally, it takes a straight-laced member of society to weed him out and prevent him from acting on his depraved instincts. Scorpio adopts the peace sign to prove to onlookers that he has peaceful intentions when he enters the playground. Yet this apparently wholesome image is smashed in the following scene, where he is tailed by Callahan to a strip club that specializes in college-age women, reinforcing the link between the counterculture and loose sexual morals. Concealing his eyes with sunglasses, Callahan chooses to remain after Scorpio leaves, presumably to ensure that no further depravity occurs. Callahan's almost impassive response to this sexuality is partially a consequence of Eastwood's acting style but also reflects the emotional vacuum created by the death of Callahan's wife prior to the film, which is revealed to the audience soon afterward. So, while Callahan rejects the politics of the counterculture, he is prepared to take vicarious advantage of its free attitude toward sex and (hetero) sexuality, albeit in a way that appreciates women only for their physical beauty and willingness to parade for men.

Eastwood's biographer Patrick McGilligan calls Scorpio a "hippie-gone-sour," calling attention to his long hair and androgynous appearance.[34] The hippies and the counterculture are indeed close reference points for Scorpio. Sporting shabby clothes and long hair, having no fixed abode, expressing an extreme distaste for authority figures, and showing an unhealthy interest in children and naked women, Scorpio is a clichéd image of a countercultural figure. His taunting of Callahan uses common terms of abuse associated with the countercultural critique of modern policing: "pig bastard" and "rotten oinker." He seems unconcerned that he lives in squalor and, as numerous commentators have suggested, exhibits certain nihilistic tendencies in living an "unlivable" life, rejecting liberalism and social niceties while thumbing his nose at law enforcers and pursuing a futile campaign against the city of San Francisco.[35] The entire counterculture was often accused of nihilism in the pages of the national press. Indeed, it was relatively simple for mainstream Americans to perceive the entire counterculture as a nihilistic rejection of traditional American values. It was, for many right-wingers, but one short step from dropping out to taking up arms against the United States.[36] It is therefore possible to interpret Scorpio's first murder as a metaphorical assault on mainstream American values. The woman—clearly wealthy, since she is swimming in a rooftop pool—is enjoying the leisure time that wealth brings. Scorpio/the counterculture wishes to destroy all that the American mainstream holds dear. The murder is thus also an attack on wealth, beauty, and leisure, a demonstration that the counterculture is prepared to use the great institutions of American capitalism in its quest to corrupt the United States from within. Scorpio's nihilism and cynicism is further magnified when he heads to an underground location to hand some money to an unidentified African American man. He is then tied to a chair and beaten almost to the point of unconsciousness. As he is being dragged outside, he rouses himself to slur, "You black son of a bitch." He is thrown out after a valedictory stomp "on the house." The purpose of this peculiar incident is made clear in the next scene, where a heavily bandaged Scorpio is being wheeled through a hospital while giving a television interview at which he identifies Callahan as the perpetrator, and complains, "I'm supposed to be innocent until proved guilty, but just look at me." Naturally, this media interest results in Callahan being pulled off the case, although the detective insists that he intends to continue to follow Scorpio on his own time. In being prepared to continue his investigations while nominally off-duty, Callahan confirms his dedication to his job and implicitly denounces his colleagues for their lack of commitment, a position that he maintains throughout his career.

Before this, however, he visits Gonzales at the convalescent home. After learning that Gonzales plans to leave the police force and enter teaching, he talks to Gonzales's wife, Norma. She laments the fact that her husband is often denounced as a "pig" despite being a good man and then wonders aloud how Callahan's wife copes. This prompts the film's most pronounced moment of introspection, and the first point at which viewers are invited to consider Callahan's absent private life. His role as the city's guardian demands total dedication, to the exclusion of all other interests. Like Scorpio, Callahan seems to be of no fixed abode. There are no shots depicting his domestic life; he eats and drinks at the office or in diners, and he interacts with the general public only when at work.[37] He resists any form of self-analysis: mirrors—a frequent cinematic device used to connote an individual's consideration of his or her actions, as seen at the conclusion of *Bullitt*—are conspicuous by their absence, and Callahan is rarely seen in silent contemplation. The only reference to his private life comes after Norma's question, when he tells her of his own wife's death at the hands of a hit-and-run driver. The cinematography of this scene is particularly notable, and reminiscent of another San Francisco film, *Vertigo* (Hitchcock, 1958). The two characters, Callahan and Norma, descend an external staircase from the rooftop ward where Gonzales is recuperating. They are framed by the brick architecture of the building's staircase until Callahan's final line, metaphorically suggesting that Callahan's marriage constrained his ability to pursue his professional calling. When Norma asks him why he continues in his job, he responds, "I don't know. I really don't," just as the camera shifts to show him in his element on the street. The audience is thus encouraged to conclude that this is why he continues to work as a police officer. Patrolling the city offers him the chance to avenge the death of his wife, to blot out its resulting emotional trauma, and to replace one marriage with another—hence his withering comment to the earlier suggestion that he put in for overtime: "That'll be the day," a line made famous when used as a catchphrase by John Wayne's Ethan Edwards in *The Searchers*

(Ford, 1956). Callahan's job has become his life; San Francisco is his city, in both senses—it belongs to him, but he also belongs to and is owned by it.

The Callahan-Norma scene also sheds light on the film's gender politics. Notably, Norma is the only active female character in *Dirty Harry*. The late 1960s were a period when the feminist movement was in its ascendance. The Equal Rights Amendment was passed by Congress in August 1970, after a long-term campaign by the National Organiza tion for Women (NOW). That same month, NOW organized a national strike to call attention to the unequal pay that women had to accept in the American workplace. The second wave of American feminism moti- vated hundreds of thousands of women to become politically, socially, and culturally active, yet other than Norma, the females in *Dirty Harry* seem merely to be the object of the male gaze. Callahan, for example, is quite the connoisseur of the female form. Hot Mary's vigilante defenders clearly suspect him of being a voyeur. They may well have been correct, given Callahan's lingering gaze over the naked woman in the window during the stakeout and his preparedness to remain in the strip club af- ter Scorpio's departure. Mia Mask notes that the sexual vulnerability of women is "at the film's foundation," as demonstrated by the grisly death of Mary Ann Deacon at Scorpio's hands.[38] Women thus have no agency in *Dirty Harry* but instead are merely subjected to the actions of men. Even Norma seems to have little discernible impact on her husband's career choices.

Callahan's poignant interaction with Norma is short-lived, as the central plot returns with Scorpio hijacking a school bus, heralding the film's final scene. The bus passes the San Francisco city limits as Callahan argues with the mayor over Scorpio's ransom demands. This sequence, which moves the action to the Hutchison Gravel Quarry in Marin County, brings *Dirty Harry*'s relationship with the Western into sharp focus. The hijacked bus passes a herd of buffalo before heading under a railroad bridge on which Callahan acts as a sentinel (see fig. 6). These two classic images of the Old West reinforce the suggestion that there is now a complete absence of law and order in the Scorpio-Callahan rela- tionship. Frontier justice, as practiced by the San Francisco Committee of Vigilance, reigns, making explicit the film's suggestion that Callahan is a representation of law and order engaged in perpetual struggle with lawlessness and licentiousness. The duel to the death between protagonist and antagonist in an abandoned quarry again echoes the final showdown of many a Western (see fig. 7). This link is reinforced by Callahan's final action. Aware of the repercussions of killing Scorpio, he removes his badge and casts it into the lake behind the quarry, echoing the Man with No Name's gesture at the beginning of *For a Few Dollars More*. It also references the conclusion of *High Noon*, while containing a similar ambiguity. Despite their refusal to assist him in his ninety minutes of need, Will Kane rescues the entire population of Hadleyville from the Miller Gang. At first glance, Kane's gesture of dropping his sheriff's badge into the dirt appears to be one of disgust at the town's citizens. Yet as Peter Biskind notes, Kane is as much disgusted with the American legal system as he is with the people. Earlier in the film he is told by an aging lawman, "It's a great life. You risk your skin catching killers, and then the government turns them loose to shoot at you again." Kane's earlier work in sending Frank Miller, the Gang's most dangerous individual, to the gallows is undone at the film's outset by the federal courts in the North who set Miller free on a legal technicality.[39] Callahan's gesture implies a similar disgust with bureaucracy and positions him within the Western tradition, as another frontier gunslinger attempting to curb the excesses of the frontier's lawless elements. Furthermore, it reflects Eastwood's own ideas. *Life* reported him arguing while shooting *Dirty Harry* that "there's something wrong with the people who make the movies. If we could do away with . . . some of those studio people, those men in their black suits sitting at their desks, who've been around for a hundred years . . ."[40] In 1985 he complained to an interviewer, "Individual independence is becoming an outmoded dream. We're overwhelmed by paperwork, administrative formalities, committees and subcommittees. . . . Harry takes a position against this because, by the time you've finished the paperwork, the criminal's committed more crimes."[41] The inability of the liberal elite to police the city with the interests of the people foremost is combined with the knowledge that he will have to file even more paperwork once he returns to the office, and so Callahan concludes that he should continue to play by his own rules.[42] That Callahan is now alone is reinforced by the return of the soundtrack clip that first appeared as Mary Ann Deacon's body was exhumed.[43] There is a suggestion that Callahan now sees himself as a true vigilante, bound by no rule of law and free to defend San Francisco using any means he sees fit.

* * *

Eastwood later suggested that Callahan's position was born of frustration with the attitude of the media and the country's political elite toward crime in the late 1960s. Such comments indicate that Eastwood considered the film a comment on American society and that its diegetic world was not far removed from the real one: "There wasn't much thought of the victims of violent crime. Most of the news media was obsessed with the rights of the accused, as they should be. But there was also an underlying thing within society out there in general that felt that maybe there was so much accent put on the rights of the accused that they weren't taking care of the rights of the victim."[44] Later he went further, suggesting that "everybody was just, sort of, sick about worrying about the accused. . . . How 'bout let's worry about the victims for a while?"[45] While acknowledging that Callahan was a callous man who potentially "provided simple solutions to horribly complicated problems," Eastwood argued that Callahan represented a necessary, perhaps even heroic, bulwark against criminals who were becoming adept at working the liberal system to their advantage.[46] Scorpio's pleas for a lawyer in the Kezar Stadium scene reveal his awareness of his *Escobedo*-guaranteed rights as well as his privileging of these rights above Mary Ann Deacon's simple right to life. His horror at the pain that Callahan is prepared to inflict is compounded by his awareness that his nemesis is not playing by the liberal rulebook. The film's ending demonstrates Callahan's final alienation from the system that has frustrated his crime-fighting instincts and talents at almost every turn.

Far from straightforward right-wing propaganda, but certainly not as liberal as Don Siegel suggests, *Dirty Harry* is perhaps most suspicious of bureaucratic liberalism and the permissive attitude toward the counterculture in California. This is not to deny the brutality of Callahan and the film, but rather to place this brutality within context. Callahan is a working-class male who finds himself assailed from above by bureaucrats and careerist politicians. Forced to work alongside police who are either overeducated, undermotivated, or plain incompetent, he sees a city below him overflowing with debauchery and criminality. Over-worked, he has to protect his city using the most efficient means pos-sible. Hence a punch in the face works for the potential suicide—it is quicker, easier, and less of a bureaucratic headache than an attempt to talk him down. In this, Harry Callahan and Clint Eastwood are kindred spirits. Both conduct their work with the minimum of fuss, abiding by strict deadlines and working within tight budgets.

Although much of *Dirty Harry*'s political commentary relates to na-tional issues, awareness of the local context enables a reading of *Dirty Harry* that fully appreciates the causes of Callahan's conservatism and that buttresses the film's conservative political stance. Callahan's city is a key reference point for understanding his film, and San Francisco's historical and political geography is central to the film's political subtext. The conservative bias of the D.A. scene, for example, is reinforced by the judge's identity as a representation of Berkeley and compounded if view-ers link this to Callahan's distaste for college-educated police. Similarly, the history of African Americans in the city exposes Callahan's opinions as far from race neutral (a conclusion that could be drawn if the film's location and class politics were to be ignored).[47] Furthermore, the lo-cal approach reveals how the film comments on the tensions between liberals such as the mayor, conservatives such as Callahan, and products of the 1960s such as Scorpio. The film's conclusion is that men like Cal-lahan are needed to clean up the mess left by men such as the mayor in their inability to quell the criminality of men like Scorpio. While the film does not offer complete approval of Callahan's methods, it acknowl-edges that they are the most commonsense option. Callahan's conserva-tive credentials are constant themes, and they are presented in such a way that viewers are implicitly encouraged to conclude that the United States needs a "commonsense" Callahanian approach to crime.[48] Spe-cifically, then, Harry Callahan is a San Francisco man. We see Callahan both dominating and, to a lesser extent, being dominated by "his" city. His immersion in San Francisco enables him to overcome almost all the obstacles set before him: his knowledge of its culture means that he does not punish Hot Mary's vigilante defenders; his knowledge of its recent history helps to save the jumper; and his knowledge of its geography ensures that he is able to follow Scorpio's wild-goose chase. His relation-ship with his city is underscored by his nonexistent private life. Callahan, as suggested by the opening scene, *is* San Francisco's police and the city's moral and physical guardian. His distaste for Scorpio derives not simply from Scorpio's crimes but also from Scorpio's relationship with the counterculture, which Callahan has presumably been tackling for some time. His position as the city's lone hero means that he must use any means necessary to bring Scorpio to justice.

Although there is more than a suggestion that San Francisco represents the American frontier, *Dirty Harry* most explicitly presents the city, in the words of Martin Rubin, as "a charged urban inferno."[49] Whereas Frank Bullitt polices a modernist metropolis, Callahan's San Francisco is decaying and debased, a postmodern city in the making. This decay, the film suggests, is the result of liberal complacency and bureaucracy. The film, then, prompts viewers to side with Callahan in his battle over how San Francisco will be policed: either following liberals' assumption that criminals will play according to their rules, or following Callahan's awareness that codes of decency, fair play, and liberal conceptions of individual rights no longer apply. This position is underscored by the relative absence of shots from Callahan's point of view. Instead, the camera is almost always looking up to him. These low shots exaggerate Callahan's physical height and also reinforce the notion that he is the city's higher authority.[50] Viewers are encouraged to admire him, even treat him with awe—after all, he does things that no sensible member of the public would consider—while appreciating his dominance of San Francisco's criminal underbelly from a safe distance. It comes as little surprise to discover that the film was extremely popular among actual San Francisco police officers.[51]

Dirty Harry also confirms San Francisco's position as a key location for the struggle between liberalism and conservatism in the 1970s. Callahan's battles with the local power structure are useful indicators of the frustrations felt by conservatives at liberal bureaucracy. Enveloping *Dirty Harry* in San Francisco suggests that the film is best approached through analysis of its presentation of urban transformation in the second half of the twentieth century and the escalating tensions between liberals and conservatives in the nation's cities. Callahan's rejection of bureaucratic liberalism allows him to fall back on a more primitive and perhaps more authentic form of justice, one that has deep roots in San Francisco's history, namely, a form of frontier justice that acknowledges the twin concepts of vigilantism and individual power. Callahan's relationship with his city is deepened by its position as a cradle of social libertarianism and as a site experiencing the last throes of New Deal bureaucratic liberalism. Thus Callahan is painted as a traditionalist conservative, harking back to San Francisco's roots in the Old West and in some respects anticipating the national political dominance of anti-statist conservatives such as Ronald Reagan and George W. Bush.[52] *Dirty Harry*, then, reveals that the conservative backlash responded not only to liberal lawmaking but also to urban transformation and the perceived problems brought to the cities by the counterculture which itself emerged in part as a consequence of social liberalism. That all of this occurs in a liberal stronghold cements *Dirty Harry*'s position as an agent of backlash, suggesting that conservative individualism could triumph over liberal bureaucracy and permissiveness. This places the film, and indeed the city, at the forefront of the debate concerning the future of the United States, suggesting that like the San Andreas Fault, Harry Callahan is an unwelcome yet permanent feature of San Francisco's landscape.

Figure 1. *Dirty Harry*, 4m23s. Callahan surveys his domain from the Bank of America; Holiday Inn at center.

Figure 2. *Dirty Harry*, 7m51s. Callahan is outwitted by the technocrats in the mayor's well-appointed office. His disgust at their bureaucratic solutions to crime is palpable.

Figure 3. *Dirty Harry*, 1h07m11s. "I have rights!" Callahan tortures Scorpio at Kezar Stadium as the audience's view retreats into fog.

Figure 4. *Dirty Harry*, 1h07m43s. A rare moment of reflection: Callahan gazes down at his city from Marin County after the exhuming of Mary Ann Deacon.

Figure 5. *Dirty Harry*, 1h11m49s. Callahan is being upbraided by the D.A. (*left*) and Judge Bannerman. Again, his hatred of the bureaucrats is clear to see. This is a rare shot in which Callahan appears to be shorter than his antagonists.

Figure 6. *Dirty Harry*, 1h31m14s. Callahan acts as sentinel on the railway bridge. The Wild West surroundings indicate that frontier law now operates.

Figure 7. *Dirty Harry*, 1h36m31s. Callahan surveys Scorpio's final resting place. Height equals mastery.

Figure 8. *Magnum Force*, 35m18s. Early Smith kneeling in front of a racist robber, shot from Callahan's point-of-view.

Figure 9. *Magnum Force*, 1h53m18s. "You guys don't have enough experience." Callahan confirms his mastery of the death squad.

Figure 10. *The Enforcer*, 18m59s. Callahan (suggestively positioned closest to the American flag) questions Moore (*right*) in the presence of the offscreen Ms. Grey and members of the SFPD.

Figure 11. *The Enforcer*, 20m23s. The PRSF does it "for the people" in their stolen van.

Figure 12. *The Enforcer*, 31m21s. Callahan is in typical pose, talking with his SFPD superior officer.

Figure 13. *The Enforcer*, 33m51s. Callahan's hand rescues Moore from a bazooka's discharge.

Figure 14. *The Enforcer*, 1h29m03s. Callahan uses a bazooka to dispense with the PRSF's leader and "fucking fruit," thus cleansing San Francisco of its gay population.

Figure 15. *Sudden Impact*, 8m34s. Callahan outlines his philosophy to a recently acquitted criminal.

Figure 16. *Sudden Impact*, 12m04s. Callahan (with added phallic weapon) invites the African American population to *make* his day. Note the astonished expressions.

Figure 17. *Sudden Impact*, 17m52s. Callahan condemns the waves of corruption that threaten his city.

Figure 18. *Sudden Impact*, 32m15s. Horace King (Albert Popwell) admires Callahan's Magnum.

Figure 19. *Sudden Impact*, 32m50s. Callahan explains why his Magnum is so powerful.

Figure 20. *The Dead Pool*, 28m58s. Callahan admires the scenery in the gym while Al Quan (*right*) struggles with his weight.

Figure 21. *The Dead Pool*, 1h00m10s. A sweaty Quan cannot keep up with the virile Callahan.

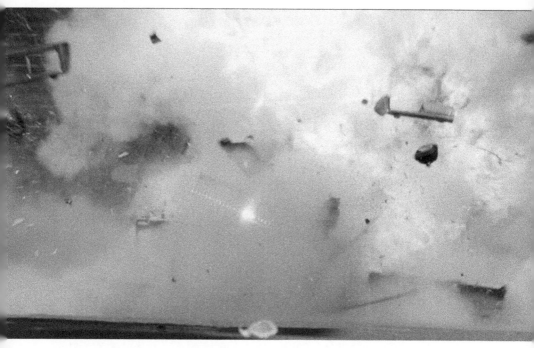

Figure 22. *The Dead Pool*, 1h10m09s. Callahan's car is destroyed, but he escapes unscathed.

Figure 23. *The Dead Pool*, 1h23m01s. "You're shit out of luck": Callahan and his large weapon.

Dirty Harry's Sequels and the Backlash

I don't want to do a character just to continue it.

Clint Eastwood, 1976

I don't know why anybody would want to look for political ramifications in any film.

Clint Eastwood, 1988

The *Dirty Harry* sequels have largely been dismissed as mere box-office fodder, ranking among Eastwood's less interesting films despite all grossing more than the original. Although none were as critically or creatively successful as *Dirty Harry*, they demand consideration for a variety of reasons, not least because there has been increasing interest in the concept of "sequelization" in recent cinema studies. They conform to the expectations attached to movie sequels by being somewhat disappointing in comparison with the original film.[1] More important, however, they reconstruct the narrative of *Dirty Harry*, bringing the tale of Harry Callahan to different conclusions, each of which refracts and contributes to the popular memory of the original film and its eponymous antihero. Thus, as Carolyn Jess-Cooke points out, they encourage us to "meditate" upon the original film, compare and contrast the lead character's past and present, and think of the sequel as "both a natural progression from and return to the past."[2] Jess-Cooke and Constantine Verevis note that "the sequel does not prioritize the repetition of an original, but rather advances an exploration of alternatives, differences, and reenactments that are discretely charged with the various ways in which we may reread, remember, or return to a source."[3] The *Dirty Harry* sequels both challenge and confirm this notion. True, they place Harry Callahan in different situations, supposedly casting new light on him. Indeed, Deborah Allison argues that each sequel was specifically designed to rebut criticisms of the previous film while reprising its successful elements.[4] Yet they also conform to the template by replicating the formula of the original, including key themes and characteristics of the original.[5] All introduce the major antagonists soon after the main credits, while Callahan is reintroduced during a slyly humorous foiling of a crime. The major plot then takes place in which the criminals' threat to society is revealed and Callahan is drawn to investigate. After numerous skirmishes with his superiors, Callahan solves the crime and kills the criminals in a final shootout. Their traditional style is both a reflection of their pulpy origins and a metaphoric representation of their underlying messages. Moreover, Callahan remains such an immovably conservative figure that they must also be considered as repetitions of the original.

Made during a period of American cinema characterized by critiques of the myths on which many cinematic genres were based, the *Dirty Harry* sequels are unabashedly traditional in form. Unlike *The Long Goodbye* (Altman, 1973) or *Chinatown* (Polanski, 1974), they do not challenge and reconstruct the detective genre; none are as compelling a character study as *Serpico* (Lumet, 1973) or *Taxi Driver* (Scorsese, 1976), as peculiar as *Badlands* (Malick, 1973), or as spectacular as *Apocalypse Now* (Coppola, 1979). In essence they are B movies, designed to provide the maximum thrills and violence for minimum financial investment. Relying in part on Eastwood's star persona, the films offer little of interest to the student of what might be called "high cinema" (such as the movies mentioned above). They are, however, worth approaching as what might be termed "pulp cinema." Like the detective author Dashiell Hammett, Eastwood did not see such works as art but as a means to an end. Hammett's hard-boiled thrillers were written predominantly to get paid; for Eastwood, they were designed to maximize profits in order to obtain leverage with his studio for more creatively satisfying work that he wished to pursue. John Milius acknowledges as much, claiming that Eastwood once told him, "These things don't have to be that good; they just have to be cheap."[6]

Their "pulpiness" is intensified by the relatively anonymous directors attached to each project. Robert Kapsis and Kathie Coblentz note that when acting Eastwood preferred to work with a director who would be open to his suggestions.[7] The well-documented tensions between Eastwood and director Philip Kaufman on the set of *The Outlaw Josey Wales* (Eastwood, 1976), which led to the removal of Kaufman, also contributed to Eastwood's decision to work with more malleable and easygoing men in the later films.[8] With the exception of the Eastwood-directed *Sudden Impact*, none were directed by high-ranking directors. Ted Post (*Magnum Force*, 1973) remains chiefly renowned for television work, particularly for *Rawhide*, on which he first worked alongside Eastwood. He directed Eastwood in the post-Leone Western *Hang 'Em High* (Post, 1968), and following *Magnum Force* his greatest success was *Go Tell the Spartans* (Post, 1978), which commented on the futility of the American presence in Vietnam during the early 1960s. James Fargo (*The Enforcer*, 1976) was previously an assistant director on a number of Eastwood movies and later directed the Eastwood vehicle *Every Which Way But Loose* (Fargo, 1978). Buddy Van Horn (*The Dead Pool*, 1988) directed two other Eastwood vehicles but remains best known for his work as a stunt coordinator. These selections for director suggest that Eastwood was happiest on the *Dirty Harry* films with someone who had already proved his worth to Malpaso and would not prove too demanding a taskmaster. They also reinforce the notion that Eastwood was the films' dominant creative individual.

A number of key themes unite the *Dirty Harry* sequels. All are set in the San Francisco Bay Area, enabling an analysis that emphasizes the films' representation and refraction of local politics, culture, and society. They try to dull Callahan's rough edges by having him accept partners of different ethnicities and gender while attempting to position him as a bulwark of moderation against rogue cops, political militants, and revenge killers: an ironic yet populist reversal of his original characterization. Whereas Callahan once seemed to be leading a single-handed crusade to bring down the liberal criminal justice system, he later seems to uphold this very system. His methods, once considered by his superiors brutal and unnecessary, later seem harsh but fair. He forges friendships with non-white characters, most notably a succession of characters played by the African American actor Albert Popwell, who appears in all but the final film. He noticeably softens before women, becoming more attractive to them as he ages. The later films also become increasingly self-reflexive. This process reaches its apogee in *The Dead Pool*, which comments on Callahan's "celebrity" status and enters the debate about the influence of violent films on present-day society.

Callahan appears to become increasingly invulnerable as the series progresses, both to ensure that further sequels are possible and to conform to audience expectations. This runs in tandem with one of the series' least-acknowledged features: the development of Callahan into a metaphor for a form of traditional American conservatism that gained traction in the 1970s and attained the highest office when former California governor Ronald Reagan was elected president of the United States in 1980. The increasing macho overtones of the series buttress Callahan's conservative credentials even as the sequels attempt to soften the explicit political edge of the first film and emphasize Callahan's romantic side. The gap between Callahan and his colleagues continues to animate the plots of the films, with the SFPD's staff regularly expressing disgust at Callahan's Paleolithic attitudes toward policing. In presenting him as such the films suggest that Callahan represents traditional American values, ones that were central to post-1960s conservatism. Combined, they develop an ideological message which suggests that crime is everywhere in American cities and that powerful individuals in the legal system such as Callahan are necessary to prevent crime destroying the fabric of the postmodern American city. They thus present San Francisco as the nation in microcosm and are best approached as an ongoing conservative rebuttal to 1960s liberalism.

Plots

Written by John Milius and Michael Cimino, the police procedural *Magnum Force* (1973) is, according to Milius, the "flip side of the coin" to *Dirty Harry*.[9] It echoes its predecessor in emphasizing the corruption of San Francisco's elites, although the focus shifts to the corruption within the higher echelons of the police department and San Francisco's criminal population. Working alongside an African American partner, Callahan gradually realizes that a series of brutal murders in the criminal underworld have been planned and executed by an SFPD "death squad" led by Callahan's boss, Lieutenant Briggs. This squad comprises a number of new recruits who met while serving in the Vietnam War. After discovering the squad's identity, Callahan is kidnapped by Briggs, who compares the squad to the San Francisco Committee of Vigilance, noting that history "justified" the vigilantes' actions.[10] This renders the link between Callahan and the Committee explicit, drawing on the hidden links in *Dirty Harry* and encouraging audiences to reconsider their understanding of the Callahanian approach to crime. Callahan retorts that police vigilantism is but one small step from lawless anarchy, a highly ironic comment given his treatment of Scorpio in *Dirty Harry* and a clumsy attempt by the scriptwriters to defend Callahan's position and present him as one of the centrists in the SFPD. He might "hate the goddamn system," but as he points out, "until someone comes along with some changes that make sense, I'll stick with it."

Magnum Force might be approached alongside other mid-1970s detective films that explore corruption among political or economic elites, although its exploration of this theme is tentative and simplistic.[11] Some commentators consider it a liberal riposte to *Dirty Harry*, but this is a superficial reversal.[12] A lifetime member of the National Rifle Association and self-confessed gun enthusiast, Milius was, according to Eastwood, obsessed when writing the script with news reports about right-wing police groups in Brazil who were executing opponents of the country's military junta.[13] Milius opined in his audio commentary on the DVD release of *Magnum Force* that the police death squad was "do[ing] the Lord's work" in killing gangsters before concluding that "society *needs* Dirty Harry."[14] As if the extremism of the death squad is not enough, their dress—black uniforms, knee-high leather boots, white helmets, and sunglasses—encourages viewers to think of Nazi Stormtroopers; thus is the supposedly fascistic Callahan crudely juxtaposed with some truly fascistic characters.[15] Dismissed by Judith Crist in *New York* magazine as "pure garbage," *Magnum Force* grossed nearly $45 million, significantly more than *Dirty Harry*.[16] Pauline Kael was disgusted enough by the movie to lament that Eastwood had replaced the John Wayne archetype with a figure "who essentially stands for nothing but violence," ultimately destroying any notion of the cinematic good guy.[17]

In *The Enforcer* (1976), written by Sterling Sillifant and Dean Reisner from an idea originally pitched by two Eastwood fans, Callahan tackles left-wing political extremists. As the People's Revolutionary Strike Force (PRSF) terrorizes the city, Callahan contends with the rise of feminism, embodied in his first female partner, who appears to owe her position on the force to affirmative action. Like the *Magnum Force* death squad, the PRSF contains Vietnam veterans, thus reminding knowledgeable viewers of the violent legacy of the war and obliquely suggesting that a conservative icon is needed to clean up the mess left by meddling liberals. The PRSF kills one of Callahan's colleagues and later kidnaps the mayor of San Francisco. In a slight retread of *Dirty Harry*, the chief of police agrees to pay ransom, but the city's finances are saved by Callahan, who thwarts the plot. The PRSF is a hugely clichéd group based loosely on the Symbionese Liberation Army (SLA), which during the 1970s styled itself as the Bay Area's left-wing revolutionary vanguard. Its members look like hippies and employ leftist rhetoric (see fig. 11), although it becomes clear that greed drives the group's ringleaders. The SLA achieved international notoriety through a series of violent incidents, including the kidnap of Patricia Hearst, but failed in its attempt to lead a mass uprising. The PRSF seems to hold similarly confused aims and its final disintegration comes as a result of its members' ineptitude and Callahan's superior skills. Callahan thus again appears as the scourge of a hypocritical left. Despite its pedestrian direction by another self-identified "gun nut," *The Enforcer* matched *Magnum Force*'s success at the box office, grossing $46 million.[18]

Gender politics are central to the plot of the third sequel, *Sudden Impact* (Eastwood, 1983). Here, Callahan is temporarily exiled to the fictional Bay Area town of San Paolo to investigate another serial killer. His reckless behavior has damaged one too many SFPD operations and appears to be threatening the force's relations with the press, so the "walking freaking combat zone" is encouraged to relocate. In a plot featuring certain similarities to the notorious horror film *I Spit on Your Grave* (Zarchi, 1978), the serial killer is a woman who adopts Callahanian tactics to avenge a gang rape. Matters become complicated when she and Callahan become romantically entangled. Eastwood's direction, coupled with Bruce Surtees's cinematography, renders the film the most stylistically interesting of the sequels. *Sudden Impact* features many noirish touches, from its oppressive cinematography to the frequent allusions to the killer's precarious psychological state, Callahan's isolation outside the city he knows, and the "suppressed but very present sexuality."[19]

Vincent Canby of the *New York Times* denounced *Sudden Impact*'s "ridiculous" screenplay, although his poor review did not prevent the film from becoming the highest-grossing Dirty Harry film, at over $67 million.[20]

The final, perfunctory sequel, *The Dead Pool* (1988), depicts a visibly aged Callahan thwarting a serial killer who suffers from a personality disorder. After watching too many violent movies the killer becomes convinced that a film director, Peter Swan, has stolen his ideas for future movies. He steals Swan's "Dead Pool" list, part of a game in which players bet on which celebrities they think will die next. The killer sets about realizing Swan's list, which happens to include Harry Callahan. *The Dead Pool* is the most self-reflexive of the Dirty Harry movies, and challenges many of Eastwood's own statements concerning the relationship of popular film to the real world. It explores the role of the media and celebrity culture through the figure of Samantha Walker, a local news reporter who becomes romantically involved with Callahan. Callahan's education in racial diversity, meanwhile, is continued by his new professional partner, Al Quan, a Chinese American police officer who has a sadly predictable expertise in martial arts. An SFPD lieutenant with a public-relations brief muses on this new partnership: "Personally, I think teaming Callahan with a Chinese American would be very good for the department's image." As Deborah Allison notes, the notion that ethnic diversity is a public-relations exercise could equally be applied to the film series itself.[21] *The Dead Pool* grossed under $38 million, suggesting that film audiences were tiring of Callahan's antics. Eastwood was fifty-eight at time of the film's release, past the normal retirement age for San Francisco police officers, reinforcing the suggestion that the time was ripe for "Dirty" Harry to hand in his badge for good. Eastwood commented soon after *The Dead Pool* reached the cinemas that "every time, whenever I do a Dirty Harry picture, I say that's enough. But as I said, Harry's become an old friend to me, and I like to look in on him now and then."[22] Five years later, however, and freed from the necessity to publicize the film, he reflected on the series somewhat differently: "Sequels were OK at one time in my life, but now I feel that if I do a film . . . maybe it should then be left alone. . . . I don't know where I'd take Harry any more."[23]

Race

As suggested by Al Quan's character, racial politics in the sequels essentially follow the template set by *Dirty Harry*. A minority partner is assigned to Callahan in order to educate him in diversity issues. Gradually, these partners learn the Callahan style of policing while allowing Callahan to demonstrate that he is no racial bigot, before they are caught in the crossfire between Callahan and the criminals. The overwhelming message of these characters is that American minorities have much to learn from natives and are ultimately expendable. The sequels pay very little attention to the particular problems that face the multiple minority groups in either San Francisco or California; instead, they are simply treated to lessons in Callahanian patriotism.[24]

Intriguingly, one of the recurrent actors in the series is Albert Popwell, whose characters gradually soften as the series continues. He first meets Eastwood in *Coogan's Bluff*, where he plays a drug user who threatens Coogan with a flick knife, and first encounters Callahan during the "Do I feel lucky" monologue in *Dirty Harry*. His appearances in the sequels gradually bring him closer to the action, although he remains an essentially passive character. In *Magnum Force* he plays a murderous pimp who, much to Milius's delight, is the third victim of the death squad.[25] Subsequent appearances see him on the other side of the law. In *The Enforcer* he plays "Big" Ed Mustapha, the leader of an African American militant group called Uhuru (lampooned by Callahan as the VFW: "Very Few Whites") and the only Popwell character to survive unscathed. His organization, he claims, is simply "waiting for all you white honkies to blow each other up so we can move right on in." His inner-city office is furnished with African trinkets that Callahan identifies as stolen goods from various American hotels. In so doing, Callahan reveals the ersatz Africanism that characterizes opportunists like Mustapha. Metaphorically, this scene suggests that Mustapha's appropriation of African style and politics is as false as his ornaments. More perniciously, neither belongs to him. Both are therefore as false as each other, and Mustapha is revealed as a charlatan. After being exposed, Mustapha strikes a deal with Callahan, allowing him to maintain his militant facade while cooperating with Callahan's investigation. This prompts the two to develop an understanding based on their shared outsider status: "Callahan, you're on the wrong side," Mustapha points out. "You go out there and put your ass on the line for a bunch of dudes who wouldn't even let you in the front door any more than they would me." Callahan responds that he does not do his job for those people. "Who then?" "You wouldn't believe me if I told you." Popwell's transition from criminal to integrationist sidekick is completed in his final appearance, in which he portrays Horace King, a friend, fellow gun aficionado, and onetime partner of Callahan (see fig. 18). Horace allows Callahan to stay in his apartment in San Paolo and even gifts him "Meathead," a flatulent and incontinent bulldog who becomes Callahan's guardian angel. King's reward is to be killed by hoodlums who are targeting Callahan.

Popwell's characters encapsulate the sequels' representation of blackness and the difference between the surface appearance and the underlying meaning of the Dirty Harry series. At first glance, Popwell's growing centrality suggests that the films are becoming increasingly aware of the African American presence in San Francisco and American life in a wider sense. He moves from criminal through informant to trusted sidekick, gradually integrating himself into Callahan's world. Yet beneath this, Popwell remains marginal. Even though Mustapha appears to detest the system, Callahan is able to outwit him and suggest that his best interests are served by cooperating with the white detective who himself distrusts the system but is firmly enmeshed within it. Mustapha is thus drawn into Callahan's world and eventually becomes one of its defenders when he gives Callahan some important information about the PRSF and encourages his new partner to "do 'em in." Consequently, his militancy— and that of Uhuru—is denuded by his realization that the system can protect people like him, despite its failure to offer more than lip service to his ambitions (it is notable that Uhuru operates out of a shabby office in a deprived area of San Francisco). Thus the film proposes a bond between Callahan and Mustapha: as Paul Smith suggests, they are both outsiders who reject the meaningless platitudes of San Francisco's liberal hierarchy but who ultimately acknowledge that it is the least-bad option.[26] More perniciously, Horace King's role is merely to die in order to save his white friend, placing Popwell's final role firmly within a tradition of African American sacrifice in twentieth-century American cinema: Sidney Poitier playing Tommy Tyler in *Edge of the City* (Ritt, 1957) comes instantly to mind when King is murdered. Notably, upon discovering

King's body, Callahan seems more distressed that the hoodlums have injured Meathead. Popwell's absence from *The Dead Pool* offers another reflection of conservative ideology: just as the Reagan administration allowed black Americans to become the forgotten minority, Popwell becomes the forgotten character.

King essentially suffers the same fate as Callahan's African American partner, Early Smith, in *Magnum Force*. In the first sequel, Smith is taught the ropes by Callahan in a basic reprisal of Chico Gonzales's learning experience. Yet whereas Gonzales is injured in his attempt to protect Callahan, Smith dies because he chooses not to answer Callahan's urgent telephone call and opens a booby-trapped mailbox. As troublingly, Smith is earlier sent undercover to root out some armed robbers at a hardware store. The white criminals racially abuse Smith, and one of them orders him at gunpoint to kneel in front of them. Callahan, meanwhile, observes from behind a two-way mirror (see fig. 8). "Right here is where I kill me a nigger," sneers the robber. The camera turns to a point-of-view shot, looking down the barrel of the gun toward Smith as he lowers himself to his knees. It is only at this point that Callahan emerges to shoot the criminal, initiating a shootout in which two of the other robbers are also killed. There are numerous disturbing racial signifiers in this scene. Importantly, of Callahan's partners, only the African American Smith is forced to kneel before a white man on camera. This degrading position has distant but very real echoes of black submission during slavery. Furthermore, Smith is only saved after being placed in this position, and after he is racially abused, even though there are ample opportunities for the gun-happy Callahan to intervene beforehand. Smith is therefore reminded of his subordinate position before being saved by his white master, a thoroughly demeaning experience that merely serves to reinforce his reliance on Callahan. His fate offers a further reminder that Smith needs the protection of his white master in order to live.

Al Quan, the series' belated attempt to acknowledge the Far Eastern presence in San Francisco, suffers no such indignities.[27] Callahan's acceptance of him is indicated as soon as he appears: whereas his colleagues refer to Quan only by his surname, Callahan immediately calls him Al. Quan's usefulness is illustrated in the partnership's first set piece. They spot a robbery in progress at a restaurant in Chinatown. Quan calls for backup while Callahan enters the restaurant to apprehend the robbers. Only one escapes, and he is promptly drop-kicked by Quan. Quan proceeds to use martial arts to subdue the robber before arrest. Elsewhere, Quan is subjected to similar indignities to Callahan's previous partners. At one point, the two are at the police gym. Callahan spots Quan while he does some bench presses, although Callahan's attention wanders to a woman working out nearby just as Quan begins to struggle (see fig. 20). Later, the two head for a run along the Embarcadero. It soon becomes apparent that Callahan is in far better shape than his younger and more agile partner (see fig. 21). Luckily, Quan only suffers wounded pride in these two episodes, which seem designed to remind viewers of the aging Eastwood's virility. Inevitably, however, like all of Callahan's partners, Quan must be injured in the line of duty, allowing Callahan to fight the final showdown alone. When their car is destroyed by a car bomb, Quan suffers a few broken ribs thanks only to a bulletproof vest that he was advised to wear by Callahan.

Elsewhere, San Francisco's minority population simply seems to be present to reinforce Callahan's mastery of any situation. In *Magnum Force*, some "dark swarthy types" (in Milius's words) hijack an airplane but are thwarted and killed by Callahan, who happens to like the hamburgers served at one of the concession stalls in the airport.[28] The film's death squad massacres a poolside party of Italian Americans, described by Milius as "goombahs . . . [who are] living too well to be honest citizens."[29] In *The Enforcer*, Callahan is informed that the "minority community" has grown tired of his antics. "I suppose you're talking about the hoods?" responds Callahan. Later, some of Mustapha's Uhuru members leer at Callahan's partner Kate Moore when she enters their headquarters. "Don't worry, pig—we'll see that she don't get lonesome," smirks one of them, confirming that while they might appear to be political organizers, they are never far from succumbing to their base instincts as stereotypically hyper-sexed black bucks. Most famously, the gang that is robbing Callahan's favorite diner in *Sudden Impact* is entirely African American. Callahan dispenses with three of them with minimal fuss before the last man standing grabs a hostage. "Go ahead—make my day," snarls Callahan as he aims his Magnum at the criminal's head, once again echoing George Wallace's threat to rioters: "We just want to see you pick

up one of them bricks, now!"[30] Callahan's day would be made by the opportunity to kill another black man rather than merely averting the robbery (see fig. 16).

A nuanced depiction of race and ethnicity in San Francisco is clearly
not a priority for the sequels' directors and screenwriters, but even so,
their films fail to liberalize the message of the original. Racial and ethnic minorities remain either criminal or expendable, collateral damage,
or even cannon fodder within the wider struggle between Callahan, the
criminals, and the elites. Genre considerations naturally inform the
deaths or injuries of his partners, since Callahan must prevail alone in
order to reinforce his heroic status and his uniqueness. Although a form
of mutual respect eventually develops between Callahan and his partners, audiences remain aware that this partner must be either killed or
sacrificed in order for Callahan to demonstrate his mastery of the criminals. Thus Callahan's whiteness is an indication of his superiority; their
otherness a reminder of their subordinacy.

Gender and Sexuality

The sequels' gender politics are similarly deceptive. Callahan's masculinity most obviously manifests itself in his frequent use of his long-
barreled .44 Magnum. As significant is his sexuality and relationships
with women. In *Magnum Force* he beds a comely neighbor. In *The Enforcer*
he learns to respect women in the SFPD, and in the final two films his
romantic involvements with women are major plot points. The women
in the sequels conform to one (and occasionally two) of three character
types: love interest, professional partners, or criminals. The first type
formed part of an attempt by the filmmakers to "soften" Callahan by
making him more available to women; the second attempted to challenge Callahan's macho traits; and the third tried to challenge Callahan
in a different manner. All, however, end up being submissive characters
who become reliant on Callahan for their survival.

In attempting to make Callahan more attractive to women, the filmmakers hoped to improve the box office while also demonstrating that
the "new" Callahan was far from the brute of the first film. Of course,
this conception of what appeals to a woman is highly conservative in
its assumption that women will only respond to Callahan as a romantic

figure, hinting at one of the underlying themes of the films. In contrast to the outlaw Josey Wales, Callahan is not searching for or attempting to re-create a simulated family.[31] *Magnum Force* presents the audience with its first glimpse into Callahan's love life. Carol, who is married to an embittered and depressed colleague of Callahan's, flirts with Callahan when he visits to express concern about her husband. After asking why he has never made a pass at her, she attempts to kiss him but is interrupted by her children, who seem to be a source of great frustration: "With all those kids, do you think I'll ever get laid?" she laments. Callahan's gentle rebuff of her advances at once demonstrates his appeal to women but just as importantly reinforces his respect for the family unit, one of the central pillars of society for conservatives. His refusal to cuckold his colleague reminds viewers that Callahan stands for family values, that he has matured since *Dirty Harry*, and that he has moved far beyond the priapic Walt Coogan. As an upstanding member of society, not to mention a widower, he will not undermine the sanctity of marriage.

He has not been neutered, however. Soon after Carol's proposition, Callahan is approached in his apartment block by Sunny, a young Asian American woman who simply asks, "What does a girl have to do to go to bed with you?" "Try knocking on the door" comes the insouciant reply. After inviting her into his spartan apartment, Callahan is called into work, but Sunny settles in to await his return. As they head to bed, she tells him that he's her first cop. He replies, "This'll be two firsts tonight." The meaning of this remark is not clear. Callahan retains a photo of his wife on his bedside, so Sunny could be his first sexual partner since the death of his wife, although she could equally be the first non-white woman whom he has bedded. Sunny becomes Callahan's partner for the rest of the film, adding a layer of domesticity to his life by, for example, filling his bare refrigerator with groceries. Yet she survives only because Callahan has spotted that his mailbox has been booby-trapped, thus preventing her suffering the same fate as Early Smith. According to Milius, the scenes with Sunny—including an "efficient" love scene—were incorporated into *Magnum Force* in response to a large number of letters to Eastwood from women who wanted to see other women "coming on" to Callahan.[32] Whether or not this is true, Carol and Sunny seem to serve no other purpose than to underline Callahan's heterosexuality, since Carol is quite prepared to risk her marriage for a quick dalliance with Callahan, and Sunny simply presents herself to him as a sexual plaything. In the context of the early 1970s aftermath of free love and the vogue for sexual promiscuity, these actions might have appeared progressive, yet like Callahan's gaze at the naked woman in her apartment during *Dirty Harry*, they simply reconfirm male dominance and female submission. Neither Carol nor Sunny is sexually satisfied without Callahan; neither has a life outside the domestic sphere; finally, and most perniciously, Callahan is so attractive that he merely has to be in the presence of these women for them to swoon.

This romantic side is emphasized further in *Sudden Impact* and *The Dead Pool*. In the former, Callahan falls for a woman who turns out to be the film's major criminal; in the latter, he enters a relationship with Samantha Walker, a local television reporter. Walker first appears as a self-assured, independent woman, albeit one with a faulty moral compass. Later scenes show her coming to the realization that television ratings are not as important as respecting a moral code, a lesson that she learns from observing Callahan at close quarters. Her character seems to regress through the film as she becomes increasingly reliant on Callahan for moral guidance and physical protection. Significantly, after Callahan shoots and kills the film's serial killer with a ludicrously phallic harpoon gun, she refuses to acknowledge the media as onrushing cameramen crowd around the impaled body. Enveloped in Callahan's arms at the film's conclusion, she has lost all vestiges of her independence.

Sudden Impact offers a slightly more nuanced female character. Jennifer Spencer is the victim of a gang rape that has also rendered her sister comatose. She is initially unimpressed by Callahan but soon realizes that they are kindred spirits: "This is the age of lapsed responsibilities and defeated justice," she opines after learning of Callahan's profession. "Today, 'an eye for an eye' means 'only if you're caught.' And even then it's an indefinite postponement and 'let's settle out of court.' Does that sound profound or just boring?" She pauses, then apologizes: "Sorry, I'm sure you get that sort of thing all the time." "No," he responds, "I don't hear it enough." Later, despite suffering from trauma following a sexual assault, Jennifer invites Callahan to spend the night. In the film's final scene, she realizes that ballistics tests will link her gun to the earlier murders in the film. "What exactly are my rights?" she questions Callahan. "And where was all this concern for my rights when I was being beaten and mauled?

And what about my sister's rights when she was being brutalized? There is a thing called justice. And was it justice that they should all just walk away? You'll never understand, Callahan." He does, however. Conveniently, the gun was stolen from her by one of the dead gang members, allowing Callahan to tell to the other police officers that he was the serial killer since his fingerprints will be on it. Jennifer is therefore innocent according to legal standards of proof, and Callahan demonstrates that he knows exactly what constitutes justice, even though he overlooks Jennifer's earlier suggestion that criminals should be made responsible for their crimes. In a conclusion that holds faint echoes of *Dirty Harry*, Callahan reconfirms the inability of the legal system to bring true justice to the streets of California and the triumph of his commonsense approach to criminality.

While Spencer fulfills elements of the love interest stereotype, she is also the series' major female criminal. Adept at using a pistol, she has been considered by some to be a female analogue for Callahan: a Dirty Harriet, in some critics' words according to Richard Schickel.[33] Certainly, her understanding of justice echoes the early Harry Callahan and her chosen method of revenge—castrating her victims with a gunshot—is Callahanian in its cruelty and ironic aptness. Her rarity is not that she relies on Callahan for a certain amount of protection—after all, she can clearly protect herself—but that she does not bend to Callahan's moral will. She already shares much the same moral code, and it is Callahan who is forced to repudiate his defense of the legal system in *Magnum Force* and *The Enforcer* and return to the type of frontier justice that was central to *Dirty Harry*. Yet Spencer is a disturbed character. She paints anguished self-portraits that call to mind Edvard Munch's *The Scream of Nature* and seems to enter a different consciousness when she arrives at decisive moments related to the rape. Whereas the previous killers in the series seem to be pathological or simply misguided, Spencer has a clear and potentially justifiable motive. Her demons might render her a more troubling character, but her final escape seems to absolve her of any real guilt. In this, she can be positioned alongside Callahan as a righteous vigilante and another embodiment of frontier justice.

By contrast, *The Enforcer's* female criminals possess less agency. The PRSF includes two female terrorists who appear to be radicalized former prostitutes. In contrast to their male leaders they seem genuine, if naive and misguided, in their aim to bring power to the people. Both suffer similar fates. After one apparently leaves the PRSF to become a nun, she is shot by Callahan's partner Kate Moore when Callahan appears to have uncovered that her conversion is not genuine, revealed by the scandalous fact that she has painted her fingernails. The echo of *Two Mules for Sister Sara* is perhaps unconscious, but in reminding audiences of the duplicity of women it touches on a central theme of other Eastwood films such as *Play Misty for Me* and even *The Beguiled*. As important, it echoes *Dirty Harry* in presenting Callahan and Moore as the protectors of another pillar of conservative society: Christianity. The other female PRSF member is executed by a PRSF leader in *The Enforcer*'s most shocking scene, a moment that powerfully articulates both the ruthlessness of the PRSF and the widespread misogyny of the time. Her death is not mentioned again in the film, let alone becoming part of the revenge motif of the film's final act. Yet in foreshadowing the film's final suggestion that women are expendable, this scene reinforces the masculinist ideology that permeates the series.

This ideology is, at first glance, challenged by the major female figure in *The Enforcer*, Callahan's affirmative-action partner Kate Moore. She declares early on that she considers her sex "absolutely irrelevant," but the film attaches great significance to the fact that she is a woman. Although she goes through the same orientation process as Gonzales and Smith, Moore is humiliated to a far greater extent than Callahan's male partners and is presented as far less equipped for regular police work. This begins at her job interview, at which Callahan discovers that she has never made a felony or a misdemeanor arrest during her nine years in the police department. "What the hell gives you the right to become an inspector, when there's men who've been out there ten or fifteen years?" he demands, before telling her that on the streets she'll "get her ass blown off" and likely that of her partner as well. Moore only wins his approval when she displays her knowledge by correctly evaluating and solving an obscure legal conundrum (see fig. 10). Later on, her sickened reaction to a gruesome autopsy is played for comic relief. Finally, in perhaps the film's most sexist moment, Moore is saved by Callahan when it becomes apparent that she is unaware that bazookas are dangerous pieces of weaponry and that she must avoid standing behind one when it is about to be used (see fig. 13). Whereas Callahan's love interest and criminal partners all conform to similar physical types—very thin and attractive women with long hair—Kate Moore is decidedly frumpy and reminiscent of Barbara Bel Geddes's Midge in *Vertigo* (Hitchcock, 1958). She is stocky, somewhat ungainly, sports an unfashionable haircut, and there is never a hint that she could be attractive to Callahan. She must run—or more accurately trot, since she often wears high-heeled shoes—to keep up with him as he strides around San Francisco. Her major skill seems to be paperwork: she has already researched Callahan's background before being assigned to him, and she helps Callahan with some research when he is temporarily suspended. While she saves Callahan's life by shooting the fake nun and kills one of the terrorists in the final showdown, like Early Smith and Horace King she must be sacrificed, enabling Callahan to avenge her death at the same time as restoring justice to San Francisco. Like Gonzales, then, she best demonstrates her usefulness by becoming a woman of action. Her dying words to Callahan are "Get him," indicating that she has adopted the Callahanian tenet of justice through revenge killing. Ultimately, her death reinforces the notion that women are the weaker sex and allows Callahan to reinforce his position of masculine authority and dominance.

Callahan and Moore seem to be equals in only one scene. Soon after his suspension, they visit San Francisco's Pioneer Park and discuss their reasons for joining the police force. Moore turns to the Coit Tower and comments on its "vaguely phallic" appearance. Callahan witheringly replies that he has never considered it as such. They then talk guns, and Moore asks flirtatiously why Callahan needs such a large weapon. Unwilling to pick up on the double entendre, Callahan argues that the .38 "pings" off windshields, which is distinctly problematic in a densely populated city. "I see," comments Moore. "So it's for the penetration." Somewhat taken aback, Callahan nearly flirts back: "Does everything have a sexual connotation with you?" "Only sometimes" comes the cheeky response. Callahan is mildly amused by the retort, and they retire to a nearby bar to continue the discussion. Although seemingly innocuous, the scene is deeply ideological. While Callahan is prepared to sleep with attractive women, he fails to respond to Moore's flirting and invites her for a beer, as he would a male colleague. Much like the interplay about bra designs between Scottie Ferguson and Midge in *Vertigo*, this is a sexless conversation about sex, serving to reinforce the male's superiority.[34] Callahan here is able to resist any undesirable sexual advances. In contrast to the lecherous Uhuru members, he cannot see Moore as a sexual being. This reinforces the series' message that, whereas women cannot resist him, Callahan is fully able to assert his right to pick and choose whom he deems worthy of his sexual attention. Following the Coit Tower scene Callahan seems to treat Moore as an equal, but he has denuded her of her sexuality, despite her attempts to reveal it through witticisms and flirtatious language. Thus she remains a comic foil for Callahan's Paleolithic politics, a muted challenge to his monocultural and patriarchal worldview, and a cipher through which the audience is reminded that Callahan is an equal–opportunity bigot. Once Moore has proved herself capable of her job, not least through adopting Callahanian gunplay ideology, she is sacrificed to give Callahan further motive for destroying the film's key villain. Even in death, however, her gender is relegated to a secondary consideration: she is avenged because she is a police officer.

Elsewhere, women seem to operate simply as antagonists for Callahan or are reduced to mere stereotypes. Moore is assigned to Callahan at the behest of a female representative of the mayor's office, the aptly named Ms. Grey. Gray-haired, middle-aged, and shortsighted, her title is an indication of her independence. She talks of "winnowing the Neanderthals out of the department" in an attempt to bring the SFPD into line with "the mainstream of twentieth-century thought." When Callahan objects, she challenges him: "The woman's place is in the home, is that what you're trying to say?" Callahan's reply is caustic and no less stereotypical: "What do you think this is—some kind of an encounter group?" This contemptuous reference to one of the most important driving forces of the second wave of feminism tells the audience everything it needs to know about Callahan's attitude toward women. Callahan's position as the series' hero encourages the audience to treat feminism with the same disdain, a political position that is reinforced by Grey's link to the SFPD hierarchy. Viewers are prompted to conclude that the hierarchy is so in line with women's interests that it has promoted someone who is clearly unfit for the role. It also effectively feminizes the mayor's office. Just as Jimmy Carter was lambasted by some conservatives for being a weak (and thus less manly) president, the mayor is therefore weak for allowing mere women to dictate the SFPD's future.[35] Conversely, Callahan represents decisive masculine strength and not equivocating femininity. More unpleasantly, his masculinity is challenged by a grossly stereotyped lesbian woman gang member in *Sudden Impact*. Hard-drinking, obnoxious, unattractive, and domineering, she dominates her gang by force of will and is even so strong that she metaphorically emasculates Callahan, who is reduced to punching her and kicking her in the posterior rather than using his Magnum. As befits anyone with supposedly deviant sexuality in the *Dirty Harry* films, though, she is not allowed to live: she is shot by Jennifer Spencer for her role in orchestrating the gang rape. That she has clearly derived sexual pleasure from watching a heterosexual rape adds a further layer of unpleasantness to her characterization, suggesting that lesbianism is closely associated with deviancy, cruelty, and criminality.

The only other notable female character in the series is the movie critic in *The Dead Pool*, who appears in a distasteful episode that fortifies the sequels' masculine ideology. Molly Fisher, a famous film critic, is threatened in her condominium by a burglar who announces that he is a film director. She complains of having a weak heart, which prompts him to sneer that it is rare to see a critic with a heart before he kills her, ostensibly because she gave his work poor reviews. This scene, which echoes the Vincent Price chiller *Theatre of Blood* (Hickox, 1973), in which an actor murders every critic who has criticized his performances, is apparently the filmmakers' riposte to the *New York Times* film critic Pauline Kael. Kael was the most prominent film writer to identify Harry Callahan as a fascist and was a resolute critic of Eastwood throughout the 1970s and 1980s.[36] According to Patrick McGilligan, Eastwood read her reviews "religiously" and was stung by every one of her barbs. He even approvingly quoted a San Francisco–based psychiatrist who claimed that her vitriol was actually a reflection of how much she was attracted to him (Kael chortled in reply, "Eastwood's response is perfect . . . in fact, it's sublime").[37] Just why Eastwood was so animated by Kael's long-standing antipathy toward Harry Callahan is unclear. After all, the previous *Dirty Harry* films grossed extremely well despite her protestations. Perhaps he secretly craved her approval.

As suggested by *Sudden Impact*'s lesbian gang leader, the sequels are blithely inattentive to the gay culture of the Bay Area. In *Magnum Force*, Callahan and Smith discuss a group of young officers (who unbeknownst to them are the death squad). Smith recalls that they were at the academy the year below him and "stuck together like flypaper" to such an extent that the other recruits thought they were "queer for each other." "I'll tell you something," responds Callahan, "if the rest of you could shoot like them, I wouldn't care if the whole damn department was queer." Callahan's views are crystallized more clearly in *The Enforcer*. During the heat of the final battle, Callahan bellows "fucking fruit" at the PRSF's leader immediately before shooting the criminal with a bazooka (see fig. 14). Delivered in the wake of the passage of Assembly Bill 489, which decriminalized sodomy in California to the dismay of many conservative groups, this homophobic insult gives a clear indication of Callahan's stance on homosexuality. Kael lamented that this might represent the "last outpost of the Western hero—killing homosexuals to purify the city."[38] The obvious phallic imagery of the bazooka adds a slightly lewd symbolism to the scene, with Callahan's shot—metaphorically, the representation of male heterosexual San Francisco—obliterating the section of society that Callahan believes to be homosexual. Consequently, the only two mentions of male homosexuality in the sequels form a derogatory quip and an offensive insult. This, of course, is within the geographical context of San Francisco, perhaps the most sexually liberal city in the United States: the first American city to elect an openly gay man to public office, the home to the first lesbian rights organization in the United States, and the unofficial capital of gay America. In this context, Callahan's final act in *The Enforcer* offers a cruel and unfortunate foreshadow of the fate of the city supervisor and gay-rights activist Harvey Milk.

The sequels thus present a conservative racial and gender ideology. White male heterosexual dominance must remain unchallenged. Heterosexual women must find Callahan irresistible, although he may reject their advances if they do not conform to his ideal of physical beauty. Even when he allows a level of intimacy to develop, he remains the dominant protector. Ethnic and racial minorities must toe the line if they are not to be criminalized and then wiped out. Any potential alternative ideologies are either destroyed, neutered, or must integrate themselves into the Callahanian world. Outsiders are not allowed to exist in parallel with the mainstream: they are either deviants who must be punished or oppositionists who must realize that Callahan's way offers them the best chance to thrive. In essence, they must buy into Dirty Harry's America and not challenge its hegemony.

Physical Power

As suggested by the sequels' gender and racial politics, a steely core remains beneath Callahan's apparent softening. In *Dirty Harry*'s bank robbery, he is shot and wounded but in the heat of battle seems impervious to the pain, although his confrontation with Scorpio following the wild-goose chase reveals that he is not invincible. The sequels tend to deemphasize Callahan's physical vulnerability, instead amplifying the first film's suggestion that he is a superhero (or, more specifically, an *Übermensch*). This manifests itself in numerous ways, from Callahan's sexuality to his increasing indomitability and the fetishizing of his gun.

The .44 Magnum has become as indelibly associated with Callahan as the longbow has with Robin Hood or the Walther PPK with James Bond.[39] This is emphasized in the opening sequence to *Magnum Force*, which is a close-up shot of Eastwood's hand wielding the Magnum in front of a plain red background. The sequence closes as the gun turns to aim directly at the audience. The soundtrack shifts from the opening theme to Callahan's "lucky" monologue, and the gun is fired. Such fetishizing of Callahan's Magnum extends to the promotional material for the films. With the exception of *Sudden Impact*, each film's promotional poster is dominated by Callahan wielding a Magnum. By the time of *The Dead Pool*, the Magnum is in fact the most prominent feature, emphasizing its centrality to the character of Harry Callahan. In the films themselves, Callahan is rarely seen without his Magnum holstered or at hand. He declares his admiration for the *Magnum Force* death squad's abilities with firearms. In *Sudden Impact* he demonstrates to Horace King the superiority of his Magnum over King's shotgun, which leaves victims identifiable only by their fingerprints. "If properly used," Callahan states, the Magnum "can *remove* fingerprints." Aside from the racial subtext in this scene, in which King is reminded that he will always be second best to the white man, Callahan's Magnum becomes an object of fetish. From the loving close-up as the gun is removed from its velvet-lined case through the point-of-view shot as it is thrust into King's face to the sunlight glinting off its barrel as Callahan conducts target practice, the Magnum is the focal point (see figs. 18 and 19). Its superiority to other handguns is a metaphoric representation of Callahan's physical, moral, and political superiority, another reminder that he is the ultimate authority in this San Francisco and that any miscreants he encounters will not just be apprehended but may well be obliterated.

Callahan's authority is reinforced in the original film through numerous low-angled shots that emphasize his height. There are far fewer instances of this type of shot in the sequels; instead, Callahan's power is reinforced through other means. His final line to the death squad members in *Magnum Force* is significant: "You guys don't have enough experience." Shot from below in a deliberate echo of the finale to *Dirty Harry*, Callahan here appears to be the manifestation of the *Übermensch* (see figs. 9 and 7). In finally refusing to allow the law to bring the death squad to justice, Callahan returns to his roots as the ultimate arbiter. Indeed, after he has killed the remaining members of the death squad he is approached by its leader, Lieutenant Briggs, who informs Callahan of a potentially ironic conclusion to the case: "You killed three police officers, Harry. And the only reason I'm not going to kill you is because I'm gonna prosecute you with your own system. It'll be my word against yours. And who's gonna believe you? Because you're a killer, Harry. A maniac." Unfortunately, Briggs has not realized that Callahan has rigged his getaway car to a bomb. Briggs might think that Callahan is protecting the system, but Callahan is acutely aware of this system's limitations. Callahan's final line—"A man's gotta know his limitations"—is not just the repeat of an ironic quip. Earlier in the film, Callahan commented to Briggs that "a good man always knows his limitations." The reprisal undercuts the suggestion that Callahan believes in the system. He is not a traditional good guy but a man unbound who is in the process of becoming San Francisco's unassailable protector.

In similar fashion the conclusions of the other sequels are demonstrations of Callahan's power. The PRSF leader is annihilated when Callahan uses a bazooka in lieu of his Magnum (see fig. 14). In the final shootout of *Sudden Impact*, Callahan shoots the last remaining gang member, causing him to fall onto and be impaled by a fairground unicorn's horn. In *The Dead Pool*'s denouement the killer is skewered by a harpoon (see fig. 23). Aside from the phallic imagery, genre requirements inform all of these final confrontations. As the lone hero, Callahan must prevail in man-to-man warfare in order to provide a satisfactory and order-restoring conclusion. And yet in each case, Callahan's partner must be sidelined in order to remind us of Callahan's strength and power. Women and ethnic minorities must not be able to have the final shot, since that would challenge white heterosexual dominance and Callahan's triumphant status. Thus genre expectations, in this case the necessity for the film's protagonist to prevail over his antagonists, become part of the series' political ideology.

Callahan's power is reinforced by his imperviousness to physical injury, which increases as the series progresses and also offers a link to the Man with No Name. Just prior to the conclusion of *A Fistful of Dollars*, he fashions a metal breastplate. At the subsequent shootout, his foes realize that their bullets do him no harm and conclude that he is invulnerable. Callahan becomes similarly invincible toward the end of his career. Despite engaging with fully armed terrorists, he emerges from an attempted airplane hijacking during the opening act of *Magnum Force* without a scrape. In *The Enforcer's* opening crime in a liquor store, the only injury Callahan suffers is some slight scuffing to his sports jacket. By the last two films, Callahan is indestructible. In *Sudden Impact*, he rescues the owner of his favorite diner (in the famous "Go ahead—make my day" scene) from four gun-toting robbers, none of whom seems able to operate his weapon quickly or accurately. Later, three machine gunners fire on him, destroying a car in the process; Callahan is not scratched. He casually retrieves a Molotov cocktail that is thrown into his car before tossing it at his assailants. Upon his arrival in San Paolo, he hijacks a bus carrying the residents of a retirement home to chase a criminal ("Shag his ass," "Yeah, get that sucker," "You gotta nail that son of a bitch," the pensioners cheer). Despite having shot another police officer, the criminal is too terrified to use his gun on Callahan. "The best damn day trip I had since they dropped me in that damn home," declares one of the bus riders as they decant onto the sidewalk. Callahan is only moderately harmed in two scenes, the first when Meathead attacks him, the second when two goons beat him and drop him in the harbor. Callahan is not out of his depth, however: he quickly recovers and returns to the case. His invulnerability in *The Dead Pool* is even more absurd. In the opening sequence, four gunmen riddle his car with bullets. Despite this fusillade, he manages to extricate his car from the trap, crash it, and flip it onto its side. He emerges unhurt from a side window and proceeds to dispense with assailants with a couple of well-aimed shots from his

Magnum. Later, two criminals pepper a glass-fronted elevator compartment with bullets, but Callahan is not even scratched by the falling glass. Even more implausibly, toward the end of the film, a bomb destroys his car (see fig. 22). Callahan is again unscathed. This absurdity is reinforced by the sequels' use of quotable lines, derived from the popularity of the "Do I feel lucky" peroration of *Dirty Harry*. As David Tetzlaff suggests, the use of such humorous asides emphasizes the cartoonish elements of violence in such mid-1980s films as *Commando* (Lester, 1985).[40] Whereas "Do I feel lucky" is both an important plot point and a commentary on Callahan's brutality, later quips seem to be designed to prompt laughs rather than any deeper consideration. Thus "Make my day" is designed to undercut the racial overtones of the diner scene and to encourage viewers to chuckle at Callahan's definition of a good day. When taunted by a recently acquitted criminal in *Sudden Impact*, Callahan grabs him by the collar and delivers the following threat (see fig. 15): "Listen punk. To me, you're nothing but dog shit, you understand? And a lot of things can happen to dog shit. It can be scraped up with a shovel off the ground. It can dry up and blow away in the wind, or it can be stepped on and squashed. So take my advice: be careful where the dog shits you." In *The Dead Pool*'s restaurant scene, Callahan calmly informs one of the criminals that he has forgotten to read his fortune cookie. After crumbling the dessert, Callahan states the robber's supposed fortune—"You're shit out of luck"—before shooting him and his accomplices dead. Such quips have a distancing effect, encouraging audiences not to consider the violence and the destruction but instead to admire Callahan's almost self-conscious way with words. Crucially, the humor in these incidents does not destabilize Callahan's control, or indeed his character. His insouciance in these events reinforces his invincibility: even when faced with death he has the presence of mind to make a joke, such is his certainty that he will prevail.

In contrast to the near-human Callahan of the first film, the later films present him as an invulnerable superhero of almost mythic proportions, reminiscent of Micky Spillane's Mike Hammer, a similarly invincible conservative detective who lives in a nightmare world. This link begs further consideration of Callahan's roots in hard-boiled fiction. It is possible to draw parallels between Callahan and classic fictional detectives such as Sam Spade or Philip Marlowe. The literature scholar Megan Abbott notes that hard-boiled fiction focuses on "the solitary white man, hard-bitten, street-savvy, but very much alone amid the chaotic din of the modern city. Generally lower-middle or working-class, heterosexual, and without family or close ties, he navigates his way through urban spaces figured as threatening [and] corrupt."[41] This equally applies to Callahan. Like many fictional tough guys, Callahan is deeply suspicious of bourgeois values, having seen them weaken colleagues like Di Giorgio or prevent good police work as in the case of the innumerable bureaucrats who bother him. His rejection of these values is fundamental to his success as a detective and keeps him acutely aware of the importance of justice to the ordinary man on the street. His belief in justice begs comparison with Raymond Chandler's Philip Marlowe. Marlowe saw himself as a knight in shining armor in a world that cared nothing for his chivalrous values. Callahan echoes this chivalry in his protection of Sunny, Moore, Spencer, and Walker. Like Marlowe, Callahan has few attachments and is not concerned with wealth. He lives and works in run-down locations and retains a freedom of thought and speech that distinguishes him from his peers.[42] Whereas Marlowe uses humor to distance himself from others and as a form of self-defense, Callahan uses it to humiliate his antagonists, which produces a different distancing effect, encouraging his cinema audience to gaze at him in awe, since like Marlowe but unlike the audience, he is not cursed by Denis Diderot's *esprit d'escalier*. Yet Callahan emerges as a more hardened cynic than Marlowe. Perhaps more importantly, whereas private investigators such as Marlowe were regularly on the receiving end of a beating, such episodes are extremely rare for Callahan, who thus becomes a new archetype of the tough guy. Whereas Marlowe's toughness was underscored by his ability to take a beating and come back for more, Callahan is so tough that he rarely takes a beating. In this he almost becomes a force of nature, a phenomenon that criminals cannot comprehend, let alone defeat.

This connection with hard-boiled detectives might even be read into other aspects of the *Dirty Harry* series. Megan Abbott argues that the detective is often also a "patroller of borders . . . [since] the burgeoning ethnic diversity of his environs and of urban space more generally offers a lurking danger. . . . Just as he expresses an urgent need to shore up his masculinity in the face of feminization, the tough guy must assert his whiteness."[43] Callahan is strengthening white hegemony, just like Hammer, Marlowe, and the other tough guys who wish to ensure that their moral code prevails. That his two most significant speeches are directed at San Francisco's African American population is only the most obvious signifier of the racial politics in the series. Ultimately, Callahan's whiteness melds with his invulnerability to render him more than simply a detective with a large gun: he is the supreme arbiter and dispenser of justice in postmodern San Francisco.

The Unchanging Callahan

Callahan's unbending moral code is rooted in conservative ideology and remains constant throughout the series. As suggested by his morality, he remains staunchly conservative, even reactionary, chafing at almost every change placed in front of him. In each film he is denounced by one of his superior officers for being behind the times. In *The Enforcer* he is called a "Neanderthal" for his antiquated gender politics; in *Sudden Impact* he is a "dinosaur" and "the one constant in an ever-changing universe." He is rebuked in *The Dead Pool* for refusing to play the modern PR game. Callahan, meanwhile, remains steadfast in upholding his ideals, as if to embody the declared mission of William F. Buckley's *National Review* to "stand athwart history, yelling Stop."[44] His moral certitude remains solid and unbending. Despite being upbraided in the first film for conducting illegal searches and detaining suspects without probable cause, he continues these activities. Notably, he spends much of the last two films shooting at suspects with impunity, much like a classic Wild West hero.

In a more subtle fashion, Callahan becomes an almost monolithic presence in the movies. As Matt Wanat observes, the films become "increasingly self-assured about the goodness of their hero."[45] At almost every juncture his crime-fighting instincts are proved correct. Despite Briggs's repeated attempts to confuse and distract him, Callahan discovers the identity of *Magnum Force*'s death squad. When the police captain and the mayor become convinced that Ed Mustapha's Uhuru organization is behind the terrorist activities in *The Enforcer*, Callahan instinctively knows that they are wrong. More than anyone, he understands the distinction between the law and justice as experienced by Jennifer Spencer. Finally, he shows Samantha Walker the error of her media-obsessed ways. Like Mike Hammer he has hardly any friends, only recognizes his own conception of the law and justice, and is quite prepared to see violence as an end itself, as evidenced in the relish with which he shoots his enemies in the later movies. It is not particularly difficult to imagine a retired Callahan thinking the same thoughts as Hammer: "I lived to kill so that others could live. . . . [M]y soul was a hardened thing that reveled in the thought of taking the blood of the bastards who make murder their business."[46]

The film scholar Eric Patterson argues that Eastwood's police movies produce a cinema experience that is "fundamentally without political meaning" since it inspires "no concerted action."[47] The *Dirty Harry* sequels might not have inspired a great deal of political action (although *Sudden Impact* provided a rallying slogan for conservatives) but they certainly hold great political meaning. As the films progress Callahan becomes a metaphor for a form of traditionalist American conservatism that relies on a "common sense" outlook which laments the decline in morality, individual responsibility and traditional lines of authority. He becomes a representation of a simpler time in American history that was beloved by conservatives like George Wallace and Ronald Reagan who wished to turn the clocks back to this golden age. It comes as no surprise to learn that Eastwood was "warmly accepted" into the Reagan White House.[48] As Michael Schaller points out, in the late 1970s and early 1980s, Reagan "tapped a popular yearning to restore a sense of community, real or imagined, that had been lost since the 1960s."[49] For Reagan, this Arcadia was a "mythical turn-of-the-century Dixon [Illinois] he never quite inhabited and spent his lifetime escaping."[50] Callahan is similarly harking back to a time before the 1960s when minorities and women knew their place and crime was something that happened to other people. Like the neoconservative quest to rid the United States of red tape, Callahan fiercely resents bureaucracy, deeming it a needless intrusion that prevents vigorous action. He represents the kind of people who agreed with Reagan's 1976 statement that the United States should "start treating 17 yr old muggers, robbers, rapists & murderers like muggers, robbers, rapists & murderers."[51] He provides the kind of strong, decisive leadership that American right-wingers cried out for during the Ford and Carter administrations. He would not have led such a lily-livered campaign as Ford's Whip Inflation Now or made such a startling U-turn on granting federal loans to stave off the bankruptcy of New York City. His response to the *Magnum Force* hijackers renders it easy to discern what Callahan would have done when faced with the Iranian hostage crisis during the sorry decline of Carter's presidency. His execution of the criminals echoed (perhaps consciously) the attitude of the outspoken conservative Los Angeles chief of police Ed Davis. In 1972, Davis quipped semi-seriously, "I recommend we have a portable gallows, and after we have the death penalty back in, we conduct a rapid trial for a hijacker out there, and hang him with due process out there at the airport."[52] Callahan, presumably, would have considered this too cautious a policy, although he doubtless would have agreed with Davis that police should be crime fighters rather than "button-down-collar boys who were community-relations types."[53]

One might also suggest that Callahan played a role in the culture wars, helping to divert American attention from economic problems to other issues. Even though the urban centers of the United States were dealing with the fallout from spending cuts and other supply-side economic policies that characterized the post-Nixon administrations, the *Dirty Harry* films still blamed liberals for this malaise. In this filmic world, liberalism continued to facilitate the tides of scum that fill the streets. The location of the films here is crucial. All are based in San Francisco, with *Sudden Impact*'s San Paolo a thinly disguised Santa Cruz.[54] Whereas *Dirty Harry* explicitly confirms the position of San Francisco as a key location for the battle between conservatism and liberalism in the 1970s through its location shots, the sequels do not belabor the point that Callahan is a San Francisco native. Yet the thematic links between the five *Dirty Harry* movies and the regular setting in the Bay Area means that the audience is encouraged to accept San Francisco and its surrounding area as the site of the metaphorical battles within each movie.

San Francisco held a reputation during this period for being a hotbed of liberal politics. Nancy Pelosi, sixtieth Speaker of the U.S. House of Representatives, stated in 1988 that San Francisco is "the capital of the progressive movement in this country."[55] Even as the country at large drifted rightward, San Francisco's electorate consistently returned Democrats to office in both local and state elections.[56] Callahan's presence in the belly of the liberal beast allows the films to present conservatives as an oppressed minority, fated to struggle against both crime and the liberal bureaucracy, despite the conservatives' gradual, and by *Sudden Impact* total, domination of the ideology of both major American political parties. In 1980, following Jerry Brown's failed bid for the presidency, Brown's supporters managed to elect Charles Manatt as Democratic National Chairman. According to the California historians Joel Kotkin and Paul Grabowicz, this represented "the institutionalization of [conservative] California's ideological dominance over the second of the nation's two parties."[57] The California that Kotkin and Grabowicz refer to is the swath of conservative opinion that dominated the southern and eastern parts of the state and which failed to gain a foothold in San Francisco. Soon afterward, Manatt urged the Democratic Party "to leave behind the New Deal traditions and move toward the more businesslike approach advocated by [Jerry] Brown." "No one," Manatt argued, "is going to vote Democratic in 1982 just because we ran FDR fifty years before. . . . We must convince people we can manage government as well as create it. We cannot be viewed as dewy-eyed spendthrifts or incompetent administrators."[58] San Francisco, by contrast, remained liberalism's western outpost, becoming the focus of Callahan's quest against the failures of the liberal experiment. The films' San Francisco becomes a manifestation of Reagan's 1966 insistence that California city streets at night resembled jungles, where law-abiding citizens feared to tread; Callahan is represented as the only possible solution to this perceived problem.[59]

Callahan's conservatism is underlined by his unrelenting war with bureaucracy: a regular bugbear of modern American conservatives, including Eastwood himself. Eastwood stated in 2008 that *Magnum Force* was designed to show that Callahan merely resented how the American legal system "had disintegrated into a bureaucratical [sic] nightmare."[60] "Individual independence is becoming an outmoded dream," he claimed in 1985. "We're overwhelmed by paperwork, administrative formalities, committees and subcommittees."[61] Callahan provides a cathartic, visceral response to this burden. In *The Enforcer*, he denounces Personnel as the department for "assholes" before becoming frustrated at an administrator's failure to locate a file. "I'm coming down there in five minutes," he seethes. "You'd better have those files open you pencil-pushing son-of-a-bitch." After causing a mobster to die from a heart attack in *Sudden Impact*, he is blamed for wasting "months of surveillance and intelligence work . . . thousands of dollars, hundreds of man-hours" devoted to compiling a case against the criminal. "He would've just snaked his way out of it," comes the laconic reply. "Maybe we saved the taxpayers a little money?" Later, when Jennifer Spencer quizzes him over whether he is a police officer or a criminal, he suggests that some people consider him to be both. Inevitably, these people are "bozos with big brass name-plates on their desks and asses the shape of the seat of their chairs." Foremost in his thoughts here are the local chief of police who complains that Callahan seems to have increased the crime rate in San Paolo: "We're logging more overtime than the township can afford to pay. . . . In case you haven't noticed there's been no truce declared on the muggings, the shoplifting, the burglaries, the drunken driving, all these less headline-grabbing crimes that we face here every day! Now we're doing the best we can!" "Maybe that's not good enough," is Callahan's reply.

San Paolo was part of the new California, where Proposition 13 (1978) had restricted local property-tax rates and Proposition 4 (1979) had further limited local public-sector spending, imposing Callahanian discipline on the bloated state bureaucracy. Governor Jerry Brown continued his predecessor Ronald Reagan's policy to allow the New Deal to crumble. Regulation was cut alongside government support, allowing the free market to run amok. The San Paolo Police Department was thus attempting to cope with a restricted budget and ever-shrinking resources.[62] This brings Callahan's earlier comments on saving the taxpayers' money fully into focus and also informs the bind faced by San Paolo's chief of police. Men like him were squeezed from both sides, with crime rates increasing while funding was reduced. There was, for example, a 60 percent jump in the murder rate in California and the West between 1970 and 1979. The budget for psychiatric hospitals in California was slashed, building on the cuts imposed by Reagan on California's mental health provision. Thousands of traumatized and vulnerable people were simply dumped into the community without adequate support. Jennifer Spencer (whose sister remained in a psychiatric unit for the duration of Sudden Impact) was likely one such individual. Inadequately served by mental health services and potentially suffering from psychosis, she adds to the crime statistics before Callahan intervenes. Meanwhile, the response to the urban crisis among many frightened residents threatened to compound problems: by 1980, guns were present in more than three million California households.[63]

Although Callahan is a public servant himself, his response to all this demonstrates a typically conservative attitude: San Paolo's police department must work harder, and as the familiar neoliberal admonishment to public servants dictates, do more with less. As ever, Callahan leads by example. In *Dirty Harry* he scoffs at the thought of putting in for overtime and ignores orders to refrain from harassing Scorpio by following the criminal in his off-duty time. This willingness to conduct unpaid overtime is a theme of all the sequels. In *The Enforcer* he is formally withdrawn from a case but continues to take an interest and is eventually reabsorbed into the investigating force. *Sudden Impact's* central plot is predicated on his temporary expulsion from the SFPD for the safety both of him and the city. Of course, Callahan's voluntarism is a consequence of his rejection of the bourgeois trappings of home and family, affording him the freedom to pursue cases when his colleagues with family would be putting the children to bed or spending time with loved ones or even friends. Yet it also reflects an ideological position that castigates the liberals for playing by the book and working by the clock. Conservatives will get the job done, even if they derive no financial or other benefit from it beyond the satisfaction of a job well done. Their sense of duty and commitment to voluntarism stand in sharp contrast to the indolence and avarice of their liberal counterparts.

Moving beyond mere voluntary work, Callahan's attitude has startling similarities to that of certain California free-market evangelists. Randy Knapp, founder of Orange County–based computer component manufacturer Wespercorp, said in the early 1980s, "I'll tell you, this country will be finished the day people start thinking success is a government paycheck, a Saturday football game and a can of beer," sentiments that Callahan would have applauded.[64] Years later, the Apple chairman and free-market zealot Steve Jobs even harangued President Barack Obama over the issue, claiming that Chinese factory owners were not hampered by as many regulations and "unnecessary costs" as American entrepreneurs.[65] An unnamed executive of the Fluor Corporation, an engineering company that was particularly strong in southern California, went further. Talking of his fellow members of the business elite, he raged, "We've had enough of 'what's mine is mine and what's yours is mine.' That's what has been going on in this country for the last fifty years. We should go back to 'what's mine is mine and what's yours is yours and if you step over the line, I'll blow your brains out.' That's the Western way."[66] Again, Callahan would have raised a glass to this reassertion of frontier justice.

Men such as these entrepreneurs came to maturity during the massive expansion of the New Deal welfare state that culminated in Richard Nixon's first-term expansion of government spending. The increased regulatory structure of American business during this period, combined with numerous tax increases, led them to start conceiving of government as the enemy: in the words of Kotkin and Grabowicz, it was "a bloated monster whose appetite needed to be curbed."[67] They applauded Governor Brown's faint echo of Callahan's "a man's gotta know his limitations" quip in the announcement that the late 1970s would be an "era of limits."[68] They would also have approved of Eastwood's coded attack on the inefficient (and liberal) film industry: by ensuring that his films came in under budget, he was fulfilling an urge he had held since the 1960s of "show[ing] the industry that it needs to be streamlined. . . . [A]t Malpaso, we [don't] have a staff of 26 and a fancy office. I've got a six-pack of beer under my arm, and a few pieces of paper, and a couple of pencils, and I'm in business."[69] This also aligned Callahan with California Christian conservatives like Robert Grant of Christian Voice, who outlined his group's ideology in simple terms: "We're *tired* of seeing our nation's wealth squandered . . . of seeing our very sustenance being destroyed by inflation and wasteful big-government spending. We want to return to the old values of hard-work, thrift, and obedience to the laws of God."[70]

These were the type of people who agreed that the anti-tax propositions constituted a popular reassertion of traditional American notions of freedom in the face of bureaucratic liberalism. According to the historian Simon Hall, the tax revolt constituted a protest against modernization, specifically of the assessment process.[71] The old system had been reliant on human tax assessors who were elected by popular vote and thus vulnerable to corruption. San Francisco's assessor Russell Wolden, for example, was exposed in 1965 for accepting kickbacks and bribes from various commercial sources while also valuing residential property at unfeasibly low levels. The tightening up of the system through the 1966 Petris-Knox Act and the computerization of the assessing system sparked the coalescing of the anti-tax movement and brought a Callahanian opposition to liberal bureaucracy to the fore of California politics. Led by Howard Jarvis, a businessman, Republican stalwart, and self-styled "rugged bastard who's had his head kicked in a thousand times by government," the campaign for Proposition 13 (1978) comprised a forthright rejection of California's political elite and a manifestation of the popular shift to the political right.[72] Whereas lower-income supporters wished to keep more money in their pockets, their more affluent counterparts had become increasingly resentful of the fact that their tax dollars were benefiting welfare recipients and other "takers" rather than the affluent "makers" themselves. Jarvis himself was convinced that taxation itself was "un-American and illegal" and couched his opposition in simple terms that the electorate embraced.[73] For Pepperdine University president William Banowsky, Proposition 13 promised not only to rein in high taxes but also to roll back and impose discipline on government bureaucracy.[74] Ever one to sense the importance of shifts in public mood, Reagan offered a public renunciation of his previous opposition to property-tax limitations by signing the petition to place Proposition 13 on the ballot.[75] As Thomas and Mary Edsall point out, the tax revolt "shap[ed] an anti-government ethic" within the conservative movement, providing it with "a powerful internal coherence" and a popular support base.[76] This was helped in part by the simple appeal of a petition that promised to lower everyone's taxes without identifying which services would need to be cut in order to balance the budget. That a number of large corporations, the governor's office, and the state legislature united behind the opposition to Proposition 13 reinforced the idea that this was the average Joe fighting the privileged and the powerful.[77] Indeed, one of President Carter's aides called the tax revolt in California more of a "revolution against government" itself.[78] Furthermore, the spread of the tax revolt outside the state's boundaries suggested that this was not simply a Golden State concern. Callahan's beliefs thus chimed with a significant shift in American public opinion. By 1980 only 24 percent of Americans supported increased government spending to assist the African American population. Meanwhile, the Republican Party's vision that bureaucracy should be rolled back was gaining widespread acceptance.[79] As important, this new conservatism had a distinctly alabaster tint. The tax revolt and its attendant assault on the liberal welfare state frequently pitched white Americans against African Americans and

Hispanic Americans, and by the time of *Sudden Impact* it was represented in the White House by Reagan himself.

Essentially, Callahan represented a core aspect of Reaganite politics. Both he and the president harked back to California's (probably mythical) golden age, before bureaucracy, liberalism, and licentiousness expelled the state from its Eden. The conservative campaigner from southern California Rev. William McBirnie commented that Reagan's early political campaigns contained "a sense of mission. He wants to drive the barbarians out. He's El Cid. He's the guy who could have taken it easy but instead chose to come out and fight."[80] Callahan did so, albeit in more spectacularly violent fashion, bringing the values of the frontier to modern-day San Francisco. This is even explicitly referenced in *The Enforcer* when he is temporarily removed from the homicide department after destroying a shop while foiling a robbery. The chief of police is apoplectic: "This little Wild West show of yours yesterday is exactly the kind of thing this department's no longer prepared to tolerate!" This retrospection also amplifies the link between Callahan and the hard-boiled detectives of Hammett and Chandler. Like Sam Spade and Philip Marlowe, Callahan is a representative of a bygone age, living in a corrupt and threatening city. Like them, he is a knight in shining armor, although his chivalrous code is highly conservative. He represents the morality of an earlier, simpler period but one that is firmly yoked to conservative political ideology.

Callahan thus becomes a near-perfect representation of modern American conservatism. His form of "conservative egalitarianism" was as problematic as Reagan's.[81] On the surface he seems to approve of equal opportunities, working happily alongside racial minorities and women. Yet a close examination of what Callahan *does* as well as what he *says* reveals that minorities remain in subordinate positions, "fucking fruits" are exterminated, and women know their place. According to this ideology, society's problems are caused by two groups. The first are the criminals who in Callahan's opinion simply enjoy breaking the law and hold no respect for society. The second are equally pernicious: public-sector bureaucrats who mistakenly seek out deeper reasons for the criminals' criminality. In attempting to understand rather than punish offenders, they facilitate rather than reduce crime. Ultimately, this contributes to another key theme of the sequels, namely, Callahan's failure to rise in the

SFPD beyond detective. There are two threads behind this subtle and eas-ily overlooked plot feature. First, it demonstrates that, while the liberals sit behind desks and pontificate, conservatives are out on the streets, solving crime. Second, it points to the supposed refusal of the liberal elite to acknowledge that conservative crime-fighting methods are most effective. Callahan's methods are cheaper, since less money and time is wasted on bureaucracy and court appeals. They are also statistically more effective, since fewer criminals are wandering the streets when Callahan is around, not least because he kills about forty of them in the course of the series.[82] Yet even though he is undoubtedly effective, he is not able to rise to a position of authority within the force. Meanwhile, Mayor George Moscone's chief of police, Charles Gain, was alienating his rank and file by attempting to liberalize the SFPD and courting controversy by being photographed at the annual Hooker's Ball in San Francisco during October 1977. That Moscone defended Gain's record rather than firing him was proof that times had changed since Tom Cahill's tenure.[83] By contrast, the single-minded Callahan remained on the streets. This al-lowed him to continue to represent frontier justice in the increasingly urbanized city, as he blew away criminals left, right and center, even shooting them in the posterior as they tried to escape the fusillade.

* * *

Callahan's political stance—and as important, the way in which the con-servative undercurrents of these films are disguised—is exemplified in a discussion with a fellow cop at the start of *Sudden Impact*. Callahan and the other detective are on the coastline of San Francisco's northwest shoulder, investigating the scene of Jennifer Spencer's first crime—a man who has had a ".38 caliber vasectomy" according to another inves-tigating officer. In a crude piece of phallic symbolism, the detective is chewing on a hot dog. As they head down to the waterfront, he asks Callahan if "all this" is getting to him. Callahan briefly ponders the ques-tion before replying: "No, this stuff isn't getting to me. The shootings, the knifings, the beatings. Old ladies being bashed in the head for their social security checks. Teachers being thrown out of a window because they don't give A's. *That doesn't bother me a bit.* . . . Or this job either, hav-ing to wade through the scum of this city. Being swept away by bigger and bigger waves of corruption, apathy, and red tape." The camera then shifts position, depicting Callahan's profile framed by the Golden Gate Bridge: "No, that doesn't bother me. But you know what does bother me? You know what makes me really sick to my stomach?" Callahan pauses, for maximum effect. His colleague has stopped eating, eager to hear this sage advice. "Watching you stuff your face with those hot dogs. Nobody, *I mean nobody*, puts ketchup on a hot dog" (see fig. 17).

Consequently, when Callahan then concludes his diatribe with the words, "I'm talking about having our fingers in the holes and the whole damn dike's crumbling around us," the audience is still processing the humor. Callahan undercuts his conservative perspective with a quip about hot dogs. It offers a fine get-out clause in suggesting that Callahan is as flippant about politics as he is about his colleague's epicurean foibles. Yet the political statement was as extreme as Reagan's comparison of urban streets to jungles. It takes dead aim at the liberal system that frustrated Callahan's instincts for over ten years. The audience, however, is encouraged not to take the politics seriously, and to excuse Callahan because he has it all in perspective. After all, he represents common sense, that most subtle and dangerous of political ideologies.[84] This "common sense" becomes most apparent in the finale to *Sudden Impact*. In an echo of the conclusion to *Dirty Harry*, victims' rights—this time, the victims of the gang rape—are elevated over all else, which makes perfect common sense. Jennifer Spencer was so traumatized by her experience that she quite literally lost touch with reality. The murders she committed could therefore be put down to diminished responsibility or even temporary insanity, but both of these explanations are far too legalistic and bureaucratic. As important, they also rely on a liberal interpretation of the law, which might suggest that the gang rape and thus society made her a criminal, that she was not fully cognizant of either her behavior or its consequences, and that prosecutors should seek to understand her motives rather than simply locking her away. Better not to enter into these murky waters and instead keep things crystal clear by placing blame on one of the gang members and allowing Spencer to walk free.

Even though he is quite prepared to punch a woman in the face, destroy Chinese restaurants, and terrorize a vicar, Callahan is a conservative, but he is apparently no bigot. The sequels conclude that the changes wrought on the Bay Area are the mistaken conclusion of decades of liberal rule. Thus they reinforce the conservative undercurrents of the original rather than, as their surface suggests, undercutting and blunting its radical edges. As time moves on, and the world of San Francisco changes, Callahan stands firm, sticking his thumb in the dike in a valiant attempt to protect traditional American values from becoming overwhelmed by the consequences of liberalism's errors. It is this that is far more important to the political ideology of the *Dirty Harry* films than the political identities of his opponents. The leftists and rightists that Callahan disposes of are so sketchily drawn that they are barely above mere caricatures of their political analogues in the real world. They are almost as simplistic as the Los Angeles cops and bikers who wear their hair in a hippy style and who sport Nazi regalia in *Every Which Way But Loose*: simply there to give Eastwood's character something to aim at. Leger Grindon writes that the foes in *Every Which Way But Loose* allow Eastwood's character to "thumb his nose at government bureaucrats and enforcers and alternately assail those who challenge the habits of common folk. . . . The hostility toward the relics of a counter-culture, the representatives of government, and middle-class decorum suggest lower-class conservatism in step with the soon-to-be-elected Ronald Reagan administration."[85] This is evidenced in the crude figures of the PRSF, based on a group—the Symbionese Liberation Army—that was itself a near-farcical and pathological echo of 1960s leftists and revolutionaries.[86] The political subtext in *Every Which Way* is thoroughly undercut—as in the *Dirty Harry* films—by comedy. Thus the sequels' politics presents two pernicious facades. First, it sets up a false dichotomy. By rendering the criminals of the right and left as extremists, the films make Callahan appear to be a centrist. This, however, is undercut when you examine exactly what Callahan says and does. Yet much of what he says appears to be common sense and slyly humorous. This humor is the second facade, since it allows Callahan to get away with expressing offensive sentiments—it's just a joke, after all. And the *Dirty Harry* movies are just that. Each is, after all, only a movie, and as Eastwood has pointed out, seeking out the political overtones in such films is a foolish exercise.[87]

Callahan's Legacy

I know what you're thinking. . . . You want to make my day? . . . Go ahead—

Clint Eastwood, speech to Republican National Convention, Tampa, Florida, August 30, 2012

MAKE MY DAY!

Delegates at Republican National Convention, Tampa, Florida, August 30, 2012

The relationship between Callahan and the conservatives arguably peaked in Eastwood's nationally televised speech on the final day of the Republican National Convention in August 2012. Here, Callahan's most famous quotation became a rallying cry that animated many thousands of Republicans. Eastwood strode to the platform at the Tampa Bay Times Forum in front of a primetime television audience. Backed by a recolored image of him playing Josey Wales standing before a town engulfed in flames while the unmistakable theme from *The Good, the Bad, and the Ugly* played in the background, Eastwood looked every one of his eighty-two years.[1] The audience chanted "Make my day!" as if the wisecrack had become a political slogan akin to "Four more years!" or even "Tippecanoe and Tyler too!" "I know what you're thinking," Eastwood started, citing Harry Callahan's first major peroration. Eastwood proceeded to hold an imaginary conversation with Barack Obama, who supposedly occupied an empty chair to his left, which at one point involved Eastwood clowning, "What do you want me to tell Romney? I can't tell him to do that . . . to himself. You're crazy." This peculiar, unplanned rhetorical device was the most noted and memorable feature of the address.[2] Yet the speech also reminded listeners of the centrality of Harry Callahan to Eastwood's persona. Opening with the monologue from *Dirty Harry* and closing with the most famous line from *Sudden Impact* indicated that Callahan was firmly in the conservative camp, partnering Mitt Romney and Paul Ryan in their quest for the White House.

"He just made my day," gushed Romney immediately afterward, even though the furor surrounding Eastwood's appearance partially obscured Romney's own address.[3] While some conservatives were delighted at the speech, others were less effusive. One unnamed Romney aide dismissed it as "weird."[4] Voices from the Democratic side of the political divide were almost unanimous in their derision, illustrating the extent to which Eastwood's screen persona had become yoked to the American conservative movement. The Democratic senator Tom Harkin argued that Eastwood's appearance was "perfect": he was "an angry old white man spewing incoherent nonsense."[5] The *New York Times* described the speech as "the most bizarre, head-scratching 12 minutes in recent political history."[6] For the satirical commentator Jon Stewart, Eastwood spent "twelve minutes on the most important night of Mitt Romney's life yelling at a chair," in an event that gave Stewart "the most joy I've gotten from an old man since Dick Cheney non-fatally shot one in the face."[7] Stewart's fellow satirist Stephen Colbert went one stage further, engaging the empty chair in a heated debate on *The Colbert Report*. (The chair prevailed.)[8] Obama himself even weighed into the discussion on his Twitter feed, posting a photo of the president's White House chair and pointing out that it was "taken."[9] Despite Eastwood's claim that he was "aiming for people in the middle," it seems that the speech did very little to challenge party lines in the 2012 election.[10]

The equivalent speech at the Democratic National Convention the following week offers an instructive contrast. President Bill Clinton, looking trim and a young sixty-six thanks to a vegan diet, launched into a bravura forty-eight-minute fact-filled debunking of the Republican platform before endorsing Obama. There were no gimmicks in Clinton's speech; just the former president, his unparalleled skill for talking to large audiences as if each individual was the only person in the room, his ability to reduce knotty political issues to their essence, and his refusal to appeal to base instincts.[11] It set the terms of battle: the gut versus the head. Dirty Harry versus Slick Willie, two of the most charismatic and recognizable individuals from the red and blue sides of the political divide. The instinctive renegade cop versus the intellectual former president. Two near-mythical icons outlining their responses to the Obama administration and their hopes for the next four years of American history. This was arguably the definitive image of Dirty Harry in America.

Callahan's two indelible quotes are central to Eastwood's cinematic persona, and their citation at Tampa Bay begs further evaluation of Callahan's resonance in American politics and culture in the post-1960s period. As the 2012 convention suggests, despite his attempt to separate his life from his screen persona, Eastwood remains unable to escape Callahan's shadow. His campaign for mayor of Carmel, California, in 1986 attracted huge media interest. The prevalence of *Dirty Harry*–themed puns in reportage of the election and Eastwood's mayoral term is revealing of the extent to which Callahan was conflated with Eastwood. "Make my day" was also appropriated by Ronald Reagan in the 1980s, demonstrating that Callahan had become not only a bona fide pop cultural phenomenon but also a conservative icon and the embodiment of the strong leader craved by the conservatives of the 1970s. Eastwood quoting Reagan quoting Callahan thus becomes a feedback loop, underscoring the relevance of the film series to modern American conservatism. An evaluation of conservative rhetoric in the Reagan and Bush eras illustrates the parallels between Callahan's fictional world and the world that American conservatives saw and intended to remold.

Such rhetorical echoes also accentuate the extent to which Eastwood's cinematic persona was reliant on Callahan. Eastwood continued to play variations on the Callahanian archetype through his films of the 1970s and 1980s. By the 1990s, however, and as suggested by *The Dead Pool* (Van Horn, 1988), he was simply too old to convince as an action hero. His acting roles shifted to incorporate Eastwood's own aging into the characters he played, at first subtly as in *The Rookie* (Eastwood, 1990) and then decisively as in *Unforgiven* (Eastwood, 1992). His later roles add further nuance to his screen persona, not least through referencing Callahan himself, as in the case of Wes Block in *Tightrope* (Tuggle, 1984) or Walt Kowalski in *Gran Torino* (Eastwood, 2008). His final major role as Kowalski, a disguised Callahan transplanted to Detroit, brings Callahan's story full circle. *Gran Torino* begins by poking gentle fun at Kowalski's antediluvian attitudes. As the film develops, however, Kowalski realizes that they have prevented him understanding that his Hmong neighbors face many of the same struggles that he does. Their attempt to retain their traditional culture echoes his maintenance of traditional masculine values. He ultimately allows his xenophobia to wither away as he gradually realizes that the future of the neighborhood rests with the Hmong youngsters. He chooses to align himself with the Hmong rather than his own family, a transcendent rejection of Callahanian attitudes and a conclusion that doubtless appealed to the people in the middle far more than Eastwood's 2012 speech.

Go Ahead, Make Me Mayor

Eastwood's mayoral campaign in Carmel provides insights into the extent to which the Callahanian worldview permeated American politics in the 1980s. Eastwood ran successfully for mayor in April 1986, receiving 72 percent of the vote, and served a single two-year term, for which he earned $4,800.[12] His major successes included ending a ban on downtown ice cream parlors, concluding a deal with the Monterey Peninsula Water Management District to increase the city's water allocation, providing more public toilets and stairways to the city's beach, and expanding the children's library. He also solved a potentially controversial problem by using $5 million of his own money to secure the future of the local Mission Ranch complex from developers, echoing William F. Buckley by commenting that "maybe the world doesn't allow you to keep things the same, but we can try."[13] His final meeting involved minor amendments to the city's General Plan, discussion of a zoning change, and the passage of laws prohibiting skateboarding on one street and reducing the speed limit in another.[14]

A small town with a population of less than five thousand in 1986, Carmel sits in the Fifth District of Monterey County, which had offered its majority approval to only one Democratic presidential candidate between 1948 and 1988. Despite its history as an artistic colony, it was no haven for beatniks or other countercultural dropouts: according to *Chicago Tribune* journalist William Rice, it once passed an anti-hippie ordinance, banning people from sitting on the city's grass.[15] The median age of a Carmelite in 1986 was fifty, and they lived in a city that had no fast-food outlets but an abundance of fancy boutiques and stores stocking gourmet produce.[16] As Robert Lindsey noted in the *New York Times* soon after Eastwood's victory, much of Carmel's political history was characterized by struggles between residents and business interests over commercial development, generating festering resentments that animated local voters and manifested themselves in a conservatism that Eastwood was able to exploit:

> Many people said today that Mr. Eastwood appeared to have tapped an unexpected lode of resentment from ordinary home-owners, whose plans for remodelling or expansion had collided with the Council's policy of controlling all manner of construction here to preserve Carmel's beauty and charm. . . . [He uses] the same "let's-get-government-off-our-backs" approach to campaigning that . . . Ronald Reagan used with remarkable political success.[17]

In some respects, Carmel, with its aging population, dislike of Demo-crats and hippies, and resentment of big government and slackers, pro-vides an ideal symbol of the conservative backlash against 1960s liberal-ism. The resentment identified by Lindsey might have focused on issues pertaining to property, but it reflects the key conservative tenet that strong government is inimical to the interests of the individual and only works to restrict individual freedom. That Eastwood was on record stat-ing that "we live in a welfare-oriented society, and people expect more, more from Big Daddy government. . . . That philosophy never got you anywhere," likely did little to harm his popularity in his adopted town.[18]

Although Eastwood campaigned and later governed in a style that deliberately ignored his celebrity status and instead emphasized his lo-cal connections and ambitions, commentators could not resist the obvi-ous temptation. "The campaign turned surreal," wrote Lloyd Grove in the *Washington Post*, "as hordes of journalists from around the world descended on the city and commenced hectoring the candidates about 'Dirty Harry' and who would make whose day."[19] "Eastwood Asks Carmel to Make His Day," wisecracked the *Los Angeles Times* in similar fashion.[20] The *Chicago Tribune* mused on the apparent paradox of Dirty Harry, who famously treated San Francisco's mayor with a cynical disdain that came close to open contempt, declaring his ambition to become a bureaucrat: "The more one thinks about it, the less sense it makes. Clint is a killer, on screen and off."[21] The *Tribune* thus refused to acknowledge that Harry

Callahan was merely a fictional construct and instead insisted that he and Eastwood were one and the same. The *Washington Post*'s Ruth Marcus went to town in her commentary. Eastwood's campaign found him "in a shoot-out"; his candidacy had a "Sudden Impact" on the community and had "not exactly made [incumbent mayor] Townsend's day"; Townsend reportedly complained that Eastwood "has spent 'A Fistful of Dollars' on the race"; meanwhile, some of the locals were not "'Beguiled' by Eastwood's candidacy."[22] At the end of an interview with the *Chicago Tribune*'s John Hubner, Eastwood supposedly "walked down those mean Carmel streets, searching for voters who have what it takes to stand beside him in the battle against the forces of Charlotte Townsend."[23] Gary Trudeau's *Doonesbury* comic strip even joined in the fun. Lacey Davenport, the strip's Republican representative for San Francisco, campaigned for Eastwood. Her stump speech questioned, "What's the greatest problem facing municipal governments today?" eliciting from Eastwood the Callahanian response: "punks." Davenport demurred in her trademark style: "Uh, no, deficits. Oh, dear, is this a law and order campaign?"[24] On the flight back to Washington, D.C., Davenport's assistant Joanie Caucus dreamed of a mysterious stranger entering her bedroom as she slept. "Make . . . my . . . night," he drawled.[25] The locals themselves made similar links. "It's a real shock to open the door and see Dirty Harry there, but he's doing it," said Bill Brown, co-owner of the local newspaper, the *Carmel Pine Cone*.[26] Predictably, "Go Ahead, Make My Day, Clint for Mayor" T-shirts were sold in a local shop, and "Go Ahead, Make Me Mayor" bumper stickers were also available.[27] The managing editor of the *Pine Cone* grew so tired of these quips that he issued the following threat: "If I hear another 'make my day' take-off, I'll scream. Or worse yet, write a long, involved editorial on the sewage capacity of [Carmel's] facilities."[28] This shorthand, however, continued in the national reportage on his mayoral administration. "His no-nonsense style of government was a touch reminiscent of the character traits of the hard-nosed cop he played in his 'Dirty Harry' movies," mused the *Washington Post* toward the end of his term.[29] "Clint Eastwood Fires Away in His New Role," chortled the *Chicago Tribune*. "The star [had] lost a showdown" in the previous year, which led to his candidacy, the *Tribune* punned.[30] "Unmaking His Day," sniggered the *Washington Post*'s examination of Mayor Eastwood's first inbox. "Okay," it warned Eastwood, "there's a backed-up sewer in Carmel,

Calif., with your name on it."[31] The new mayor even received a congratu-latory phone call from President Reagan, during which they exchanged quips and quoted each other's most famous lines.[32]

When asked what Callahan would think of Eastwood's new role, the mayor said, "Well, Dirty Harry has always been angry with the mayor. He's always been fighting bureaucracy, and I guess in real life I'm fighting bureaucracy too."[33] Eastwood's comment demonstrates that he essen-tially advocated Callahanian concepts of government and offers insight into the motives behind his decision to run. The catalyst for his campaign was his disgust with the refusal of the city bureaucracy to allow him to erect an office block next to his bar on San Carlos Street. He told John Hubner of the *Chicago Tribune* that this led him to think: "If this can hap-pen to me, who has visibility and access to the press, imagine what hap-pens to the little guy who is trying to get a project through. . . . Imagine if that project was my whole life, if my whole life savings and my family's future were riding on it. . . . You're dealing with people's lives, and they deserve respect."[34] Thus his decision to enter the bureaucracy was both to humanize it and to deconstruct it from within, as demonstrated by his position on ice cream, which was defined as a battle of ordinary folks fighting an overweening and oppressive bureaucracy, much like Calla-han's perpetual struggle with his superiors.[35] That similar sentiments had animated Reagan's gubernatorial campaign twenty years earlier demonstrates the extent to which Eastwood was drawing on the parallels between his screen persona and the modern conservative movement. Soon after his election, Eastwood argued that his purpose was to "take the community out of the hands of the few and put it in the hands of the many."[36] Adding a revenge motif to the early days of his mayoralty, one of his first actions was to sack four commissioners who had opposed his office plan. Arguing that the bureaucrats were no longer in touch with the people and had corrupted the concept of public service, Eastwood confirmed that Callahanian attitudes, leavened with elements of Jack-sonianism, were central to his political views, although it was a little-known fact that the office plan was settled out of court after Eastwood used a bureaucratic maneuver and sued the city.[37] Like Callahan, though, he took a low-paying job out of a sense of duty to his community, at-tempted to cut levels of bureaucracy in order to allow residents more freedom, and even worked extra hours without complaint much in the same manner as Callahan refused to claim the extra income he was due for overtime.[38] And when election time came around in Carmel, he declined to run again, telling the city, "A man's gotta know his limitations": the final lines from *Magnum Force*.[39]

Toward the end of Eastwood's term, Pope John Paul II was scheduled to visit, prompting the production of a poster that featured a likeness of the pope and Eastwood with the caption, "Thou Hast Made My Day."[40] That it was unclear who had made whose day indicates how highly Eastwood/Callahan had risen in the affections of Carmel's citizens. His increased political profile even compelled *Chicago Tribune* columnist and military affairs expert David Evans to reveal that he considered Eastwood to be ideally qualified to be George H. W. Bush's new secretary of defense. After all, through his movies he had "shown a consistent appreciation for cost-effective firepower and plenty of ammunition"; his Cold War anti-communist thriller *Firefox* (Eastwood, 1982) demonstrated that there would be no need to fear the Soviets stealing American technology; and his mayoral stint demonstrated his management expertise and record of service. Evans concluded, not completely tongue-in-cheek, that Eastwood was a "certified hawk, with guts and credibility to match."[41] He was not alone in considering Eastwood to be ideal for the Republican Party. A letter to the *New York Times* thought Eastwood should have partnered with Bush in the 1988 presidential campaign:

> If Mr Bush really wanted to pick a staunch conservative that many women would find attractive [rather than Dan Quayle], why didn't he choose Clint Eastwood? . . . [H]e is a well-preserved specimen. . . . Gov. Thomas Keen said chidingly of the Democrats in his key-note address: "They try to talk like Dirty Harry. But they will still act like Pee-Wee Herman." Implicit in this is the corollary that being Dirty Harry comes naturally to the Republicans. So why didn't Mr. Bush just go for the real thing?[42]

One reason for this was Eastwood's awareness that his extracurricular activities, which included numerous affairs and children with multiple partners, would have been a severe impediment to his electoral chances on the national level. As important was his continued film career, which continued to reference Callahan despite the final *Dirty Harry* movie appearing in 1988.

Callahan and Eastwood's Films

Eastwood's films since the early 1970s can be split into two distinct periods. In the first, which lasted until the release of *The Rookie*, he is in essence a pseudo-superhero. Many of these films follow *Dirty Harry*'s template in presenting Eastwood's character as an honorable loner often in conflict with his superiors. By the 1980s, his attempt to defy age and obsolescence became increasingly unsuccessful. The poor response to Eastwood's depiction of Callahan in *The Dead Pool* highlighted the beginning of a new phase in which aging and redemption became clear themes in his role, to the extent that scholars now freely discuss Eastwood's "senior persona."[43] Such films contain numerous themes related to age and its effects on the male body, but key characteristics of Callahan remain even as Eastwood headed toward retirement age.

In *The Gauntlet* (Eastwood, 1977), Eastwood plays a hybrid Callahan-Coogan in Ben Shockley, an embittered, borderline-alcoholic cop. Shockley is given one last chance to prove his value by escorting a prostitute to a court hearing at which she will testify against the Mafia. It is a setup, however: his "spit-and-polish" police commissioner and the assistant district attorney are in cahoots with the mob, and Shockley's dirty job is to be collateral damage.[44] During a lull in the chase Shockley declares that he learned as a young man that "the only people I knew that stood for something were cops," but events drew him to the conclusion that the system was thoroughly corrupt and that it worked only to beat down honorable police like him. Shockley and his ward develop a deep relationship defined by her feistiness and his physical protection. In the film's finale, they run the gauntlet of the entire Phoenix Police Department protected only by a hijacked Trail Lines tour bus. The quest allows him to develop from a schmuck into a Callahanian hero and demonstrates a far more sympathetic approach toward Eastwood's female charge, perhaps because she was played by his partner, Sondra Locke. Locke also co-starred in the Eastwood comedies *Every Which Way But Loose* (Fargo, 1978) and its sequel, *Any Which Way You Can* (Van Horn, 1980), both of which revel in anti-authoritarianism. Denounced by *Newsweek* as a "plotless junkheap," the first presents Eastwood's Philo Beddoe as a working-class force of nature who rejects the trappings of success.[45] The film's celebration of an authentically American working-class culture is announced early on when Beddoe plays a practical joke on a pretentious undergraduate student, revealing her disgust for the "real" America and encouraging the audience to sympathize with Beddoe's relaxed attitude toward life. Just as Chico Gonzales is chided for possessing a college degree, the undergraduate is derided for attempting to intellectualize country music. Meanwhile, Beddoe's Ma assails the California Department of Motor Vehicles for its absurdly bureaucratic regulations, which prevent her from obtaining a driving license. In refusing to win the film's climactic bare-knuckle fight, Philo reinforces the Callahanian notion that honor is more important than success, a theme that is reprised in the sequel when Beddoe and his opponent decide to fight for their personal satisfaction rather than the financial gain of others (although quite how much satisfaction they derived from the injuries they sustain in the fight is not made clear). Distant echoes of Callahan's insubordinate behavior appear in Beddoe's pet orangutan Clyde's wild antics and disregard for social niceties. In *Any Which Way*, Clyde regularly defecates in a police car and at the film's conclusion knocks out a police officer with a single punch: a literal extension of Callahan's attitude toward authority. The sequel also contains an odd piece of political editorial. When his love interest, Lynn, rebuffs his offer of his spare room and declares that she doesn't need a "handout," Beddoe corrects her: "Handouts are what you get from the government. A hand up is what you get from friends."

The anti-authoritarian streak continued in Eastwood's reunion with Don Siegel, *Escape from Alcatraz* (Siegel, 1979), which holds faint echoes of Siegel's *Riot in Cell Block 11* but includes an unlikely denouement that plays to Eastwood's star status. *Bronco Billy* (Eastwood, 1980) and *Honkytonk Man* (Eastwood, 1982) saw Eastwood playing against type, undercutting his own persona by playing men who essentially failed in life. Relics of a bygone age, like Callahan, these men struggle to contend with an America that has passed them by.[46] *Tightrope*, on the other hand, is best viewed as an unofficial Dirty Harry film. As the Eastwood scholar Howard Hughes suggests, it builds on and deepens the Callahan caricature in many ways.[47] Richard Schickel notes that *Tightrope* was relocated from its original San Francisco to New Orleans in part because Eastwood wanted to minimize any parallels between Eastwood's Wes Block and Callahan.[48] It is, however, almost impossible to approach Block without thinking of a Callahan who has settled down into domesticity, found to be lacking the skills necessary to maintain a marriage, and then acting out his many private sexual fantasies while attempting to preserve the image of a good father and dedicated cop. Block wallows in the swampy, licentious atmosphere of New Orleans conjured by Bruce Surtees's characteristically low lighting. The city's reputation for loose sexual morals, which echoes that of San Francisco, encourages further consideration of the parallels between Block and Callahan. Block's predilection for extreme sexual activity offers him a curious empathy for the film's villain while simultaneously placing him under suspicion, a situation that is not helped when he pays a prostitute for her services immediately after questioning her about the case. The film thus echoes *Dirty Harry*'s suggestion that only a fine line—a tightrope, even—separates the hero from the villain, as made explicit when Block tells a forensic scientist in Callahanian style that the killer was enjoying himself just before he killed his first victim.

Eastwood felt that Block was a richer and potentially more provocative character who moved beyond Callahan's single-minded obsession with the law. For example, whereas Callahan's sexuality was relatively bland, Block's was dangerous and potentially harmful to his case, his career, and his family. In Eastwood's view, this added a new dimension to his character and to Eastwood's screen persona.[49] Notably, as Drucilla Cornell observes, Block's use of handcuffs as a sexual aid reflects his thirst for control, which gradually ebbs as he matures during the film.[50] Whereas Callahan's inner struggles seem to find expression in violence, Block's considerable turmoil, which emanates from his divorce, takes flight in brothels and bars and with numerous sexual partners. Yet the film's presentation of sexual activity relies on appeals to red-blooded heterosexuality and thus does not ultimately represent a great departure from the Callahanian blueprint.[51] The film's brief suggestion that Block might have had a homosexual experience (including a knowing wink to *Dirty Harry* when Block is propositioned by a man who calls him "Alice") is overwhelmed by the naked female skin on display, often entwined with Block's, and the regular propositions Block receives from female sex workers.

Tightrope's only major deviation from the Callahan archetype is Block's integration with the New Orleans Police Department, where he is never in conflict with his superiors. In *Heartbreak Ridge* (Eastwood,

1986), however, Eastwood was again the outsider given a final opportunity to atone for knowing better than his superior officers. That Eastwood was clearly far too old to play the role was dismissed in the face of
his star power. Eastwood's Gunny Highway is tasked with training a platoon of the Army's worst recruits in advance of the invasion of Grenada.
Just as Grenada offered Reagan the opportunity to banish the failure of
Vietnam from memory, it offered Gunny another chance to demonstrate
the value of the instinctive warrior while facilitating his reconciliation
with his wife.[52] Many of the familiar Callahan tropes recur in *Heartbreak
Ridge*. Highway has a decidedly tense relationship with the top brass,
aside from fellow Vietnam veteran Sergeant Major Choozoo and Colo-
nel Meyers, whom Highway impresses with his willingness to abide by
the code of the Marines and preparedness to adapt to changing battle-
field circumstances on the fly. The men bond because each has proved
himself in deed rather than through thought. After chafing at Gunny's
harsh methods, the men in his platoon eventually develop respect and
loyalty for him when they realize that he gets things done. He treats the
college-educated Lieutenant Ring with disdain, most notably when the
lieutenant announces that he will miss a combat exercise because he has
a doctor's appointment. Most significantly, his chief antagonist, Major
Powers, has risen to his position from supply and logistics rather than in
the field: he is another "pencil-pushing son-of-a-bitch" who denounces
Highway as an "anachronism" before insisting on the completion of the
correct paperwork when dispensing equipment.[53]

Eastwood's advanced age received its first major acknowledgment in
The Rookie (Eastwood, 1990), after the largely forgettable comedy *Pink
Cadillac* (Van Horn, 1989) presented Eastwood as the scourge of a white
supremacist group and suggested that he was no longer suited to all-
action roles. Veteran Los Angeles detective Nick Pulovski (Eastwood)
schools David Ackerman (Charlie Sheen) in Callahanian crime-fighting
techniques, leading *Variety* to complain that the film should have been
called "*Dirty Harry 5½*."[54] Eastwood's biographer Patrick McGilligan
later dismissed it as a "regrettable *Dirty Harry* pastiche," yet it is best
approached as a key moment when Eastwood's cinematic persona decisively shifted to acknowledge the actor's age.[55] Alongside the regulation
wisecracks, shootouts, and scenes of mild peril, *The Rookie* plays with
certain *Dirty Harry* tropes. "Don't mind Pulovski," the lieutenant tells

Ackerman. "He's an asshole but you'll get used to him after a while." "Flattery will get you nowhere," responds Nick. Ackerman, initially denounced by Nick as an "uptight, regulation-spouting Boy Scout," is partnered with Nick because his test scores are perfect. Like Gonzales, he gradually learns the way of the instinctive police officer, a transformation that is symbolized when he begins riding his motorbike without a helmet. He finally adopts the man-of-action mantle in setting out to rescue Nick from a criminal gang. In contrast to the lily-livered mayor of San Francisco, Los Angeles's mayor refuses to pay ransom for Nick, leading Ackerman to rely on the private enterprise of his father's company for the money. After the climactic shootout at Los Angeles airport, Nick nods to *Dirty Harry* when observing that a security guard only had five bullets in his gun. *The Rookie*'s final scene, with Pulovski now confined to a desk job, establishes that the baton has passed to a younger generation of detectives.[56]

Aging continues as a theme in *In the Line of Fire* (Peterson, 1993), which featured Eastwood as a former bodyguard to John F. Kennedy, consumed with guilt at his failure to prevent the president's assassination and initially derided by his new partner for his senescence. Prior to Eastwood successfully exorcising his past by saving the current president from assassination, he takes time out with his love interest on the steps of the Lincoln Memorial while the phallic Washington Monument stands in the middle distance: Sergio Leone's block of marble is finally in its natural home. Planting Eastwood in the midst of the great presidents seemed to suggest that the actor had entered the American pantheon, a representation of the American way and potentially the one man who might have saved Lincoln from John Wilkes Booth.[57] As significant, Eastwood's Frank Horrigan is noteworthy in accepting his physical frailties: here he is denounced as a dinosaur not for his political attitude but for his advanced age and physical weakness. Again, however, his instinctive reactions to criminal activity prove more effective than his superiors' bureaucratic approach.

As *Heartbreak Ridge* and *In the Line of Fire* suggest, redemption for past sins—often those committed by Callahanian characters—is a leitmotif of the later Eastwood roles. As Eastwood himself acknowledged, the tale of *Unforgiven*'s William Munny is defined by his attempt to redeem himself.[58] Here, as an aging former gunslinger, he appears to be doing penance for the violent sins of the past before righting Big Whiskey's wrongs through an outburst of extreme violence. A morally ambiguous work, dedicated to the memory of Eastwood's directorial mentors Leone and Siegel, *Unforgiven* meditates on the impact of violence on the United States and its role in the settling of the West. Elements of *Dirty Harry* also poke through. The town's lawman, Little Bill Daggett, seems to keep the peace through controlling the presence of guns. This apparently liberal man reveals himself to be as sadistic and violent as the criminals he hopes to keep out of the town. Thus liberal bureaucracy fails and is arguably a subterfuge obscuring deeper, more problematic urges. As important, the film's final gunfight confirms the value of violence to keeping the peace in the United States. So, much like Harry Callahan, Eastwood's Munny demonstrates that a willful disregard of the rule of law bolstered by moral righteousness is necessary to maintain social harmony, even as his motivation—money rather than revenge—presents him as an avatar of a more complex Americanism than Callahan.[59]

Other late-period Eastwood vehicles unite the themes of redemption and responsibility. As former Air Force pilot Frank Corvin in *Space Cowboys* (Eastwood, 2000), Eastwood is asked by NASA to collect a rogue satellite, despite the administration's concerns that he has a Callahanian problem with authority and is no team player, having waged a long-term feud with the project's leader. After a serious accident disables its propulsion systems, Corvin pilots the Space Shuttle back to Earth without recourse to its computer navigation systems, thus saving the lives of his remaining colleagues. Throughout the mission his instinctiveness is juxtaposed with the rigidly bureaucratic trained skills of his junior colleagues. Yet the gradual humanizing of Eastwood's cinematic persona is reflected in Corvin's heroic and successful attempt to save his colleagues from certain death. The themes of redemption and Eastwood-as-savior also animate the plot of *A Perfect World* (Eastwood, 1993). As Red Garnett, Eastwood is assigned to apprehend Butch Haynes, an escaped convict who has kidnapped a young boy. Garnett previously sent Haynes to juvenile hall in order to save the future criminal from an abusive father. He is accompanied in his new mission by a female criminologist assigned to him by the publicity-hungry Texas governor. Although he initially assumes that she is the new office secretary, he gradually learns to learn from her. At the film's conclusion, an FBI marksman kills Haynes. Red's

faith in humanity, defined by his early contact with Haynes, is contrasted
with the FBI's methodical and inhumane approach to crime when Red
knocks the FBI agent out with a single punch. Red sees the criminal's
humanity; the FBI only sees a target to be eliminated. Like Red, Eastwood's boxing trainer Frankie Dunn in *Million Dollar Baby* (Eastwood,
2004) learns the true meaning of kinship as he ages. After reluctantly
training Maggie Fitzgerald and seeing her reduced to a quadriplegic in a
title fight, Dunn takes responsibility for her life and ultimately her death
as per her request. In the face of ethical dilemmas that would never have
troubled Callahan, Dunn demonstrates a deep emotional understanding of human relationships. Retired FBI agent Terry McCaleb in *Blood
Work* (Eastwood, 2002) even receives a new heart, allowing him a second chance in life. This heart, he is told, belonged to a murder victim.
Her family implores him to investigate the unsolved case, a process that
helps guide him toward further salvation and a new family. *True Crime*
(Eastwood, 1999), set across the San Francisco Bay in Oakland, continues
the redemptive theme. Eastwood's Steve Everett, a journalist, serial adul-
terer, and recovering alcoholic, is charged with covering the final hours of
Frank Beechum, a death-row prisoner in San Quentin. Everett is another
post-Callahan character with a keen sense of integrity whose healthy
hostility toward authority has prevented him from rising through the
ranks. Everett's hunch about the prisoner's innocence is another demonstration of pure instinct and brings him into further conflict with his
family, his editor, and the warden of San Quentin. It ultimately costs him
his marriage, house, and job but prevents the prisoner's death, which is
presented in the film's conclusion as a perfectly satisfactory quid pro quo.
In the film's key scene, Everett is berated by an African American woman
for failing to investigate her son's murder in a local park. Everett thinks
her son was the real killer in the crime for which Beechum was convicted.
The mother is unaware that Beecham is also black and a Christian (the
latter being a key signifier of his innocence). She initially refuses to assist
Everett, thinking that this is another case of white society protecting its
own while allowing black Oakland to fester in poverty, drugs, and murder. Unlike Callahan, Everett seems genuinely moved when faced by his
complicity in white Oakland's neglect of the city's black population. In
saving Beechum he offers a certain level of salvation, helping to place a
sticking plaster over Oakland's racial wounds. *True Crime* thus reinforces

the suggestion that honorable, race-neutral whites like Everett are able to solve the problems facing black America. Like the *Dirty Harry* series, then, it fails to dig beneath the surface of the Bay Area's racial politics.

These roles aided the softening of Eastwood's screen persona and presaged Eastwood's final major acting role as Frank Kowalski, the character who definitively overthrows Callahan's notion of retribution with the ethos of redemption. Callahan is more than a spectral presence in *Gran Torino*, as acknowledged by many reviewers.[60] At the film's outset, the Korean War veteran Kowalski shares numerous values with Callahan. Like Callahan, he is antagonistic toward those he encounters. His contempt for his neighbors, family, and the dwindling number of friends he retains—embodied in a guttural growl that seems to emerge from the core of Kowalski's acidic viscera—is perhaps the logical outcome of Callahan's misanthropy. Like Callahan, he has little faith in the local police department to prevent or solve crimes in the neighborhood. He echoes Callahan's equal-opportunity race hatred in openly airing his disgust at the multiculturalism of his neighborhood as his fellow whites flee Detroit. He frequently calls his Hmong neighbors "swamp rats" and "gooks" while attempting to herd them off his property each time they step on his lawn. Initially, he has no time at all for liberalism and his gender identity is as stereotypical as Callahan's. As the film historians John Gourlie and Leonard Engel observe, Kowalski "is equally adept at the traditional male rituals of domestic home life and at the warrior rituals of violence."[61] Just like Callahan, he is perfectly prepared to use heavy artillery when necessary, and initially at least, he erects verbal, attitudinal, physical, and corporeal barriers around him to ward off friendship.

Released mere weeks after the election of Barack Obama supposedly ushered in a post-racial era, *Gran Torino* immerses itself in the divisions that white racial attitudes brought to the United States. Kowalski begins the film as an unapologetic racist, resentful of the loss of white community cohesion in his neighborhood. Matters are not helped when the teenage son of his Hmong neighbors, Thao, unsuccessfully attempts to steal Kowalski's beloved Ford Gran Torino, which is itself a symbolic representation of Kowalski's traditional white-working class masculinity. This theft, a metaphor for the decline of white racial superiority and white anxieties about American multiculturalism in the twenty-first century, drives the film's plot. As the attempted theft suggests, Thao is challenged to become a "real man" by the gang, a task that mirrors the pressures placed on him by his family members, who are steeped in a highly traditional Hmong culture. Thao is offered a chance to redeem himself by working for Kowalski as penance. This is as redemptive for Kowalski, however. Thao first impresses Walt when he helps an old lady retrieve fruit that has spilled from her shopping bag. His recourse to a traditional vision of masculinity offers Walt an opportunity to develop the kind of empathy for Thao that he initially reserves for his drinking buddies. Thao then deepens Walt's connection with the local community when Walt charges him with fixing up neighboring houses as part of his restitution. The two men develop a strong bond as Walt instructs him in traditional American male activities. A visit to the barbershop for the two even includes distant echoes of Callahan's race-baiting in *Dirty Harry*. "Perfect! A Polack and a Chink!" jokes Kowalski's barber as they enter. Kowalski greets his old friend in similar fashion: "How you doing, Martin, you crazy Italian prick?" "Who's the nip?" inquires the barber. "He's a pussy kid from next door," says Kowalski before turning to his young friend: "You see, kid? That's how guys talk to one another." Thao is then invited to greet the barber, but his citation of Kowalski's ethnic gibe prompts the outraged barber to whip out and target his rifle. The scene resolves with Thao humorously attempting to absorb the codes of American male conversation. The casual ethnic and racist slurs remain unchallenged, in order to demonstrate that Thao, like the barber and Kowalski, must simply shrug them off as part of the daily grind. Instead, the scene focuses on masculine rituals of good-natured back-slapping abuse, designed to conceal the friends' deeper feelings for one another.

Kowalski's character development and redemption offer a hopeful and traditional coda to Callahan's career and, as Sara Anson Vaux notes, redefines Eastwood's notion of masculinity by supplanting the code of violence with a new code of fatherhood and linking personal salvation and spiritual peace.[62] He learns, firstly, to accept the presence of his neighbors, then to respect them, and after realizing that he has more in common with them than he does his own family, he finally arrives at a relatively deep philosophical understanding that the future of the neighborhood rests with them. After promising Thao to "man you up a little," he helps his new friend by teaching him important manual labor skills and encouraging him to invite a girl on a date. Kowalski's death at the hands of a local gang is as inevitable as it is tragic. After Walt beats and threatens a member of the local gang, they take revenge on Thao's older sister, Sue. Sue's beating leads Walt to conclude that this destructive cycle of violence threatens to overwhelm both the neighborhood and Thao's life. The film's final scene essentially brings the tale of Callahan full circle: an act of senseless violence—the death of his wife—arguably begins his career as an angel of vengeance, and Kowalski's final rejection of this code enables him to be reunited with his wife in the hereafter. For in goading the gang members while refusing to carry a gun himself, he enables the community to move into the future. Most significantly, though, at a personal level, he finally questions and ultimately rejects the assumptions that defined his career, revealing an understanding of common humanity that Callahan failed to appreciate. He bequeaths Thao his Gran Torino, a highly symbolic decision that underscores his new understanding of the future of the neighborhood and the nation itself. As important, he allows the rule of law to win, with the police apprehending the gang members and proving more effective than vigilantism in securing the future of the neighborhood, and, in this highly metaphorical movie, the United States.

The Reagan Presidency

In March 1985, Ronald Reagan spoke to the members of the American Business Conference on the subject of tax: "I have my veto pen drawn and ready for any tax increase that Congress might even think of sending up. And I have only one thing to say to the tax increasers: Go ahead, make my day."[63] Reagan liked the line so much that he repeated it at a gala celebrating his eighty-third birthday in 1994, this time in a wider-ranging sense: "I must say that returning to Washington today really brought back memories. . . . Up on Capitol Hill, I saw that big, white dome bulging with new tax revenues. I instinctively reached for my veto pen and thought to myself, 'Go ahead, make my day.'"[64] His use of Callahan's threat transformed the detective into the lone executive fighting the massed ranks of the legislature, his line a Reaganite clarion for the overthrow of Democrat tax-and-spend politics.

Eastwood considered this citation "kind of amusing."[65] The Callahan citation, however, was no mere quip. More than simply reflecting

Reagan's populist way with words or his speechwriters' grasp of the zeitgeist, it includes numerous revealing signifiers. Most obviously, it paints an image of Reagan the president as doer, rather than thinker. While Congress dithers, Reagan draws his veto pen: like Andrew Jackson, he is ever prepared to enact the people's wishes. It suggests that the tax battles could be won by the gunfighter president, although in this case, the pen is mightier than the Magnum. It also reinforces Reagan's insistence that, despite decades in Republican politics, he remains an outsider heroically battling the system on behalf of the ordinary Joe.[66] As important, it presents the liberals as the bad guys, threatening the stability of the country with their economic policies, and cloaks the Reagan administration's economic policy—which worked to the benefit of society's richest people—as the moral quest of the good guy. Almost paradoxically, however, Reagan's citation confirms Callahan as a mainstream icon. By buttressing his conservative credentials, Reagan demonstrates that Callahan is no longer the outsider but that he now has friends in high places. Eastwood's approval of the citation offers further endorsement, confirming Callahan as a Reaganite. Like Callahan, Reagan might tread the same floors as the bureaucrats in the same institution, but his aims, methods, and beliefs are inimical to those of the insiders. So whereas this impersonal bureaucracy retains a tyrannical control over the people's finances, Reagan represents the very human impulse to fight for liberty, justice, and American individualism, even as he pushes for a regressive tax regime. In approvingly quoting a fictional character, Reagan used the symbolism of the presidency to elevate Callahan beyond a near-mythical status and into one of the guiding lights of his struggle to overcome the Democrats' bureaucratic hegemony. His citation also erodes the nastiness of Callahan's line. In *Sudden Impact*, Callahan is goading an African American criminal into offering him an excuse to do something that only the thin blue line of the law is preventing. Reagan, by contrast, is not threatening to kill but simply to prevent taxes rising: apparently, the thoroughly moral quest of the conservative.

As Reagan's quip suggests and David Doherty argues, presidential rhetoric is often allusive on matters of policy but can offer useful insights into more abstract ideas such as the values held by individual presidents. Hence it might offer clues as to policy inclinations and goals, not least because the general public is at liberty to connect the expressed values to policy.[67] Or more pithily, as James Druckman and Justin Holmes state, "[w]hat the president says matters."[68] The pulpit of the presidency is a hugely symbolic and powerful tool for the communication of ideas and for directing the public to issues that the president and his party might consider politically advantageous. The annual State of the Union address and campaign stump speeches are but the most obvious of the opportunities afforded (aspiring) presidents to direct attention to their (proposed) policies. The choice of words, which can range from the consciously selected material of prepared speeches through unconscious improvisations, can be analyzed in order to demonstrate certain parallels between Callahan's worldview and some of the ideas expressed by the conservative presidents Reagan, George H. W. Bush, and George W. Bush. Echoes of Callahanian attitudes also informed California's politics during this era. The gubernatorial election following Governor Gray Davis's recall in 2003 was characterized by Republican candidate Arnold Swarzenegger repeatedly citing his post-Callahan role as the Terminator. Yet Schwarzenegger's time in office revealed the limitations of such posturing, illustrating the extent to which macho Republicanism was unattuned to California's peculiar brand of politics.

As Jonathan Schoenwald notes, Reagan was the figure who pushed conservative ideology into the background, replacing it with a personality who could "expound on such ideas without seeming fanatical."[69] Stuart Spencer, one of Reagan's 1966 gubernatorial campaign managers agrees: "In his '66 campaign, he said everything Barry Goldwater said, but he said it better—not as harsh. . . . They said the same things, basically, but Reagan said them very nice and pleasant."[70] This demeanor certainly attracted working-class voters who were to bear the brunt of Reagan's harsh economic policies.[71] To voters in 1980, Reagan's sunny disposition, self-deprecating jokes, and apparent lack of rancor appealed to citizens who considered Goldwater too extreme, Nixon too sinister, Agnew too menacing, and Carter too gloomy.[72] His image as a "do-er," bolstered by his rhetoric, attracted those disappointed by Ford's and Carter's perceived feebleness. He was, according to Republican National Chairman Frank Fahrenkopf, a leader who (like Callahan) offered "discipline and certainty" to a nation that craved such things.[73] He was thus the ideal individual to popularize a tough and uncompromising conservative ideology that appealed strongest to winners and so-called strivers by focusing on their shared cultural values. In essence, Reagan offered Callahanian rhetoric wrapped in a cheerful, can-do manner that encouraged rather than threatened its listening public. Reagan's words might read harshly on the page, but when presented by the actor-turned-president they lost their uncompromising tone. The message might appear to be written by Harry Callahan, but it was delivered by Mr. Rogers.

Importantly, both Reagan and Callahan felt that straightforward answers were available to address the problems that beset their societies. In 1994, Eastwood stated that Callahan offered simple solutions to problems facing American cities in the 1970s.[74] Perhaps unwittingly, this referenced two lodestones of California conservatism. John Wayne once complained, "They tell me everything isn't black and white. Well, I say, why the hell not?"[75] More famously, Reagan argued in his January 1967 inaugural address that "the truth is, there are simple answers—there just are not easy ones."[76] He might have been referring to fiscal struggles and budget deficits, but his policies suggest that this apparently populist quip offers a deep insight into his worldview and approach to his job. To Reagan, simple answers were the most instinctive and consequently most appropriate response. Too much bureaucracy? Cut down government. A sluggish economy? Reduce taxes. Striking workers? Attack the unions. Too much crime? Impose harsher sentences. Callahan's approach was very similar: combat crime using the only techniques that criminals feared, whether they be extralegal or not.

This concept of straightforward answers revealed itself in the Reagan presidency's almost Callahanian approach to the victims of crime and a similarly anti-liberal attitude toward the roots of criminal behavior. As Eastwood pointed out, *Dirty Harry* emerged from a general sense that criminals and suspects were receiving more attention and care than their victims.[77] This attention to victimhood became a central pillar of Reagan's criminal policy as president. Within months of his inauguration, he was identifying crime as an "American epidemic."[78] He unrolled a list of depressing statistics to the International Association of Chiefs of Police, commenting that the figures painted a portrait of "a stark, staring face . . . of a human predator, the face of the habitual criminal. Nothing in nature is more cruel and more dangerous."[79] This face he contrasted with the "innocent victims of crime [who] . . . have needed a voice for a long, long time, and this administration means to provide it."[80] Warming to his theme, he told the doubtless supportive audience of his plans to "redress the imbalance between rights of the accused and rights of the innocent."[81] Any country that allowed guilty men and women to go free on trivial technical errors was committing a "grievous miscarriage of justice" every time it failed an innocent victim, sentiments that echoed Callahan's response to the release of Scorpio in *Dirty Harry*. Reagan used the example of a search of a drug dealer's property in San Bernardino to illustrate the absurdity of the situation as he saw it. After failing to find any evidence in a search of the property, one of the officers searched in the diaper of a sleeping baby who was present at the scene, which led to the case being thrown out on the grounds that the baby had not consented to being searched.[82] This possibly apocryphal tale would equally have outraged Callahan. "I would suggest the time has come to look reality in the face," Reagan opined after recounting the anecdote. "American society is mired in excessive litigation. Our courts today are loaded with suits and motions of every conceivable type. . . . Our legal system has failed to carry out its most important function—the protection of the innocent and the punishment of the guilty." The criminal justice system, he argued, was no longer working. "All too often, repeat offenders, habitual law-breakers, career criminals, call them what you will, are robbing, raping, and beating with impunity and, as I said, quite literally getting away with murder. The people are sickened and outraged. They demand that we put a stop to it."[83] Such words would not have been out of place in the heated discussion between Callahan and the district attorney in *Dirty Harry* or in one of his regular arguments with his superiors. Reagan's conclusion was similarly Callahanian: crime control was not merely about throwing money at the problem but was "ultimately a moral dilemma" that called for a moral solution: "The war on crime will only be won when an attitude of mind and a change of heart takes place in America, when certain truths take hold again and plant their roots deep in our national consciousness, truths like: right and wrong matters; individuals are responsible for their actions; *retribution should be swift and sure* for those who prey on the innocent."[84] For Reagan, as for Callahan, the law was an extension of the country's moral code and the problem was simple: "It's a problem of the human heart. . . . [M]en are basically good but prone to evil, and society has a right to be protected from them." Only moral courage would enable individuals to resist the criminal impulse, and it was only by allowing the police and the courts to carry out their duties efficiently that they would be able to complete their work effectively. This commonsense approach to crime, he claimed in 1984, "is beginning to pay off. . . . The liberal approach of coddling criminals didn't work and never will."[85] Justice was best served through retribution rather than rehabilitation.

The failing American criminal justice system, which was at the core of the *Dirty Harry* series, was also a recurring theme in Reagan's rhetoric. Reagan's thought was straightforward: the system's overriding function should be to protect the innocent and punish the guilty.[86] The crime epidemic, which affected nearly a third of the population, resulted in the death of more than twenty-two thousand people in 1981 and cost the nation nearly $9 billion per year. The government's duty, Reagan said, was to make the country safe, especially for those most in need of protection: its female and elderly population. This gendered notion of men as the protectors was, of course, central to the *Dirty Harry* series. The president's answer was to crack down on the career criminals who committed the most serious offences, and he urged Congress to pass the anticrime bills that were then being debated.[87] Robert Bork's commonsense attitude to sentencing and the Constitution was a prime example of the Reaganite approach in action.[88] When supporting Bork's nomination to the U.S. Supreme Court, Reagan argued that Bork would "take a tough, clear-eyed look" at criminal justice and join the president's war on crime.[89] "The American people do not want judges picked for special interests," Reagan declared. "They do not want to return to leniency in the courtroom and unsafe streets. They want judges and laws that reflect common sense attitudes about crime."[90] Judges like Bork, who advocated strong executive action—and who would have received Callahan's approval—were the answer to the crime epidemic.[91] During his ultimately unsuccessful confirmation hearings, Bork appeared to be a defender of traditional morality, declaring that he opposed numerous recent Supreme Court decisions that acknowledged marital rights and abortion rights and outlawed racial and sex discrimination.[92] Reagan clearly felt that Bork would extend this doctrine into the realm of law and order. Edward Kennedy's opinion of Bork's nomination was unequivocal and offers a useful insight into the way in which liberals recoiled from Bork's conservatism: "Robert Bork's America is a land in which . . . rogue police could break down citizens' doors in midnight raids . . . and the doors of the federal courts would be shut on the fingers of millions of citizens."[93] Detectives like Callahan would no longer live in fear of liberal judges curbing their freedom to crush their foes. For Reagan, on the other hand, Bork was purely and simply a "champion of individual freedom."[94]

Reagan consistently argued that the crime wave was a direct consequence of 1960s liberalism and permissiveness, two ideals that he rejected unhesitatingly.[95] This, of course, echoed Callahan's disgust with the system's respect for Scorpio's civil rights at the expense of May Ann Deacon's right to life. It also offered a post hoc response to Jennifer Spencer's killing spree, implicitly offering a critique of the failure of the California legal system to bring her tormenters to justice and offering tacit approval of her actions. From Reagan's perspective, the liberal intellectuals of the 1960s made two major mistakes. First, they considered crime to be a consequence not of poor choices or a lack of basic morality but an outcome of poverty and disadvantage. Second, liberal social policy was simply too lenient on criminals and was similarly mistaken in attributing social problems to material environment.[96] For Reagan, the crime wave was rooted in the same mistakes as the sluggish American economy of the 1970s: "The same utopian presumptions about human nature that hinder the swift administration of justice have also helped fuel the expansion of government."[97] Government spending, he argued, could not tackle social ills, and such social engineering simply ignored the base issue at hand. By denying the existence of any absolute truths about human nature, these liberals falsely thought that they could be the harbingers of a "great new era" in American history. The consequences of this hubris were manifold: "runaway inflation, soaring unemployment, impossible interest rates. We've learned," Reagan opined, "that Federal subsidies and government bureaucrats not only fail to solve social problems but frequently make them worse."[98] He noted that the 1960s and 1970s witnessed huge rises in crime and declared that a "failure to administer prompt and sure justice" was a major causal factor.[99] "Excessive government spending, taxing, and regulating," he concluded in 1985, "is a formula for disaster."[100] The War on Poverty was an utter failure whose only result was the creation of a "great new upper-middle class of bureaucrats" whose avowed intention was to keep vast swaths of the population impoverished in order to justify their own existence.[101]

While extolling the virtue of the legal system in keeping the hordes at bay, Reagan argued that a prime goal of his administration was to "help revive America's traditional values: faith, family, neighborhood, work, and freedom."[102] Government could play no role in this; indeed, it was the liberals' folly to assume that government could steer the nation's tiller rather than simply set the nation adrift. Government spending was thus indicted not only as economic folly but as cultural malaise; its beneficiaries similarly condemned for their moral failings.

Reagan held an almost Manichaean view of the world that was startlingly similar to Callahan's view of San Francisco. The full force of the law should be brought to bear on the perpetrators of crime. The police—those who had presumably successfully suppressed their proclivity for evil—represented civilization's good guys, pitched against the barbaric hordes of the jungle, who thanks to liberal mollycoddling were prepared to overrun the country in an orgiastic crime spree. Reagan simply proposed to swing the pendulum of justice away from the accused and toward the victims—in essence, offering his full backing for the police and letting them get on with their job, a little like George Wallace promised back in the 1960s. There are also hints in Reagan's rhetoric which suggest that vigilantism was not necessarily problematic. He lauded the members of the NRA for taking the initiative in fighting crime, by organizing patrols in their own neighborhoods, supporting their local police departments and "insisting that justice be carried out."[103] More chillingly, in 1988 he declared that "truly effective law enforcement demands our reliance on one of our great historical strengths as a Nation: the willingness of our people to band freely together, in local communities, in defense of lives, homes, and property."[104] Although outwardly a nod to the constitutional right to form well-regulated militias, such a statement also hinted that he was prepared turn a blind eye to vigilante action, especially now that his presidential term was about to expire.

Reagan concluded his remarks to the International Association of Chiefs of Police in 1981 with a typically folksy encomium to his hosts: "I commend you for manning the thin blue line that holds back a jungle which threatens to reclaim this clearing we call civilization. No bands play when a cop is shooting it out in a dark alley."[105] In reprising a core theme of his 1966 gubernatorial campaign and Nixon's 1968 presidential campaign, Reagan reminded his audience of the Manichaean world in which they lived while also outlining its racial parameters through the metaphor of the struggle between the jungle and civilization. The fears that the cities were turning into lawless zones that were prevalent among certain sections of the populace became a regular theme of Reagan's oratory. Speaking to the nation in September 1982, he revealed that the White House had received numerous letters from citizens who claimed that they were afraid to "walk the streets alone at night."[106] Nearly eighteen months later, he lamented that "too many of our friends and loved ones live in fear of crime. And there's no mystery as to why. For too many years, the scales of criminal justice were tilted toward protecting rights of criminals. Those in charge forgot or just plain didn't care about protecting your rights—the rights of law-abiding citizens."[107] By the mid-1980s, and with hardline policies being enacted in many states, Reagan was able to dismiss liberal suggestions that the declining crime rate was a consequence of demographic shifts. This, he argued, was coincidence, not causality. More criminals were in jail now, and this was "happening because we're doing more to protect the innocent and punish the guilty. And that's why, today, our homes, our families, and our societies are safer."[108] Callahan would have nodded in agreement. He would also have been impressed with Reagan's July 7, 1984, radio address to the nation. The address focused on the president's dissatisfaction with Congress, which had mired his bills in committee. Reagan urged his listeners to use their initiative and contact their representatives to tell them to push for a vote on the omnibus bill that would break the bureaucratic stranglehold of the liberals. "Americans want this anticrime legislation," he concluded in populist fashion, "and they want it now."[109] To him, the public was "fed up" with what he called "liberal leniency and pseudointellectual apologies for crime." They wanted the courts to return to a simpler concept of the law by affirming values "that teach us right and wrong matters, and that individuals are responsible for their actions, and retribution should be swift and sure for those who prey on the innocent."[110] As important, they—or rather, he—wanted the liberal bureaucracy to be overthrown, and the most effective antidote to this suffocating liberal establishment was tough executive action.

The Reagan-Callahan parallels even extend beyond politics. On March 30, 1981, Reagan was hit in the arm by a ricocheting bullet from an assassination attempt. He was pushed into his limousine before he was aware that the bullet had lodged in his chest. Code-named "Rawhide" after the Eastwood television series, Reagan was sped to George Washington University Hospital and attempted to walk into the examination room, unconsciously echoing Callahan's blasé reaction to being shot at the outset of the *Dirty Harry* bank robbery.[111] After being stabilized, Reagan found time to josh with his surgeons before being anesthetized, pleading with them to confirm that they were Republicans.[112] To Nancy Reagan he brushed it off with the comment that he merely "forgot to duck."[113] Like Callahan, Reagan was incensed that hospital staff wanted to cut open his clothes; Reagan's aide Lyn Nofziger put this down to Reagan being "kind of a tightwad."[114] Like Callahan, Reagan did not let his injuries divert him from his duties: he returned to the Oval Office less than a month after the shooting, which many observers credited to his magnificent physique and health.[115]

As Toby Glenn Bates argues, Reagan persistently referenced American traditions and history, couching his references in layers of nostalgia in order to create a narrative that emphasized an Arcadian past that was disrupted and traduced by the tumult of the 1960s.[116] Like Callahan, he grew to political maturity during this period, and his experiences indelibly marked his attitude toward the relationship between government, the law, and the people. Callahan, too, was forged by the various political and social movements of the 1960s. Both seemed utterly certain of the rectitude of their views toward the upheaval that they witnessed at first hand, and both worked assiduously to unmake the world constructed by the 1960s. While Reagan only explicitly referenced Callahan once, the "make my day" quip is indicative of the deep parallels between the worldview of the president and the police detective. There is no evidence to suggest that Reagan watched the *Dirty Harry* films and then decided on his policies. He might have watched *Rambo: First Blood Part II* (Cosmatos, 1985) and concluded that "next time I'll know what to do," but the *Dirty Harry* series seems not to have resonated as explicitly.[117] Instead, the similarities suggest that Callahan and Reagan tapped into similar strains of conservative ideology; that Callahan expressed many of the frustrations of mainstream conservatives in the 1970s and 1908s; and that while the movies were fictional, their refraction of recent American history was not far removed from the world outlined by the president.

The Bush Dynasty

Republican Callahanianism appeared to skip a generation following Reagan's final bow, although key continuities remained. According to *Newsweek*, the Great Communicator's successor, George H. W. Bush, was fighting the "wimp factor" even before he was elected, despite his war record and background in the CIA.[118] Depicted on *Newsweek*'s cover in October 1987 piloting his speedboat in determined pose, Bush seemed to be overcompensating even twelve months prior to the presidential election. It was precisely this overcompensation for his public image of weakness that contributed to his fateful promise at the 1988 Republican National Convention: "Read my lips: no new taxes."[119] Deliberately enunciating each word carefully and leaving a distinct pause between them, Bush was clearly hoping to mimic John Wayne or Callahan promising to bring justice to some petty criminals, although his preppy diction somewhat undercut the threatening tone of the statement. In the same speech he also talked of his life and political career in terms of his many "missions," both civilian and military, and derided the liberals in familiar terms: "The fact is, they talk—we deliver. They promise—we perform. . . . I respect old fashioned common sense, and have no great love for the imaginings of social planners. . . . I'm the one who says a drug dealer who is responsible for the death of a policeman should be subject to capital punishment." It is often forgotten, however, that earlier in the same speech Bush cited a fictional detective who was perhaps more reminiscent of the future forty-first president: Joe Friday of *Dragnet*, whose catchphrase, "Just the facts, ma'am," was used as the template for Bush's approach to his speech.[120]

The 1988 election campaign was arguably defined by the most notorious exploitation of a criminal case in American electoral history, one that echoed Callahan's frustration with liberalism and allowed Bush to sidestep the "wimp" factor. While on furlough in Massachusetts during 1986, Willie Horton assaulted a man before raping his fiancée and stealing his car. The furlough program had been supported by the Massachusetts governor and Democratic presidential candidate Michael Dukakis.[121] During the presidential campaign Dukakis was demonized as a tax-and-spend governor with a fondness for radicalism, whose liberal

crime policies led directly to criminals roaming the streets and terrorizing law-abiding Americans. Even worse, Dukakis was a paid-up member
of the ACLU.[122] In the words of the *Washington Post*, Dukakis was a "tax-
spending liberal who let murderers out of jail," a phrase that Callahan
himself might have uttered.[123] Bush frequently lambasted Dukakis for
being a profligate, soft-on-crime liberal. On the stump toward the end of
the campaign, Bush even bragged "miracles of miracles[!]" when Dukakis
referred to himself as a liberal Democrat—or, according to Bush, "the big
'L.'"[124] Whereas Callahan and Reagan took on the forces of evil by urging
"Go ahead: make my day," Bush crowed, Dukakis would instead squeak,
"Go ahead: have a nice weekend."[125]

As the historian Jeffrey Tulis points out, once in office Bush retreated
from the rhetorical style of Reagan, not least because his almost "in-
articulate" style of speech was not suited to the bully pulpit.[126] Bush's
preference was for more sentimental imagery, of front porches and a
thousand points of light, a "kinder, gentler nation" populated by "quiet,
gentle, decent people," more akin to television's Walton family than the
riotous Simpsons.[127] Even when citing John Wayne, Bush managed to
end on a folksy simile: "Wayne spelled it out in his simple, all-American,
pointblank style. He said: 'There's right and there's wrong. You gotta do
one or the other. You do the one, and you're living. You do the other, and
you may be walking around, but you're as dead as a beaver hat.'"[128] Like-
wise, amid struggles with his Democratic Congress, Bush sounded less
like a leader than a back-porch politician, or even worse, a bureaucrat: "If
Congress sends me a weak [crime] bill here in the final hours, I'm going
to veto it," he said in 1990, failing even to hint at Reagan's famous promise of five years previous.[129] In Philadelphia he lauded Herman Wrice, a
local "towering mountain of a man who started a whole movement by
declaring war on a crack house with a sledgehammer," before compar-
ing Wrice to Wayne himself.[130] Yet in the same week he told a Montana
audience, "Let's face it, heroes alone can't win wars."[131] Similarly, when
on Callahanian territory Bush managed to convey discomfort: "Crime,
and crimefighting, is usually a question of right and wrong—good and
evil, if you will," he told a Houston anti-drug rally.[132] The final clause in
Bush's phrase is crucial, suggesting the unease with which he employed
Manichaean rhetoric. It reveals that Bush saw himself far more as a dot-
ing father to the nation than as its commander in chief. To police officers

in Orange County he talked more of victimhood and compassion than Reagan ever did.[133] His crime policy promised to "rededicate ourselves to responding with speed and sensitivity to the needs of innocent crime victims."[134] "If you do crime, you do time," he declared in 1989.[135] The Bush administration would "take back the streets . . . from the criminals who threaten our neighborhoods and our families—not just in the cities but all across this country. We are going to win the battle against the criminal."[136] Even so, "just punishment," he argued, "is a moral, civilized response to wrong. Punishment is necessary not only as a deterrent to future crimes but for its own sake—which is to say, for the sake of justice."[137] This talk of civility and sensitivity marked a step back from Reagan's sternness, a key factor in the difference between the Gipper and "Poppy."

On the world stage Bush faced an enemy in Saddam Hussein, who was as close to a movie villain as any scriptwriter could have imagined. When asked whether Saddam would be hunted down in the wake of his invasion of Kuwait, Bush missed an opportunity for some Reaganesque sloganeering: "No, I'm not going to say that. Not hunt him down, but nobody can be absolved from the responsibilities under international law on the war crimes aspect of that."[138] Even when he attempted a rhetorical flourish, Bush sounded unconvinced of his own power. "World opinion is saying. . . . 'Out, Saddam Hussein, Iraqi, out of Kuwait, and restore the leaders!' But you have to talk to get there."[139] His response to Saddam was animated more by his faith in bureaucracy and diplomacy than saber-rattling. "I want to see the United Nations move soon with chapter VII sanctions," he averred, confirming his faith in a bureaucratic solution to Iraq.[140] "The key is collective action," he argued, "sharing the responsibilities and the risks, the challenges and the costs."[141] Bush acknowledged that Saddam offered a particularly apposite example of the difference between "good and evil, right and wrong," but failed to hit the right note in response, stating that Saddam had provided "a whole plateful of clarity" with his actions in Kuwait.[142] Hussein's reaction to these statements is not recorded, but it was highly unlikely to have involved quaking in his boots.

As if to compensate for his father's perceived weakness, George W. Bush keenly adopted the role of the nation's Callahanian commander in chief. For Stanley Renshon, the second Bush president was a man who "embrace[d] conflict," as evidenced by his decision to spend the final hours of the 2000 campaign in his competitor Al Gore's home state.[143] According to the journalist Nicholas Lemann, the younger Bush considered the election contest in almost Callahanian terms: the "regular guy versus an archetypal member of the new elite," a true American versus a privileged insider who grew up in Washington D.C.[144] After election, Bush vowed to be a "commander-in-chief who respects our men and women in uniform, and a commander-in-chief who earns their respect."[145] The al-Qaeda hijackings of September 11, 2001, offered him the perfect opportunity to demonstrate his resolve and the nation's might:

> I want him held—I want justice. There's an old poster out West, as I recall, that said, "Wanted: Dead or Alive." . . . I just remember— all I'm doing is remembering—when I was a kid, I remember that they used to put out there, in the Old West, a wanted poster. It said, "Wanted: Dead or Alive." All I want—and America wants him brought to justice. That's what we want.[146]

His rhetoric suggests that Callahanian notions of justice and moral certainty were fundamental to Bush's worldview, and that gut instinct was essential to his decision making. Such feelings, according to a 2009 study, were also central to Bush's appeal to voters. The study revealed that, even when presented with facts which indicated that Bush's policies worked to their disadvantage, Bush's supporters relied on a variety of non-intellectual responses in order to explain their continued support for Bush. This included a dismissal of the facts and some decidedly dissonant cognition. Many argued that their continued support for Bush was based on their belief that he seemed more personable, more working-class and down-to-earth than, for example, the equally wealthy and privileged John Kerry.[147] This support, cultural studies scholar Richard Johnson argues, was a consequence of Bush's ability to articulate the concerns of many ordinary Americans in terms that they recognized, another example of the cognitive dissonance that characterized the thoughts of Reagan's working-class supporters.[148]

"I made up my mind at that moment that we were going to war," Bush said of his feelings when he was informed that an airplane had crashed into the World Trade Center.[149] He claimed that the attack made his "blood boil," and he was filled with a certainty that forever dominated his interpretation of the situation: "America is under attack, and *they will pay*," he said later. "I still feel that way."[150] "What you saw" in his address to the nation later on September 11, he recalled, "was my gut reaction coming out."[151] Bush's instinctive response continued to inform his bellicose and Manichaean rhetoric of that key month of his presidency. "I relied on instinct," he recalled.[152] Like Callahan telling his superiors that a criminal would be brought to justice, he passed a note to his adviser Karen Hughes which averred, "This is an enemy that runs and hides, but won't be able to hide forever. An enemy that thinks its havens are safe, but won't be safe forever."[153] He repeated these words to the nation the following day, adding, "This will be a monumental struggle between good and evil. But good will prevail."[154] Grief, anger, and resolve were not simply the emotions of the nation but were the emotions of the president himself. "Tonight," he told Congress later that month, "we are a country awakened to danger and called to defend freedom. Our grief has turned to anger, and anger to resolution. Whether we bring our enemies to justice, or bring justice to our enemies, justice will be done."[155]

Bush's anger led him to a simple conclusion: the perpetrators of the atrocity were to be brought to justice by whatever means necessary. As he pointed out on September 11, "We're going to take care of this. And when we find out who did this, they're not going to like me as president. Somebody is going to pay. . . . We're going to kick their asses."[156] "Boy, they really miscalculated," he reiterated in February 2002.[157] His revulsion at the act mirrored that of Callahan upon discovering Mary Ann Deacon's body, and his response similarly pushed at the boundaries between legal force and vigilante action. "Every nation, in every region, now has a decision to make," he announced. "Either you are with us, or you are with the terrorists. . . . Freedom and fear are at war."[158] On the day of the attack, he stated that the United States would "make no distinction between the terrorists who committed these acts and those who harbor them. . . . America has stood down enemies before, and we will do so this time."[159] "If he is alive," Bush said of Osama bin Laden, "there is no cave deep enough for the United States. We're going to find him."[160] And thus, when he spoke to the United Nations, nominally to ask for its backing for his plan to disarm Iraq, he did not appeal to international law, common decency, or unity, but simply urged the UN to "show backbone."[161] The United States and its "Coalition of the Willing" was prepared to ride roughshod over the UN in its fight against evil, regardless of any legal impediments. For Bush, the best way to maintain the coalition's unity was "strong leadership . . . by being clear that we are going to win."[162] Moral clarity and decisiveness were central to Bush's demeanor during this period. Like a presidential Callahan, he instinctively knew the best course of action to take, whether it abided by international law or not.

At Camp David in September 2001, Bush declared that "the United States will do what it takes to win this war. . . . [T]here is a desire by the American people to not seek only revenge but to win a war against barbaric behavior, people that hate freedom and hate what we stand for. And this is an administration that is going to dedicate ourselves to winning that war."[163] He insisted that the United States was seeking justice, but the close proximity of the two words "justice" and "revenge" in his utterances suggests a blurred boundary between the two, or even that Bush was reminding himself that as president he could not approve of revenge. He told the military in 2002, "You're delivering justice—not revenge but justice—to agents of terror."[164] Of the terrorists, he promised, "They can run, and they can hide, but they can't run and hide forever. This patient Nation will stay the course until we bring the killers to justice. We seek not revenge; we seek justice."[165] The tension between justice and revenge—which animated *Dirty Harry* and its sequels—was a regular theme in Bush's rhetoric of the time. He saw only a small line between the two: "I think it's a difference of attitude," he told reporters in July 2002.[166] What for liberals might be considered revenge was, for Bush and his supporters, justice. This constituted a rare outbreak of relativism in Bush's rhetoric. Crucially, however, this combined with his Manichaean belief in the split between good and evil, right and wrong. Those who disagreed were, quite simply, wrong.

In a broader sense, Bush's conception of his role as president and commander in chief was somewhat Callahanian: "I can only just go by my instincts."[167] According to the journalist and administration observer Bob Woodward, Bush "wanted action, solutions. Once on a course, he directed his energy at forging on, rarely looking back, scoffing at—even ridiculing—doubt and anything less than 100 per cent commitment. . . . His short declarations could seem impulsive."[168] Donald Rumsfeld went further, according to Woodward, apparently believing it "part of his [own] responsibility to *think* on the president's behalf."[169] In the course of a long interview in August 2002, Bush mentioned his instincts frequently, leading Woodward to conclude: "It's pretty clear that Bush . . . is driven by a secular faith in his instincts—his natural and spontaneous conclusions and judgments. His instincts are almost his second religion."[170] "I have not doubted what we're doing," Bush stated. "There is no doubt in my mind we're doing the right thing. Not one doubt."[171] "If I'm doubtful . . . If my confidence level in our ability declines, it will send ripples throughout the whole organization. . . . [I]f there's a kind of hand-wringing attitude going on when times are tough, I don't like it."[172] In rejecting "hand-wringing" liberals, Bush echoed Callahan. Like the detective, he led in a simple world. Thus, when considering the tense situation in Palestine during 2002, he argued:

> Look my job isn't to nuance. My job is to tell people what I think . . . and people can make all kinds of excuses, but there are some truths involved . . . and one of the truths is, they're sending suicide killers in—because they hate Israel. That's a truth and you can justify it anyway you want, nonetheless it is the role of the President, as far as I'm concerned, to stand up and tell the truth.[173]

What he deemed right or wrong was based on eternal truths and gut instinct, much like Callahan's policing style. He and his allies were quite simply on the side of good in its eternal struggle against evil, representing civilization and purity in a battle with barbarism and depravity.[174] So the thousands of people killed on September 11, 2001, were the victims of evil.[175] What caused him to consider the hijackers evil was simple: common sense, which was to Bush the most important and most objective means of determining policy.[176] After all, as Bush pointed out, "I don't need to explain. . . . That's the interesting thing about being president. Maybe someone needs to explain to me why they say something, but I don't feel I owe anyone an explanation."[177] Bush later told Bob Woodward, "I'm not a textbook player, I'm a gut player."[178] "*I don't take cues from anybody*, I just do what I think is right. That's just the way I lead."[179] This informed Bush's Manichaean and bellicose rhetoric, which, according to the scholar Douglas Kellner, was itself "grounded in anti-intellectualism and hatred of democracy and intellectuals . . . [playing] to anti-intellectual proclivities and tendencies in the extreme conservative and fundamentalist Christian constituencies who support him."[180]

Kellner argues that this developed into a neo-Orwellian "Bushspeak" that "involves continual repetition of simplistic slogans aimed to mobilize conservative support and without regard for truth."[181] It was potentially only a small step from declaring a war on terror to daring the evildoers to make his day. One might also suggest that many of Bush's quarrels replayed the D.A.'s office scene in *Dirty Harry*, with the commonsensical Bush railing against the legalism of pointy-headed intellectuals such as Kofi Annan or the condescension of nabobs like John Kerry.

*   *   *

Such muscular conservatism found its limits in Callahan's home state during George W. Bush's presidency. Arnold Schwarzenegger succeeded Gray Davis as California's governor following a bitter recall vote in 2003. Schwarzenegger's fame rested on his roles in two films. As the eponymous hero in the John Milius–directed *Conan the Barbarian* (1982), Schwarzenegger paraded his impressive physique while keeping dialogue to a minimum. He was even more robotic as *The Terminator* (Cameron, 1984), laying waste to vast tracts of California in his quest to end the life of a future human liberation leader. The persona shaped by these *Dirty Harry*–influenced films decisively informed his nascent political career. The initial stages of his 2003 campaign were defined by his call to Californians to "terminate" the Davis administration (helpfully, *Terminator 3: Rise of the Machines* [Mostow, 2003] was then in cinemas, reminding Schwarzenegger's audience of his fame, signature role, and crucially his masculinity).[182] Most obviously, Schwarzenegger's campaign foundations lay in knee-jerk anti-government sentiments surrounding Davis's handling of the energy crisis which led to electricity blackouts in parts of the state, and a perception that Davis was aloof from the electorate.[183] Davis's shortcomings once again suggested that the liberals were bureaucratic wingnuts who considered themselves a cut above the ordinary voter. Schwarzenegger himself placed considerable emphasis on his lack of political experience and his position outside the Sacramento bubble, despite being listed as a Republican. Davis, of course, was firmly enmeshed in the state's Democratic machine. A vote for the recall of Davis and against the Democrats' alternative recall candidate, Cruz Bustamante, might easily be interpreted as a de facto vote against the Democratic bureaucracy, and perhaps even an anti-government vote itself.

Gendered appeals were central to Schwarzenegger's political career. As one of his advisers observed, "It's like the famous Muscle Beach scene where the scrawny guy is getting sand kicked in his face by a body-builder. But in this case, everybody's cheering on the bodybuilder."[184] When his 2004 budget struggled to pass the legislature, Schwarzenegger denounced his Democratic tormenters as "girlie men." This was Schwarzenegger's first serious setback as governor, and his immediate response spoke volumes about his respect for the political process. The jibe had its roots in a *Saturday Night Live* sketch that parodied Schwarzenegger's physique and accent, but according to one of the governor's spokesmen, it was not intended to "question the virility or sexual orientation" of its targets. "It's his way of saying they're wimps," claimed Rob Stutzman without further elaboration.[185] This notion of masculinity clearly had its roots in Schwarzenegger's early bodybuilding career. Real men were like Schwarzenegger and Callahan: strong, decisive, and most likely Republican. Democrats, by contrast, were equivocal, indecisive, and worst of all, weak. The governor was prone to halting budget negotiations in order to attend political rallies at which he would disparage his opponents as children who needed to go into time-out before reminding his audiences to "terminate" them, again calling their masculinity into question.[186] Appearing at the Republican National Convention later that summer, Schwarzenegger repeated the insult, mocking the Democratic presidential and vice-presidential candidates John Kerry and John Edwards as "economic girlie men."[187] Even the widespread opprobrium for these antics failed to curb Schwarzenegger's fondness for equating good politics with hypermasculinity: during the protracted debates over the state budget in 2010, he sent a sculpture of bull's testicles to the leader of the state senate, Darrell Steinberg, in an effort to inspire the "requisite fortitude" for deficit reduction among Steinberg's peers.[188] Clearly, in Schwarzenegger's mind, all it took was *cojones*.

What must be noted, however, is that Schwarzenegger was eventually cowed by the Democratic apparatus in the state. He reined in his rhetoric, learned how to work with a Democrat-controlled legislature, and even transformed his image from the Humvee-driving "Governator" into a sandal-wearing, cycling advocate of green energy.[189] Schwarzenegger's transformation—a consequence both of his failure to develop a long-term solution to California's energy problem and of the importance of progressive environmental policies to the twenty-first-century California electorate—was highly calculated, but it also demonstrates the limitations of the Callahanian approach in such a heterogeneous state. It placed Schwarzenegger on the edge of the Republican mainstream, forever dooming his chances of advancing further within the national Republican apparatus. Although seemingly paradoxical, this new Schwarzenegger retained vestiges of the Callahanian approach to politics. By shifting with the wind, he proved not only his malleability but also his outsider status within his own party. Liberal positions on the environment, abortion, and the minimum wage ensured that he was on the Republican fringe while his opposition to gay marriage and heavy cuts in the wake of the 2008 fiscal crisis did not endear him to Democrats.[190] By proving his individualism he managed to win a second term, but his loftier ambitions were to be unfulfilled.

Years after backing Governor Reagan's gun-control plan for California, the National Rifle Association provided perhaps the most succinct and chilling articulation of Callahanian ideology. Speaking in 2012, soon after the death of twenty children and six adults in Newton, Connecticut, at the hands of a lone gunman, NRA CEO Wayne LaPierre offered a blunt response to questions about how to prevent such atrocities from recurring: "The only way to stop a monster from killing our kids is to be personally involved and invested in a plan of absolute protection. The *only* thing that stops a *bad* guy with a gun is a *good* guy with a gun."[191] It was as if LaPierre had recently watched *Magnum Force*, in which Callahan opined: "There's nothing wrong with shooting as long as the right people get shot." Similar echoes of Callahan can be found dotted throughout conservative politics in the period since the movie series began. Callahan also exerted great influence over Clint Eastwood's emergence as a conservative icon, as his 2012 Republication National Convention appearance confirmed. The detective tapped into strands of thought that resonated in the conservative section of the body politic, becoming one of the emblematic figures of the conservative backlash, despite being a fictional construction. These parallels indicate the importance of the movies to an understanding of modern conservatism, bringing high politics and popular culture into a firm embrace.

"Dirty" Harry Callahan
in American Popular Culture

I will show you the last Dirty Harry story.

Frank Miller

Trust me: I know what I'm doing.

Sledge Hammer

Callahan's afterlife expanded even as Eastwood was attempting to nuance and ultimately destroy the "Dirty" Harry caricature through his later roles. Eastwood himself has commented that the detective's status as a cultural icon is close to a bane on his life: he is so frequently assailed by people demanding that he make their day or questioning whether he feels lucky that he no longer even responds. This harassment, however, did not stop him from including the message "You made my day" on his Hollywood Boulevard paving stone in 1984.[1] That Eastwood did not need to explain his reference indicates exactly how well known Callahan is in American popular culture. This popularity generated and is reflected by reactions to and reimaginings of Callahan in various media. These productions tend to avoid the political undertones of the films to focus instead on Callahan's role as a violent angel of moral retribution. That such responses to Callahan are restricted to supposedly "low" forms of culture such as pulp fiction, cartoons, and video games metaphorically reinforces the suggestion that Callahan is an outsider, refused entry into America's high-culture canon. They also reflect the deep roots of Dirty Harry in Don Siegel's early career as a director of B movies and in Eastwood's as a jobbing actor in low-budget productions, arguably returning him to his source.

The most obvious response was a cycle of violent films featuring alienated outsiders who engaged in vigilante action. More interesting was a series of pulp novels featuring Callahan that emerged in the early 1980s. Here, Callahan becomes even more cartoonish, defeating underworld crimelords, corrupt union officials, rapists, drug smugglers, mobsters, mass murderers, and terrorists. The final novel provides the ultimate foe for Callahan: a criminal who has stolen his Magnum. Just as this literary response to Callahan focuses on his violent essence, Callahan's appearance in video games is as the champion of violent retribution. A *Dirty Harry* pinball machine allowed gamers to "shoot" pinballs through a replica Magnum; a Nintendo video game offered gamers the opportunity to kill criminals at will; and an aborted Xbox video game promised gamers the opportunity to live out Callahanian fantasies. The cartoon element of Callahan, hinted at by the games, featured heavily in the spoof television series *Sledge Hammer!* (1986–88), in which a thinly disguised Callahan wields his Magnum at the slightest provocation from antagonists ranging from ATM machines to people contemplating suicide. The irony and humor within *Sledge Hammer* emerge from the fact that Hammer's actions serve only to highlight his (and thus Callahan's) preposterousness. Elsewhere, many Eastwood fans were disappointed by *The Dead Pool.* Their dissatisfaction prompted a small number of responses that explicitly reimagined the final Dirty Harry story. The Internet allowed such fans to broadcast their own reimaginings of the conclusion to Callahan's career. These "fanfic" representations complicate our understanding of "sequelization" and demonstrate how Callahan operates as a vehicle for some Americans to express—however obliquely—their anxieties, fears, hopes, and preoccupations via acts of inquisitive engagements with the character and the franchise. Finally, frustrated at Eastwood's refusal to complete Callahan's story arc with a suitable final act, the comic writer Frank Miller created a thinly disguised sixty-year-old Callahan analogue in a section of his Eisner Award–winning *Sin City* series. On the verge of retirement, Inspector John Hartigan completes one last job that offers final proof of his moral core. Hartigan featured in the portmanteau film *Sin City* (Miller, Rodriguez, Tarantino, 2005). Portrayed by Bruce Willis, renowned for his role as the post-Callahan vigilante cop John McClane in the *Die Hard* series, the screen Hartigan forms a feedback loop within Callahan's fictional successors. Together these responses construct Callahan as a cartoonish apostle of violence whose verbal quips are almost as deadly as his Magnum.

Vigilante Films

John Wayne, stung by *Dirty Harry*'s success and regretful at his rejection of the role, responded in *McQ* (Sturges, 1974) and *Brannigan* (Hickox, 1975). Both featured Wayne as an insubordinate cop with a thirst for violence and a stern belief in law and order. Like the *Dirty Harry* movies, *McQ* was set on the West Coast, albeit in Seattle. *Brannigan*, meanwhile, sent Wayne's Chicago policeman Jim Brannigan to London to track down a fugitive mafioso played by John Vernon (*Dirty Harry*'s mayor). Vincent Canby of the *New York Times* concluded that in *McQ*, Wayne was simply following Eastwood's route from the western frontier to the city beat and that the film shared a willingness to "suspend civil rights in the name of law-and-order."[2] Gene Siskel argued that one of the film's few strengths was Wayne's ability to convey his character's almost Callahanian "contempt for the weaklings of the world."[3] Garry Wills pithily denounced both as "slightly Soiled Harry."[4] Despite such critical rejection, both films confirm that even Wayne, the quintessential hero of the Western, needed to bring his cinematic persona into the twentieth-century urban arena, thus completing the symbolic transformation of the American cinematic male hero from the cowboy to the rogue police officer.

The vigilante film cycle played on the caricature of Callahan to offer a crude legitimization of vigilante action. Callahan clones dominated the action. Like Callahan, *Lethal Weapon*'s (Donner, 1987) Martin Riggs found himself a widower courtesy of a car accident and had a decidedly terse relationship with both his colleagues and his superiors, although as Paul Smith notes, his resentment and frustration moves beyond Callahan's opposition to bureaucracy to approach "something closer to a genuine existential angst."[5] In *Death Wish* (Winner, 1974), a liberal conscientious objector, Paul Kersey, finds his values shaken to the core when his wife and daughter are raped in their own home. Walking the streets at night, armed with a Colt revolver (which resembles a .44 Magnum) and consumed with thoughts of revenge, he begins killing any violent criminals that he encounters. When the police eventually catch up with him, they merely insist that he leave town, providing tacit acceptance that he was acting morally. A series of increasingly tedious sequels placed Kersey in various situations requiring vengeful actions, including the murder of his daughter and maid in *Death Wish II* (Winner, 1982); the murder of his close friend in *Death Wish 3* (Winner, 1985); the drug overdose of his girlfriend's daughter in *Death Wish 4: The Crackdown* (Thompson, 1987); and the brutal murder of another girlfriend in *Death Wish 5: The Face of Death* (Goldstein, 1994). In the *Die Hard* movies, John McClane frequently clashes with government officials, some of whom consider him a terrorist.[6] Other retreads included the Sylvester Stallone vehicle *Cobra* (Cosmatos, 1986) and Ridley Scott's *Black Rain* (Scott, 1989). David Denby of *New York* magazine derided *Cobra* as a simple rip-off of *Dirty Harry*, an opinion that was perhaps bolstered by the appearance of *Dirty Harry's* veterans Andrew Robinson (Scorpio) and Reni Santoni (Chico Gonzales) in the cast. *Black Rain*, meanwhile, merely suggested to Denby that Callahan and his descendants should simply give up the ghost and head to the retirement home.[7]

Faint echoes of Callahan even resonated in a cycle of science-fiction films made during the 1980s and 1990s. Notably, *RoboCop* (Verhoeven, 1987), *The Terminator* (Cameron, 1984), and their sequels prominently feature fascistic robots—"Dirty" Harry stripped of the last vestiges of humanity—as their central characters. Like Callahan, the robots utter highly quotable lines in the midst of unleashing huge waves of violence. Arnold Schwarzenegger's Terminator simply drawls "fuck you, asshole" when an unwelcome janitor threatens to investigate his activities. *RoboCop's* ED-209 announces that criminals have "twenty seconds to comply" before riddling them with bullets.[8] "Dead or alive, you're coming with me" states RoboCop, a cyborg who is as uncannily accurate with his custom-built gun as Callahan is with his Magnum. After replicating Jennifer Spencer's revenge tactics in *Sudden Impact*, RoboCop taunts one of his victims: "Your move, creep." His successful campaign against crime in Detroit simply leads to RoboCop's betrayal by the corporation that built him, leading to a conclusion where he shoots and kills the company's president. Both robot films appeared during Reagan's presidency, a time during which, according to the film scholar Susan Jeffords, many film heroes were heavily influenced by the *Dirty Harry* template. Reagan's

America, Jeffords argues, would use military might to overwhelm its opponents, and would not back down when faced with any physical threats.[9] At a surface level, the robot films offer a continuation of backlash politics, yet liberal elements remain. The eponymous hero of *Robo-Cop*, for example, finally prevails after learning of and accepting that he has a human core wrapped in a robotic exoskeleton. His quest becomes one of uncovering corruption in the collusion between government and business, and his final triumph is embodied in his final insistence that he be known thereon by his human name. As for the Terminator, the robot relies merely on its physical power and is unable to compete with the resourcefulness and cunning of its human targets. Moreover, in proposing murderous robots as the logical conclusion of Callahan's trajectory, the science-fiction films constitute an implicit liberal rebuttal of *Dirty Harry*, highlighting the lack of humanity in such characters.

Dirty Harry's Pulp Fiction

According to the literary scholar Walter Nash, "popfiction is nothing if not predictable."[10] In the interregnum between *The Enforcer* and *Sudden Impact*, twelve *Dirty Harry* novels were published by the books subsidiary of Warner Brothers. Published under the pseudonym "Dane Hartman," the books were written by at least two authors who were commissioned to produce short, punchy, violent, and relatively simplistic stories that would appeal to the largest possible audience.[11] Although potentially shocking in terms of their graphic depiction of violence (heads splitting open are a frequent occurrence), the pulp novels are deeply conservative. Clive Bloom argues that pulp fiction is characterized by deliberately bland (or rather, accessible) language, teleological and predictable plotting, and an "avoidance of psychology."[12] Such books tend not to challenge societal norms, and instead merely reflect the status quo. The Dirty Harry pulps ask little of the reader beyond a willingness to be entertained and a basic knowledge of Callahan's modus operandi. They do not challenge our understanding of Callahan, nor do they provide much that is unexpected. They confirm Callahan as the individualistic pulp hero par excellence, reflecting Bloom's argument that "pulp thrives on the fantasy *representation* of authoritarian, fascistic figures and situations . . . simplified into violence and erotica."[13] Ric Meyers, a martial arts cinema expert who authored six of the novels, studied the *Dirty Harry* films in order to glean information that might be used in the stories, although he later claimed that Warner Brothers was not keen on the subtler and more psychological aspects of his work. He confirmed the exploitation origins of the novel series, stating that it was simply a revenue source and a way to continue the character while Eastwood was not making any Callahan movies.[14]

Authors of such work find themselves bound creatively by the strictures imposed by their publishers, but they retain a certain level of autonomy in determining how the stories develop. In this sense, the interest in the Callahan pulps lies not in their predictable violence and plotting, nor in their fidelity to a Callahan "mythos," but in the authors' mild deviations from or alterations to the expectations of the reader.[15] Thus we see Callahan removed from San Francisco, in an effort to add some variety (or to obviate the obvious criticism that such a bloodbath in San Francisco over such a short period of time would likely have led to Callahan's final removal from duty). In the first book Callahan relocates first to Los Angeles and then to San Antonio to tackle a crime boss following the murder of a Texan sheriff with whom he was friendly. Characteristically, he does this unpaid. In the second he tracks a corrupt union boss to the Caribbean, and in the fourth he finds himself in Mexico.[16] Elsewhere he heads to Boston, ostensibly to visit family. Events naturally conspire to have him track a murderer amid the city's notorious criminal underworld.[17] The seventh finds him in a small northern California town, and his travels extend to Los Angeles in the sixth; Chicago in the eighth; and Beirut, El Salvador, and Italy in the tenth.[18] Most significantly, the first book concludes at the Alamo, thus confirming Callahan's status as an American legend.[19] The actual Alamo now presents itself as "the shrine of Texas liberty," where the rebel Texans gave their lives in the service of the Texas Revolution.[20] Callahan might not have made the ultimate sacrifice, but in his willingness to protect honest American values from a hit man in the pay of a crime boss he positions himself alongside William B. Travis, Jim Bowie, and Davy Crockett as a near-mythological defender of the American way. That John Wayne played Crockett in *The Alamo* (Wayne, 1960) adds a further layer of significance to the novel. One of the novel's criminal hit men is a Wayne "freak" who thinks he actually lives in one of Wayne's movies; by the end of the novel, Callahan himself suspects that he had "stumbled into a John Wayne movie."[21] The book even identifies the Alamo itself as Wayne's graveyard.[22] The mantle of the Great American Hero had only recently been vacated when Wayne died in 1979; *Duel for Cannons* advocated Callahan as the next in line.

While the Callahan pulps have largely been forgotten in public discourse, they are revealing of Warner Brothers' understanding of the success of the film series. By focusing so heavily on violence, the pulps minimize the political undertones of the film series, instead encouraging the readership simply to revel in Callahan's almost superheroic actions and his ability to endure extreme pain in pursuit of criminals. *Family Skeletons* even makes this explicit, drawing numerous none-too-subtle parallels between Callahan and Superman.[23] Only rarely do the novels touch explicitly on Callahan's politics: while pursuing an African American suspect in *Family Skeletons*, Callahan wishes that it was the 1960s again, largely because it would ease his apprehending of an African American suspect: "If a negro [*sic*] had run around any major city in his underwear . . . he would have been tackled by twenty concerned citizens before he had gotten ten yards."[24] Instead, the vast majority of the books hew closely to the action blueprint established by the films. Callahan fights union bosses, a Chinese organized crime gang, a group of crazy terrorists and a left-wing terrorist cell, a demented government scientist, and finally a cop-killer who steals his Magnum, all the while shooting deserving criminals to death, gouging the occasional eye, and being shot, tortured, and verbally abused for his troubles.[25] He uncovers corruption in local unions, northern California police, and the Drug Enforcement Agency while breaking bread with a Republican opponent of gun restrictions.[26] In *Death in the Air*, he must tackle a scientist who hopes to use airborne chemicals to kill huge numbers of San Franciscans, a plot device that Ric Meyers based on real events and fears.[27] Readers are regularly reminded that Callahan refuses to endanger the public when on the job.[28] One book even predicts a central element of *The Dead Pool*'s plot by pairing Callahan with an attractive television anchorwoman.[29] All fetishize his Magnum and feature graphic descriptions of the injuries wrought on Callahan's victims when a high-powered bullet enters their bodies.

The novels ostensibly reinforce Eastwood's insistence that the films be made cheaply and that they hold no major significance beyond their ability to make money for his paymasters.[30] Yet beneath this, they offer insights into the nature of Callahan's iconic status. As cheap, undemanding, and luridly violent tales, they appeal to the broadest section of male society. They are far removed from the high-cultural leanings of modern literature, reinforcing Callahan's identity as an ordinary American. The novels also implicitly attack the elitism of the literature industry. They were ignored by the press, again a reflection of the distance between the high-cultural elite and the tastes of ordinary Americans. By ignoring the pretensions of literary fiction, the pulps aim not for the reader's head but his (and they were defiantly masculine books) heart and guts. Much like the films, they are simplistic and almost entirely predictable. Their conservatism is thus more metaphorical than explicit, rendering them a fitting tribute to Callahan's ideals.

Spoofing Callahan

Although there was never an official *Dirty Harry* television series, his centrality to American popular culture in the 1980s and 1990s ensured that it was easy for programs to reference Callahan, safe in the knowledge that the audience would pick up on the citation. *The Simpsons*, for example, ever ready to parody any aspect of American popular culture, created a spoof Callahan in McGarnagle, a television detective with attitude. McGarnagle is, according to the incompetent patriarch Homer Simpson, "the policeman who solves crimes in his spare time!" Although McGarnagle does not appear on-screen in his first appearance, his voice deliberately mimics Eastwood's diction and intonation. McGarnagle, like Callahan, is being upbraided by his chief: "Did you really have to break so much furniture?" "You tell me, Chief," McGarnagle drawls in Callahanian style, "you had a pretty good view from behind your desk." "You're off the case, McGarnagle!" bellows the chief. "You're off *your* case, Chief!" retorts McGarnagle. This truly absurd yet authentically Callahanian response provokes the chief to question, "What does that mean, exactly?" Before McGarnagle can answer, Homer Simpson offers the joke's punch line: "It means he gets results, you stupid chief!"[31] When Bart Simpson is facing a moral dilemma in a later episode, McGarnagle returns, this time in an incident where he is framed for a crime he did not commit.

The witness is a scared young boy whom McGarnagle, appearing visually for the first time, presses to tell the truth: "You gotta do this one for me, Billy." Suitably awed, perhaps by McGarnagle's resemblance to Eastwood, the boy agrees and the scene cuts to the chief's office. "Well, McGarnagle, Billy is dead," the chief booms. "They slit his throat from ear to ear." "Hey!" McGarnagle sneers, "I'm trying to eat lunch here."[32]

This satirical approach animated *Sledge Hammer*, a cult comedy show in which the show's eponymous hero was, like Callahan, a San Francisco police detective with a notorious reputation for violence, a short temper, and an ability to incense his superiors with great ease. Over two seasons, Inspector Hammer left a trail of devastation in his wake, culminating in his botched attempt to defuse a nuclear bomb which destroys an entire city.[33] *Sledge Hammer*'s creator, Adam Spencer, later testified to the significance of *Dirty Harry* to his own thoughts about creating a television show. Whereas most viewers approached the series as drama, Spencer thought the films had a "great sense of humor."[34] After watching *Sudden Impact*, Spencer concluded that the time was right to "provide a satirical look at Dirty Harry, Rambo and all those other guys," through creating a character who, like Inspector Clouseau or Agent Maxwell Smart of *Get Smart*, caused mostly damage through his actions.[35] The difference between Hammer and his bumbling forefathers was that the destruction he wrought was often deliberate and over the top. Indeed, many television executives considered the entire show to be too wild for broadcast, leaving it in the hands of the upstart broadcaster ABC.[36]

Sledge Hammer's title sequence opens with a soft-focus close-up of Inspector Sledge Hammer's beloved personalized Magnum resting on a silk pillow. After Hammer lovingly picks up and caresses the gun, he aims and utters his catchphrase: "Trust me: I know what I'm doing." He shoots, and the bullet hits and smashes the camera lens. As in the *Dirty Harry* series, subtlety was not *Sledge Hammer*'s métier. Hammer was conceived by Spencer as a sleep-deprived Harry Callahan, but David Rasche played him with a gleeful and almost hyperactive abandon. The detective's appearance cites Callahan in numerous ways. Sporting a Callahanian quiff, he often hides his eyes behind sunglasses that evoke Callahan's chosen eyewear. His suits are cheap (and often ill-matched with his ties), and he drives a beat-up green Dodge, complete with bullet holes in the windshield. Hammer lacks any self-awareness and is cheerfully oblivious of the despair that his actions provoke among his colleagues and the destruction of public and private property that he wrings.[37] For the *Chicago Tribune*'s Dusty Saunders, Hammer's behavior was so over-the-top that at times he made Callahan resemble Pee-Wee Herman.[38] Noting the affectionate tone of the satire, John O'Connor, writing in the *New York Times*, suggested that Hammer might be "the perfect hero for our time. Some viewers may understandably not know whether to laugh or weep."[39] According to Spencer, the show was subtle enough that some people did not interpret it as a satirical comment on violence in American life. For example, the National Rifle Association sent him an honorary membership in recognition of the show's good work.[40] Most laughed, however, aware that Hammer was so outrageous that he simply could not be taken seriously. When the captain denounces him as "sadistic, depraved, bloodthirsty, barbaric," Hammer retorts, "Is that why you called me in here? To shower me with compliments?"[41] A significant part of the amplification of Callahan in Hammer lies in the humorous quips that Callahan became famous for uttering: at one point, Hammer made this explicit, sneering to a criminal, "Go ahead, make my day . . . may the force be with you—forget the clichés."[42] "I grew up with my gun," states Hammer, "I could shoot before I could walk."[43] "My motto is make war not love. . . . The only thing I'm involved with is my gun—and that's a monogamous relationship."[44] He cites Callahan to his bank manager— "Go ahead—make me laugh"—before denouncing the parsimonious administrator as a "yogurt-sucking mutant."[45]

As suggested by the title sequence, *Sledge Hammer* took the fetishizing of Callahan's Magnum to its extreme conclusion. Hammer sleeps with the gun and has various accessories that he attaches to his Magnum's barrel to broaden its utility in his daily life, including a spatula and a toothbrush. In one episode he attaches to the pistol his self-designed "loudener," which amplifies its report to deafening level.[46] He even owns a hair dryer in the shape of a Magnum and has a range finder as the peephole on his apartment door.[47] Under the influence of a virus, he blissfully hallucinates that his Magnum is talking to him. The gun reassures Hammer through his catchphrase: "Trust me, you know what you're doing."[48] After a criminal steals his Magnum, Hammer becomes so frenzied and troubled that he is sent to a psychiatrist. "Alone," he tells the psychiatrist, "I'm just a cop. But with my gun I'm a *dangerous* cop."[49] "I know it sounds crazy but I love that gun," Hammer tells his psychiatrist. "No woman could ever replace my Magnum."[50]

Like Callahan, Hammer is an instinctive policeman. He apprehends suspects on the grounds that "I have a feeling he was about to commit a crime . . . this is crime prevention week, remember?"[51] Believing that "scum begets scum," he advocates locking up potential criminals at birth.[52] When an ATM machine refuses to give him money or a vending machine refuses to vend, Hammer's first instinct is to draw the Magnum.[53] He revels in the fact that he gets paid to beat people up, joyously stating that "It's more than a job—it's an adventure" and lamenting that his gun is going to rust when he is put on suspension for six months.[54] When told of the fad among office workers for team-building paintball excursions, he is bamboozled: "White collar weirdos. Why play war when you can join the police and kill for fun and profit? And use real bullets!"[55] His partner, Dori Doreau, summarizes Hammer's personality aptly: "Granted, Sledge is irresponsible, undependable, egotistical, insensitive, chauvinistic, sadistic, and cruel, but other than that, he is a terrific guy."[56] When accused of being one-dimensional, he takes umbrage: "I show a whole range of emotion: anger, rage, hate."[57] He has a poster of a machine-gun-wielding model on his locker door and has targets on his apartment walls that he shoots at regularly.[58] Like Callahan, Hammer has a dead aim, although the sensibilities of network television meant that his gunshots only disarmed rather than maimed or killed his opponents. His gun-happy behavior is so notorious in the police department that his colleagues take cover whenever he threatens to wield his Magnum. He, meanwhile, is as invulnerable as Callahan. Despite expending hundreds of bullets, the criminals he faces only manage to shoot him once, and then Hammer manages to catch the bullet in his teeth courtesy of a trick taught him by his father.[59] Hammer only meets his match when a robot gravely injures him in "Hammeroid." Luckily, modern science re-creates him as the titular cyborg, a development that merely makes him more dangerous and allows the episode to parody the then-recent *Robocop*.[60]

A confirmed anti-communist, Hammer has little time for liberals, particularly those on the police force.[61] Observing the fondness for donuts among officers, Hammer launches into a diatribe:

Now your stereotypical donut is nothing but dough and sugar fried in fat, am I right? Now, that fat gums up your arteries and goes to your brain, and you turn liberal. AND THE NEXT THING YOU KNOW BARRY MANILOW IS ON THE TURNTABLE AND YOU'RE NOT GOING TO WORK AND YOU'RE VOTING FOR GUN CONTROL! YOU SEE WHAT I'M SAYING? You see that connection? *That's* why I eat granola.[62]

When a "liberal creep" from Internal Affairs attacks him for violating twenty-five of the twenty-six amendments to the U.S. Constitution, Hammer sneers, "I missed one?" Later on he states that the Bill of Rights "stinks."[63] Like Callahan, he does not care for the *Miranda* decision, averring that he prefers to read suspects their "last rites, if you know what I mean."[64] When questioning a criminal, he swats aside the protestations about rights: "Listen, creep, I'm Inspector Sledge Hammer and I don't give a damn about the rights of criminals. The only rights I'm interested in defending are the rights of [Hammer thinks for a moment] American citizens!" "I am a citizen," protests the criminal. "Shut up!" shouts Hammer. "Don't confuse me."[65] To avoid accusations of police brutality, Hammer forces a criminal at gunpoint to punch himself in the face.[66] He is suspended so regularly that it simply becomes a relief to him, allowing him to "do what I do best," and fire his gun with impunity.[67] Yet Hammer does have a small number of liberal tendencies, albeit ones expressed via gunplay. Opposed to smoking, he happily shoots cigars out of smokers' mouths. When he spots a car illegally parked in a handicapped zone, he simply shoots its tires.[68] His literary choices are also informed by his politics: his favorite book is *War and Peace* (but only the first half).[69] Moments of introspection are rare and fleeting. "Violence doesn't solve anything," he confesses at one point before pondering and reconsidering: "What am I saying? Violence solves everything!"[70]

Sledge Hammer's relationship with the *Dirty Harry* series operates on more than simply the level of a Callahan parody. Numerous episodes also refract key moments in Callahan's cinematic life. The pilot, "Under the Gun," opens with a night shot of the Golden Gate Bridge, locating the film in Callahan's hometown. The first scene opens with a criminal kidnapping the mayor's daughter. He wears a balaclava that replicates one worn by Scorpio in the Mount Davidson scene of the original movie, and he is giggling, much like *Dirty Harry*'s villain. The parallel continues in the very next scene, set in the mayor's office. John Vernon reprises his role as the mayor, and demands that Hammer be placed on the kidnapping case. Hammer promises to bring his daughter back "dead or alive."[71] The episode closes after the kidnappers echo Scorpio's demands for a private jet and Hammer discovers that the mayor's daughter had joined their gang, much like Patricia Hearst allegedly joined the Symbionese Liberation Army—the inspiration for *The Enforcer*'s People's Revolutionary Strike Force. Elsewhere, "Dori Day Afternoon" reimagines the attempted suicide from *Dirty Harry*. This time, Hammer shoots at the ledge, forcing the jumper to shuffle across and fall into an open window.[72] *Magnum Force*'s target practice competition is spoofed in "They Shoot Hammers Don't They?" with Hammer winning despite shooting the civilian targets.[73] "Magnum Farce" follows the plot of *Magnum Force* very closely. Like Callahan, Hammer is initially impressed at the vigilantes' actions. Yet when they invite him to join their group, which they say represents its members' shared "purpose of righting wrongs through force and aggression," Hammer declines, telling them, "I'm already a registered Republican."[74] When Hammer apprehends the ringleader, she quotes Lieutenant Briggs, insisting that "history justifies the vigilante" before telling Hammer that she'll prosecute him since no jury would believe his account over hers, a word-for-word repetition of Briggs's final, hubristic threat to Callahan.[75] "Hammer Gets Nailed" even anticipates a plot strand of *The Dead Pool*. A news reporter shadows Hammer ("I don't watch the news—I make it") and Doreau for a day, which culminates with a car chase that ends spectacularly badly. The reporter's conclusion is blunt and again reflects ideas present in the *Dirty Harry* series: "We don't have police [in this city]. We have frontier gunslingers."[76]

Although it lasted only two seasons, *Sledge Hammer* gathered a cult following which ensured that its DVD release was a moderate success. The ease with which it parodied the *Dirty Harry* series and its success in doing so highlights the long shadow cast by the films. That NRA members and *New York Times* readers responded positively to the show is an indication not only of Spencer's skill but also that *Dirty Harry* had become a key referent in American popular culture. Although some of the show's humor was somewhat adolescent and obvious, that it cited Harry Callahan so explicitly reveals the extent to which all Americans could relate to Callahan.[77] Moreover, its emphasis on Hammer's (love for his) gun offers an instructive insight into public attitudes toward Callahan. This public memory is as bound up in his relationship with the .44 Magnum as it is with his position as a police inspector. Consequently, his association with a private company is as important as his role as defender of the public good; any public-service principles that he holds are as memorable as his trust in private enterprise when it comes to defending himself.

Gaming Callahan

Television was not the only medium that reconsidered Harry Callahan. A 1990 video game, simply titled *Dirty Harry*, offered Nintendo gamers the opportunity to unholster Callahan's Magnum. The game's story is relatively simple: a Colombian drug lord is attempting to take control of San Francisco's underworld. Following convention, Callahan wants to investigate but is discouraged by his superiors and so sets out to bring down this criminal on his own time. Playing Callahan, the player must first walk around San Francisco's streets, dispatching hoodlums with either the Magnum or a punch to the head. Callahan may enter buildings and search their contents by smashing up furniture. He must also explore the city's sewers and interact with certain other characters, including a prostitute who grants him extra lives, a rapper who gives him some plastic explosives, a basketball player who gives him a bulletproof vest, and a homeless woman who gives him restorative chili dogs. In later levels, Callahan must explore San Francisco's dockyard and Alcatraz Island, and eventually he comes face-to-face with the drug lord. If he is victorious, Callahan repeats the "Do you feel lucky" speech, heralding the game's end.[78] Distilling Callahan to his violent essence, the game expects players simply to shoot, punch, or kick anyone who comes within range; even the detective work inside the buildings involves only wanton destruction. With a Callahan who could be shot multiple times before dying, the game presented more violence in five minutes than the entire five movies in the film series.

As Karen Jones and John Wills write, video games are inevitably compromised by the capabilities of the hardware available to their developers. Consequently, "plot details, overarching stories and character depth

[a]re all sacrificed. . . . Narrative [i]s compromised in preference to action [which] almost always mean[s] hostile exchange."[79] While Deborah Allison critiques the *Dirty Harry* game for placing gunplay at the core of the Dirty Harry universe, as Jones and Wills suggest, video games lend themselves best to action.[80] It is difficult to imagine early 1990s production companies developing a Dirty Harry game that focused as much on investigative procedure and Callahan's interaction with the bureaucracy as on him running, shooting, and killing. Yet with the vast increase in processing power of video-game machines and the concurrent rise in complexity of games by the early 2000s, such a proposition seemed possible. In 2005, Warner Brothers announced that Harry Callahan would become the star of a new video game to be released the following year.[81] The game player would adopt the persona of Callahan and guide him through his ongoing attempt to clean up the streets of 1970s San Francisco. As in the film series, Callahan would be expected to make the distinction between justice and the law, to be tough enough with the criminals while not getting into too much trouble with the SFPD authorities.[82] To ensure fidelity to the spirit of the movies, the game was to be developed in consultation with Eastwood's Malpaso Company. The announcement was met with an excitement that suggested what fans wanted was less nuanced. The gaming journalist Patrick Garratt was almost unable to contain his glee: "The mere prospect of a game where you get to play out your most rabid, macho, lead-slinging, my-way-or-the-highway, scowling, punk-whacking, flare-wearing fantasies should be more than enough for any self-respecting game fan."[83] A trailer that offered insight into the finished product's gameplay suggested that Garratt's fantasies could be fulfilled. The trailer opens with a shot of the Golden Gate Bridge shrouded in fog, soundtracked by the end title theme from *Dirty Harry*. A man's voice denounces the SFPD for its failure to protect the citizenry from the derivatively named "Gemini Killer." "The time has come for the people of San Francisco to take matters into their own hands! If the police will not protect us, we will protect ourselves!" he declares. After panning through grimy city streets, the focus falls on a grubby diner. A customer turns off the television, which is playing footage of the speech we have been hearing. The customer is Callahan, wearing the same suit and V-neck sweater as sported in the opening scene of *Dirty Harry*. He asks the chef if "that tan Ford" is still sitting in view, referencing the diner

scene from *Dirty Harry*. Before the chef can answer, another customer threatens Callahan, who responds by punching him in the face, sending him crashing to the floor. "Somebody call the police," he cries. "I am the police," mutters Callahan as he departs the scene, just as he does in *Magnum Force* when a neighbor expresses outrage at his tampering with the mailbox in his apartment building. Callahan is then seen piloting his car at breakneck speed through the streets while brandishing his Magnum, interspersed with the legends "Good Cop" and "Bad Attitude." He is seen rescuing a woman who has fallen from the Golden Gate Bridge, crushing a man's head in a vice ("I never thought of that one before," Eastwood allegedly mused when this was revealed to him), and finally reprising his "lucky" speech while wielding his Magnum.[84] The trailer ends with the legend "Justice is Dirty."[85] Due to financial problems at the game's developers, the project was not developed any further and was canceled in 2007.[86] Yet the mere appearance of the trailer is indicative of what video-game developers felt were the essential features of Dirty Harry—San Francisco, Callahan's quips, extreme violence, and traditional gender roles.

Callahan's Fan Fiction

An interactive Callahan might not have been fully achievable through the medium of video games, but the spread of web forums as the Internet embraced user-generated content allowed fans to construct and distribute their own responses to the character and his diegetic world. Carolyn Jess-Cooke argues that film sequels are "founded upon the (somewhat false) sense of spectator interactivity." As she observes of spoofs, spin-offs, and such related texts, "the relationship between a text and its surrounding texts is marked by the particularly discursive functions of the latter in both confirming and disseminating the factuality of the former."[87] As important, such paratexts encourage reconsideration of the concept of "sequelization." Whereas Jess-Cooke argues that the "primary mechanism" of sequels is their attempt to stabilize the original while providing a more participatory spectacle for the observer (in that the observer is encouraged to reconsider the generic norms of the original), paratexts such as fan fiction and video games hold even more immersive potential, not least because they offer the prospect of placing the original text within a wider universe.[88] The aborted 2007 game, for example, offered the opportunity for gamers to shape Callahan's career after *Dirty Harry* but before the other sequels. More frequently, fan fiction offers an outlet for Callahan fans to create their own closure for him, a reflection of the weaknesses in *The Dead Pool* and their devotion to a character who appears as much a friend as a cipher for their fantasies.

The first *Dirty Harry* fan-fiction writers were arguably Gail Morgan Hickman and S. W. Schurr, whose original script titled "Moving Target" was delivered to Eastwood's bar in Carmel, presumably for Eastwood to read over a beer. His approval of this treatment led to a series of rewrites and the eventual production of *The Enforcer*.[89] Despite the weaknesses of *The Enforcer*, the fact that the film's concept emerged from the creativity of fans reveals the relationship that many devout fans and fan-fiction writers have with their chosen text. As Will Brooker argues, fans become "custodians" of the characters, policing their development through, for example, sequels, and both "rehabilitating and sustaining" their characters through self-produced responses in the form of paratexts.[90] The fans' devotion to and investment in the original product often compels them to create texts that demonstrate a far surer grasp of the universe the character(s) inhabit and that have greater fidelity to the mythos than the original texts develop.[91] The primary texts—in Callahan's case, the original film and its sequels—become the baseline from which these paratexts emerge. They establish many conventions that the paratexts adhere to and histories within which the paratexts exist. *Star Wars* fans, for example, reimagined the relationship between two central characters in the first "prequel" episode, *The Phantom Menace* (Lucas, 1999). Such reimaginings emerged from the fans' disappointment at the shortcomings of *The Phantom Menace* and their own emotional investment in and knowledge of the series.[92]

Even though only a small number of *Dirty Harry* fan fictions are available online, most follow one central generic theme: Callahan taking on one last job. Unlike the *Dirty Harry* novels, they follow the chronology of the film series and assume that an age-appropriate Eastwood continues in the role. They find Callahan in retirement, eking out an anonymous existence on a paltry pension. The most detailed of the online treatments is "Dirty Harry: End Game," which emerged from the author's disappointment at *The Dead Pool*.[93] Featuring numerous flashbacks to Callahan's youth, "End Game" allows Callahan a final moment of glory in foiling a Mafia plot to steal a secret military weapon while also rescuing a large number of hostages, including his granddaughter, from criminals hiding out on Alcatraz Island. The author's love for the series is expressed through numerous references to previous films and attempts to weave Callahan into events in San Francisco history, including the 1966 riot at Compton's Cafeteria and the bombing of the Park police station, thus cementing Callahan's position in San Francisco's actual history. In line with many fan-fiction tropes, "End Game" broadens and deepens Callahan's backstory, revealing, for example, that the Mafia actually killed his wife back in the 1960s and fleshing out the story of his adoption of the .44 Magnum as his chosen weapon, thus explicitly referencing and developing brief references in *Dirty Harry* and *The Enforcer*. The addition of Chico Gonzales as a chief FBI operative might not strictly follow the series mythos (Gonzales pledges to leave the force after being injured in *Dirty Harry*), but it demonstrates the writer's eagerness to tie up important loose ends that relate to the films' most beloved characters.[94] Another uncompleted script, "Still Dirty," brings Callahan back to San Francisco from a peaceful retirement in rural northern California. A number of murders have been committed that are linked to a politically motivated group and a banking corporation that they opposed. Callahan is drawn to the case after feeling reenergized by his foiling of an attempted armed robbery of his local store.[95] The SFPD accepts him in an advisory role and partners him with David Di Giorgio, the son of his deceased partner from *Dirty Harry* and *The Enforcer*.[96]

Amid the usual mayhem, these stories reveal how fans interpret Callahan as a moral hero. "End Game" pits him against one of the staple villains of American crime fiction, the Mafia. More importantly, he rescues a number of civilians, including some children, from death at the Mafia's hands, thus symbolically protecting the American nation from organized crime. Intriguingly, however, the fact that Callahan effectively rescues the U.S. military from an embarrassing and potentially dangerous incident places the implacable foe of "the system" as the protector of that very system. Although the Navy Seals are sent in, Callahan has little need for their extra firepower. Yet in fighting alongside them and accepting their assistance, this Callahan is absorbed into the American military. He ceases to be an outsider figure, implicitly accepting the authority of the system that he has chafed against for so many years. "Still Dirty" is as intriguing, albeit for different reasons. Written in the wake of the financial calamity of 2008 and the resultant demonization of bankers, the script focuses on the tension between a local multinational bank and a thinly veiled substitute for the Occupy Wall Street movement, the Take Back movement, which has occupied a public park in San Francisco, in an echo of the Occupy protests that began in October 2011 at Frank Ogawa Plaza in Oakland. Callahan is equally cynical toward the bank chief and the protesters, thus positioning himself between two extremes, much as he was portrayed in *Magnum Force*. Like the *City of Blood* novel, "Still Dirty" has a capitalist as one of its villains, allowing a more centrist Callahan to present himself as a force of moderation. The unfinished script also features Callahan battling with cell phones, the constant presence of surveillance cameras, and the web's interaction with such technology. "Still Dirty" promises to insert Callahan's common sense into the debate between turbo- and anti-capitalists in order to restore San Francisco to peace. His resistance to technology touches on a key theme of the sequels and adds a reactionary element to the plot. Callahan thus potentially represents a haven from the hyperdeveloped world of the twenty-first century. In fighting both Take Back and the banks, while resisting the insinuation of the web into every aspect of people's lives, Callahan continues to fight for a traditional America, reinforcing his Reaganite quest for an Arcadian retreat.

Miller's Callahan

Like the fanfic writers, Frank Miller was drawn to reconsider the denouement to Callahan's tale. Renowned for his reimagining of the DC Comics superhero Batman in *The Dark Knight Returns* (1986), Miller was among the most important comic artists of the 1980s and 1990s, a reputation that was cemented by *Sin City*, a multivolume graphic novel that was published in installments through much of the 1990s. *Sin City: That Yellow Bastard* (1996) was the fourth in the series and concerned Hartigan, a tough police officer pursuing one last case on his final day before retirement. From this clichéd premise Miller spun a story that he envisaged as the last testament of Harry Callahan: "I went to see the last Dirty Harry movie, *The Dead Pool* and I was disgusted. I went out and said, this is not a Dirty Harry movie, this is nothing, this is a pale sequel. But I walked out and said that's not the last Dirty Harry story, *I will show you the last Dirty Harry story*."[97] In 1985, not long before *Sin City* took shape, Miller expressed his admiration for the film series. "Dirty Harry is clearly larger than life; his behavior would certainly land him in jail," Miller said. "But that's irrelevant. What is relevant is that . . . Harry is a profoundly, consistently moral force, administering the 'Wrath of God' on murderers who society treats as victims. . . . [H]is work has more to do with what's happening in society than any dozen of the more hip filmmakers."[98] He later confessed that part of the inspiration for *The Dark Knight Returns* was his own speculation over how Batman would act in the angry world of the 1970s and 1980s, "the time of 'Dirty Harry.'"[99] Like Callahan, Miller's Batman reacted to the release of a criminal on a technicality via extralegal and violent means, and rejected the cowardice and puny laws of the city, labeling his antagonists punks and beating them into subjugation.[100] Building on this, Miller declared that his overarching ambition for *Sin City* was to tell the story of "heroes who emerge in this swamp of corruption and are essentially at odds not so much with organized crime as the authorities, the powers that be"—another factor that reinforces the relationship between *Sin City* and the *Dirty Harry* series.[101] Relatedly, Miller himself held somewhat Callahanian attitudes. He despised the 1960s, largely it seems because many of his schoolteachers were former hippies who were wont to soliloquize the decade of their youth. He also detested comic books of the early 1970s because the writers "load[ed] their heroes] down with all these puny, petty, snotty little emotions," all of which emerged in the comics of the previous decade.[102] "We have to fight to stay alive," he told Kim Thompson in 1985.[103] Although not sited with any specificity, Miller's biography suggests that California was on his mind when he was creating Basin City, the location for all the *Sin City* "yarns," as Miller identified them. Miller moved from New York City to California in 1982 and claimed that the state grew to influence his work in numerous ways, from speech patterns to the weather.[104] During the gestation of *Sin City*, Miller was also influenced by the California novels of hard-boiled writers Raymond Chandler, Mickey Spillane, and Dashiell Hammett.[105] Miller borrowed heavily from film noir techniques for *Sin City*, expressed in the subject matter, plots, dialogue, and his almost exclusively monochrome chiaroscuro artwork.[106]

Basin City is a dank, mysterious location populated by criminals, freaks, femmes fatale, prostitutes with hearts of gold, an ineffective police force, and numerous folk of dubious moral fiber. Riddled with corruption, it is controlled by a single family named the Roarks, whose depravity is often at the core of the individual yarns in the series and whom Miller linked explicitly to the United States' most prominent liberal dynasty. Miller stated that the Roarks were "your darkest, darkest nightmare of what the Kennedys could have been."[107] This immediately begs comparisons with the *Dirty Harry* films' representation of the liberal elite. Miller wanted his hero, Hartigan, to exhibit a vulnerability that, coupled with his old age, rendered him a more believable character, more of a hard-boiled knight in tatty armor than the invulnerable superhero of *The Dead Pool*.[108] Yet Hartigan is reminiscent of a steroid-fueled Callahan. Muscular, tall, tough, implacable, and incorruptible, plagued by chest pains and ravaged by decades on the force, he wears his hair in a buzz cut, and his scarred face suggests a monumental Eastwood carved of granite. Naturally, he sports a trench coat and wields a .44 Magnum. "Just one hour to go," he sighs at the yarn's outset, "I'm pushing papers, filling out forms, going through the motions like some old forgotten machine."[109] His thoughts turn to a young girl, "helpless in the hands of a drooling lunatic."[110] He rounds on his slothful partner for hoping to turn a blind eye to this one last case, reflecting Callahan's attitude to Di Giorgio's complacency in *Dirty Harry*. Hartigan instinctively knows that unless he becomes Nancy Callahan's knight in shining armor, she will be at the mercy of a sadistic and perverted Roark clan member whose status in *Sin City*'s plutocracy guarantees that any police intervention will arrive too late. Echoing Harry Callahan's feelings about Mary Ann Deacon, Hartigan admits that "for all I know, she's dead already" before heading off to investigate.[111]

Freed from the necessity to complete any bureaucracy by his impending retirement and willingness to embrace his own death, he beats and kills numerous henchmen in his quest to find Nancy. His instincts about Roark Junior are proved correct, and in the ensuing fight he castrates Roark with his Magnum much like Jennifer Spencer did her tormentors.[112] His violence is only quelled by his partner's intervention. Shot repeatedly, Hartigan slumps to the floor, thinking "an old man dies, a little girl lives, fair trade."[113] The Roark family has other plans, however.

Using their own medics, they keep Hartigan alive and Senator Roark Senior informs Hartigan that he will be convicted of raping the eleven-year-old Nancy and shooting Roark Junior. He will then die in prison.[114] Abandoned by his wife, friends, and colleagues, Hartigan's faith in humanity is sustained only by the weekly arrival of a pseudonymous letter from Nancy. Yet his edifice of hope collapses after eight years when her letters stop and a severed finger is delivered instead. Consumed with thoughts of revenge, he agrees to sign a false confession in order to make parole. His first action after freedom is to locate Nancy at a sleazy bar that employs her as a topless dancer. In so locating her, he unwittingly reveals her to Roark Junior, who has also been reconstructed thanks to his family's deep pockets. Theo Finigan notes that the moral depravity of *The Dark Knight*'s criminals is "ostensibly signaled by physical deformity and mental illness," a theme that returns in *That Yellow Bastard*.[115] Junior is now as physically disfigured as he is mentally disturbed. His body has been twisted almost beyond recognition and his skin recolored a putrid yellow. He emits a stench that serves as an olfactory representation of his moral degeneracy. After kidnapping Nancy, he takes her to the Roark family farm, which becomes the location for the yarn's final scene in which Roark Junior is killed, Nancy freed, and Hartigan finally released from his burden.

Hartigan's morality and sexuality are presented as two key factors in elevating him from the Roarks and separating right from wrong. Hartigan is irresistible to Nancy, and the epistolary relationship that develops between the two underpins her sexual attraction to him, thus suggesting that this is a deeper love than that produced by mere physical attraction. He spurns her physical advances while confessing that he loves her with all his heart. Hartigan's tragic and self-abnegating awareness of the massive age gap between himself and Nancy starkly contrasts with Roark Junior's attraction to underage girls and violent expression of his sexual urges (graphically presented in his inability to maintain an erection unless the object of his desire screams in pain). As important, it echoes Callahan's relationship with his romantic partners Sunny and Samantha Walker. That Hartigan repeatedly saves Nancy's life and protects her from predatory males presents the two in a heteronormative relationship, with the male representing strength and power, and the female emotionalism, subordination, and weakness.[116] Nancy is only able to demonstrate her strength when refusing to scream while being tortured by Roark Junior. Despite his physical degeneration, he is able to dominate her, ensuring her reliance on a truly masculine savior. Hartigan has already resisted the temptation to yield to his base instincts, thus confirming that he is Nancy's moral as well as physical guardian. Nancy's surname points readers to Miller's stated aim for the book. Just as Hartigan hopes to rescue Nancy and preserve her purity in the face of a society that has failed her, Miller hoped to rescue Callahan and preserve the purity of Callahan's legend in the face of a culture industry that had besmirched his memory. In essence, her tale is Miller's wish-fulfillment alternative to the murder at the core of *Dirty Harry*'s plot, and Nancy is a Mary Ann Deacon rescued and returned to safety.

Like Callahan, Hartigan is consumed by his moral quest to protect one more girl from the Roark family. He is regularly beaten by corrupt officers while in prison. In refusing either to confess or to reveal Nancy's whereabouts, Hartigan confirms his moral rectitude even as his entire world is destroyed. One prison guard even sarcastically comments, "*John Hartigan*. Mister *law and order*. Mister *by the book*. Mister *high and mighty*. Always looking down your nose at *real cops*."[117] These real cops are those who have accepted Basin City's realpolitik and turn a blind eye to the city's most egregious crimes in order not to upset the status quo and to preserve their own status within the city. In essence, they play malevolent Di Giorgios to Hartigan's Callahan and are unable or unwilling to risk their lives to protect the innocent. They are notably absent from the book's finale, which, like the climax to *Dirty Harry*, occurs at a lawless location. The Roark farm is a semi-mythical place in *Sin City*'s geography, a location that every police officer learns is beyond his control. No ordinary cop would dare enter, let alone attempt to apprehend a Roark. Hartigan knows these rules and their inevitable consequence. The Roark farm is classically western in appearance. A weather vane idly spins while Kevin, a major character from another *Sin City* yarn, silently reads the Bible on the porch. In blending *Sin City*'s noir with the Western, the denouement of *That Yellow Bastard* returns the frontier hero to the center of the narrative, offering further echoes of Callahan's roots in Westerns. The lawless farm is the location for both Roark Junior's sexual violence and Hartigan's retributive and redemptive violence. As Hartigan approaches, he reminds himself to "know your limitations," citing Callahan's final quip in *Magnum Force*.[118] He comes across a naked, flaccid Roark, whipping a silent Nancy. The ensuing fight concludes with Hartigan ripping off Roark's penis with his bare hands before pounding Roark's face into the floor, a gruesome act that Hartigan seems to derive no pleasure in performing.

Hartigan's final promise to Nancy is in the classic pulp fiction tradition. He promises to blow the case wide open and bring down the entire Roark clan after revealing all of their crimes to the authorities. He encourages Nancy to leave town and start again without the threat of the remaining Roarks or their henchmen hanging over her. Yet this is merely a temporary suspension of narrative logic. "No," Hartigan tells himself after Nancy departs. "The game is *rigged*."[119] His final action is to take a Magnum and shoot himself in the head, to ensure Nancy's freedom and his (and Callahan's) apotheosis. This near transcendent conclusion uncannily anticipates the demise of Walt Kowalski, the other major Callahan analogue. Both select highly moral deaths in the service of the freedom of youthful friends, trading their own wasted past for their friends' promising future. In adopting mutually assured destruction as the only secure conclusion, they remain true to Callahan's reputation as a moral conquistador; in dying amid a spectacular conflagration, they ensure that he has become legend.

*   *   *

In both concluding Callahan's story in triumphant and redemptive fashion while also enriching his backstory, paratexts such as *That Yellow Bastard* and Callahan's fanfic demonstrate the fans' investment in and devotion to the series. They also suggest that Callahan has become a mythological character and a vital feature of the American popular culture landscape. As important, they return to the deep roots of *Dirty Harry*. Pulp novels, comic books, video games, and fanfics are frequently considered to be among the lowest forms of culture, displaying few of the redeeming features of the American high culture canon. They are the twenty-first-century equivalent of B movies, the dross that was economical to make, designed to appeal to the lowest common denominator, and expected to hold little significance beyond the ability to keep people occupied while they waited for the A movie at the top of the evening's bill. Callahan's afterlife in these forms suggests that he remains an outsider figure, refused entry into the canon, sniping at the great art that defines what some commentators and writers feel best represents their nation. Yet close examination of these texts offers a different perspective on the significance of the response to Harry Callahan, and brings his story full circle. Don Siegel's directorial career truly took shape during the 1950s, when he directed a series of B movies. *Invasion of the Body Snatchers* was itself designed as a B movie, and its transcendence of both genre and status is testament to Siegel's genius and a convincing rebuttal to those who dismiss low culture as trash or meaningless fodder for the uncritical masses. Similarly, the *Dirty Harry* movies were not designed to be major contributions to American culture or great expressions of Eastwood's creativity but as a simple means to generate profits for Warner Brothers. As successive generations of film scholars have demonstrated, *Invasion* and many of its fellow B movies offer important insights into American politics, life and culture in the 1950s. Just as they do not deserve dismissal, the *Dirty Harry* movies and the varied responses to them should not be consigned to the dustbin of our cultural history. Analysis of them reveals the extent to which Harry Callahan has become more than simply a facet of Eastwood's cinematic persona but as a cipher for Americans' fantasies about themselves and their country. Callahan represents American strength, honor, chivalry, and righteousness while also revealing its bloodlust, lack of respect for the rule book, and fondness for guns. Harry Callahan is thus as much an American archetype as George Washington, Uncle Sam, Rosie the Riveter, and apple pie.

That said, Callahan is more than simply a pop-culture construct. His continued popularity must be understood within the context of post-1960s conservatism. The historian Jefferson Cowie argues that Richard Nixon's attempt to construct a new Republican majority in the U.S. electorate was forged through an appeal to their cultural values rather than their economic interests. This Cowie identifies as "an appeal to their moral backbone, patriotic rectitude, whiteness, and machismo in the face of the inter-related threats of social decay, racial unrest, and faltering national purpose."[120] Essentially, the Nixon-era Republicans saw the response of white Americans to the tempest of the 1960s as a search for calmness and security, a desire for respite from unrelenting change and torment, and a demand for common sense to put a stop to the madness they had witnessed during the antiwar marches, civil unrest, and youthful rebellion of the previous few years. Ronald Reagan built on this by constructing a "populist right" that offered "cultural refuge" for working-class white Americans. Callahan was a similar figure who offered moral certainties, rejected the liberalism of the 1960s and all it represented, and was prepared to defend American values with all his strength. His continued popularity might best be interpreted as an expression of a yearning for simpler times among the electorate, one that was entwined with the Republicans' focus on "patriotism, God, race, patriarchy, and nostalgia for community."[121] Their rhetorical appeals to these abstract ideas diverted attention from, for example, the economic policies of Reaganism, which resulted in higher working-class unemployment and the rapid decline of American industry. They encouraged people to forget Reagan's assault on collective bargaining and the union movement, and the decline of social cohesion in the conservative era. Americans were urged instead to focus on more emotional concepts such as national pride and cultural values than economic realities that should logically have sent workers back into the embrace of the Democratic Party. Approached from this direction, Harry Callahan's quest to clean up San Francisco thus acts as a pressure valve, enabling Americans to rejoice in the destruction of the criminal element in their cities while scoffing at the follies of the liberals in their failed attempts at social engineering. His five films encourage white viewers to forget the incoherence of their adherence to Reaganism and focus on their shared resentment of the world bequeathed to them by the 1960s liberals, while also reminding them of the Democrats' abandonment of the white working-class vote. The widespread investment in Harry Callahan might therefore become a signifier of Republican dominance of popular political and cultural discourse in the post-1960s era.

In 1993, Eastwood told Peter Biskind of his thoughts on his final days: "I figure that by the time I'm really old, somebody at the Academy Awards will get the bright idea to give me some sort of plaque. I'll be so old, they'll have to carry me up there. . . . 'Thank you all for this honorary award' and SPLAT. Good-bye, Dirty Harry."[122] Clearly aware of the lasting legacy of Callahan and the close relationship between the actor, the icon, and the character, Eastwood suspected that his most famous role was likely to be prominent in his epitaphs. While he appreciated its importance to his career, Eastwood might also have underestimated Callahan's impact on the nation. Callahan the instinctive crime fighter; scourge of bureaucrats, liberals, cheats, and punks; defender of truth; dispenser of justice; force of good in a world suffused with evil was a pure expression of an Americanism that was also reflected in the conservatism of the post–civil rights era. After all, in his heart, he knew he was right.

Notes

Introduction: Why *Dirty Harry* Matters

Epigraphs: Capitol Building quote in Kotkin and Grabowicz, *California, Inc.*, 255; Eastwood quoted in *Conservative Digest*, June 1977, in Crawford, *Thunder on the Right*, 80–81.

1. Judith Crist, "Some Late Bloomers, and a Few Weeds," *New York*, January 10, 1972, 57.

2. Gary Arnold, "Dirty Harry," *Washington Post*, December 27, 1971, B10.

3. Crist, "Some Late Bloomers," 57.

4. Ryan and Kellner, *Camera Politica*, 9.

5. "AFI's 100 Years . . . 100 Heroes & Villains," http://www.afi.com/100years/handv.aspx (consulted December 12, 2012); "AFI's 100 Years . . . 100 Thrills," http://www.afi.com/100years/thrills.aspx (consulted December 12, 2012).

6. "AFI's 100 Years . . . 100 Movie Quotes," http://www.afi.com/100years/quotes.aspx (consulted December 12, 2012); P. Smith, *Clint Eastwood*, xi.

7. Legs McNeil, "Mr. Mayor: Go Ahead, Make Me Mayor, said Clint Eastwood. And They Did," *Spin*, June 1986, 57–63. Note also the citation of another famous Callahan line in the article title.

8. Quoted in Jeffrey Goldberg, "The Deadliest Gun in Town," *New York*, September 6, 1993, 34.

9. "*Dirty Harry* (1971) Smith & Wesson 29," http://www.nramuseum.com/the-museum/the-galleries/william-b-ruger-special-exhibits/hollywood-guns-6/dirty-harry-%281971%29-smith-wesson-29.aspx (consulted May 19, 2014); Sophie Borland, "Lightsabre Wins the Battle of Movie Weapons," *Daily Telegraph*, January 21, 2008, http://www.telegraph.co.uk/news/uknews/1576154/Light sabre-wins-the-battle-of-movie-weapons.html (consulted May 16, 2014).

10. Paul Smith (*Clint Eastwood*, 91–92) also notes that the law is an impediment to Callahan's actions, but he does not relate this to the wider point here.

11. Vaux, *Ethical Vision of Clint Eastwood*, 2.

12. Crawford, *Thunder on the Right*, 41; Elizabeth Kastor, "The Cautious Closet of the Gay Conservative: In the Life and Death of Terry Dolan, Mirror Images from the Age of AIDS," *Washington Post*, May 11, 1987, B1–B3.

13. Schickel, *Clint Eastwood*, 196; Siegel, *A Siegel Film*, 373.

14. Crawford, *Thunder on the Right*, 81.

15. Wirthlin quoted in Cowie, *Stayin' Alive*, 306.

16. Rubin, *Thrillers*, 137.

17. Ibid., 139.

18. Philips quoted in Crawford, *Thunder on the Right*, 166.

19. Sides, *Erotic City*, 8, 142, 166–68; Philip Hager, "Background for Films? Often It's San Francisco," *Los Angeles Times*, December 9, 1973, box 3, folder 36, Joseph L. Alioto Papers, San Francisco History Center, San Francisco Public Library [hereafter Alioto Papers]; Don Tayer of the San Francisco branch of the Screen Actors Guild suggests that the Film Production Office was less than proactive. Tayer to Thomas J. Mellon, April 15, 1970, ibid. For an example of boosterism for San Francisco's potential as a film location see Gerald Nachman, "Coast's Bay Area Is Lure for Filmmakers," *New York Times*, August 12, 1971, 28.

20. Schickel, *Clint Eastwood*, 262; "San Francisco Facilities to Be Used in Warner Bros. Photoplay 'Dirty Harry'—3/24/71," box 3, folder 36, Alioto Papers.

21. Baker, *Masculinity in Fiction and Film*, 88; Schickel, *Clint Eastwood*, 259; Siegel, *A Siegel Film*, 357, 358, 359, 373; Judy Fayard, "Who Can Stand 32,580 Seconds of Clint Eastwood?" *Life*, July 23, 1971, 48. Eastwood pointed out in a 2001 documentary that he had "always had an affinity for this particular area," as he was born in San Francisco and raised in the Bay Area. Dirty Harry: *The Original* (2001 documentary), in *Dirty Harry* Special Edition DVD. Josh Sides claims that Siegel deliberately chose San Francisco because he thought that the city's reputation would help to create "dramatic tension" in the film, although Siegel's comments in his autobiography suggest otherwise. Sides, *Erotic City*, 167.

22. McArthur, "Chinese Boxes and Russian Dolls," 33.

23. Baudrillard's original reads: "The American city seems to have stepped right out of the movies. To grasp its secret, you should not, then, begin with the city and move inwards to the screen; you should begin with the screen and move outwards to the city." Baudrillard, *America*, 56.

24. Crawford, *Thunder on the Right*, 81.

25. Nile Gardiner, "The Top Ten Conservative Movies of the Modern Era," *Daily Telegraph*, January 11, 2012, http://blogs.telegraph.co.uk/news/nilegardiner/100126732/the-top-10-conservative-movies-of-the-modern-era (consulted December 10, 2012). See also Tim Stanley, "Clint Eastwood Was Right: Hollywood Can Be Quietly, yet Profoundly, Conservative," *Daily Telegraph*,

September 1, 2012, http://blogs.telegraph.co.uk/news/timstanley/100178849/
clint-eastwood-was-right-hollywood-can-be-quietly-yet-profoundly-conser-
vative (consulted December 10, 2012); Richard Grenier, "The World's Favorite
Movie Star," *Commentary*, April 1, 1984, http://www.commentarymagazine.
com/article/the-worlds-favorite-movie-star (consulted April 24, 2010).

26. McGilligan, *Clint*, 213, 214 (quotation on 214).

27. Grenier, "The World's Favorite Movie Star."

28. Thomson, "Cop on a Hot *Tightrope*," 93.

29. Ibid.

30. The Letterman quotation may be viewed at http://www.youtube.com/wa
tch?v=59rQjGejFyA&NR=1&feature=fvwp (consulted April 24, 2010) or http://
www.youtube.com/watch?v=fjFPTXohUFo (consulted December 11, 2012).

31. Stuart Heritage, "And Breathe: Transcendental Meditation: Does It
Work?" *Guardian*, March 1, 2014, Weekend 33.

32. Eastwood quoted in Hentoff, "Flight of Fancy," 154.

33. McGilligan, "Clint Eastwood," 28.

34. Ryan and Kellner, *Camera Politica*, 13.

35. Toplin, *History by Hollywood*, vii.

36. S. F. Anderson, *Technologies of History*, 1, 4. See also J. Monaco, *How to
Read a Film*, 217–19.

37. Wang, "'A Struggle of Contending Stories,'" 92–115; Byers, "History Re-
Membered." Note also Connelly, "*Gallipoli* (1981)"; E. Smith, "History and the
Notion of Authenticity."

38. Quart and Auster, *American Film and Society*, 2.

39. Baudry cited in E. Smith, "History and the Notion of Authenticity," 482.

40. Stuart Hall, "Encoding/Decoding."

41. Hentoff, "Flight of Fancy," 157.

42. J. Monaco, *How to Read a Film*, 224, 229–30; S. F. Anderson, *Technologies
of History*, 102.

43. Stuart Hall, "Culture, the Media and the 'Ideological Effect.'"

Chapter 1. Before *Dirty Harry*: Making Clint Eastwood

Epigraph: McGilligan, "Clint Eastwood," 29, 33.

1. *Life*, July 23, 1971, front cover.

2. Judy Fayard, "Who Can Stand 32,580 Seconds of Clint Eastwood?" *Life*,
July 23, 1971, 46.

3. See http://www.the-numbers.com/people/CEAST.php (consulted June 7,
2010). Aside from the *Dirty Harry* sequels, it took until 1977 for the gross takings
of an Eastwood film to surpass *Dirty Harry*'s receipts.

4. McGilligan, *Clint*, 34, 40, 42–52, 59–60; Schickel, *Clint Eastwood*, 21, 68–69.

5. McGilligan, *Clint*, 112; Schickel, *Clint Eastwood*, 87–88, 102–3, 107, 108, 119, 125 (quotation).

6. McGilligan, *Clint*, 110.

7. Ibid., 126–29.

8. Quoted in Westbrook, "Thoroughly Modern Eastwood," 50.

9. McGilligan, *Clint*, 133.

10. Eastwood quoted in Schickel, *Clint Eastwood*, 137.

11. Leone quoted in ibid., 138.

12. P. Smith, *Clint Eastwood*, 9.

13. McGilligan, *Clint*, 144–45.

14. Ibid., 150, 157.

15. Unless otherwise noted, all quotations derive from the film under discussion.

16. McGilligan, *Clint*, 155, 156, 158; Schickel, *Clint Eastwood*, 175, 189.

17. Eliot, *American Rebel*, 95.

18. McGilligan, *Clint*, 162; Schickel, *Clint Eastwood*, 186.

19. McGhee, "John Wayne," 11; Wills, *John Wayne*, 22, 29. See also Grant, "John Ford and James Fenimore Cooper," 207; Sarris, foreword, xi; Levy, *John Wayne*, 48–49, 53; Wills, *John Wayne*, 302.

20. Sarris, foreword, ix.

21. Levy, *John Wayne*, 52.

22. Wills, *John Wayne*, 311.

23. McGhee, "John Wayne," 17.

24. Ibid., 10.

25. Levy, *John Wayne*, xvi, 238.

26. Wills, *John Wayne*, 284, 287 (quotation).

27. P. Smith, *Clint Eastwood*, 272n10, argues similarly; see Wills, *John Wayne*, 11–12, for national polls linking Eastwood's rising star to Wayne's setting sun.

28. Schickel, *Clint Eastwood*, 168; McGilligan, *Clint*, 155–56.

29. Their final collaboration was *Escape from Alcatraz* (Siegel, 1979).

30. Schickel, *Clint Eastwood*, 221. Schickel claims that Siegel would likely also have directed Eastwood in *Kelly's Heroes* (Hutton, 1970), had his schedule allowed. Ibid., 233.

31. Grant, *Invasion of the Body Snatchers*, 43–47.

32. Siegel, *A Siegel Film*, 158, 161, 165; *Riot in Cell Block 11* theater poster, http://www.impawards.com/1954/riot_in_cell_block_eleven_xlg.html (consulted September 3, 2012).

33. "National Film Registry," http://www.loc.gov/programs/national-film-preservation-board/film-registry/complete-national-film-registry-listing (consulted July 1, 2015).

34. Siegel, *A Siegel Film*, 178.

35. Grant, *Invasion of the Body Snatchers*, 14–20; Siegel, *A Siegel Film*, 185.

36. Westbrook, "Thoroughly Modern Eastwood," 42.

37. Fayard, "Who Can Stand 32,580 Seconds of Clint Eastwood?" 48. "Offed" is slang for "killed."

38. Ibid., 48.

39. Siegel, *A Siegel Film*, 300.

40. Rubin, *Thrillers*, 140.

41. Ibid., 141–42.

42. Richard Slotkin argues that the American (Western) hero triangulates between "bureaucratic order and savage license." Slotkin, *Gunfighter Nation*, 642.

43. Eastwood quoted in R. Thompson and Hunter, "Eastwood Direction," 49.

44. These were Siegel and Eastwood's slang terms to indicate who was the driving force behind particular inclusions: a "Clintus" was a shot or dialogue that Eastwood wanted in the movie; a "Siegelini" was Siegel's equivalent. Siegel, *A Siegel Film*, 326; Schickel, *Clint Eastwood*, 197.

45. Siegel quoted in Kapsis and Coblentz, Introduction, x.

46. Kapsis and Coblentz, Introduction, x.

47. Fayard, "Who Can Stand 32,580 Seconds of Clint Eastwood?" 48.

48. Siegel, *A Siegel Film*, 357. Dick Lochte, "Just One More Hangover," *Salon*, July 11, 1997, http://www.salon.com/1997/07/11/mitchum (consulted October 20, 2013), reports that Robert Mitchum also rejected the role. Apparently, advertisements announcing Sinatra's forthcoming role as "Dirty" Harry were prepared for the press. See, for example, "Sinatra as Dirty Harry," *Box Office*, November 9, 1970, http://web.archive.org/web/20111001082114/http://www.the-dirtiest.com/sinatra.htm (consulted October 1, 2013).

49. Hughes, *Aim for the Heart*, 49; Roberts and Olson, *John Wayne*, 586.

50. Wayne quoted in Roberts and Olson, *John Wayne*, 587.

51. Roberts and Olson, *John Wayne*, 587; see also Levy, *John Wayne*, 99.

52. Wills, *John Wayne*, 201, 204–7, 212–15, 216; Levy, *John Wayne*, 259, 281, 297, 302 (quotation).

53. Levy, *John Wayne*, 254; "Operation UPSHOT-KNOTHOLE," Defense Threat Reduction Agency fact sheet, May 2014, 1, available at http://www.dtra.mil/Portals/61/Documents/upshot-knothole---2014.pdf (consulted July 1, 2015); U.S. Department of Energy, "United States Nuclear Tests: July 1945 through September 1992," December 2000, 4, http://www.nv.doe.gov/library/publications/historical/DOENV_209_REV15.pdf (consulted May 22, 2014); Defense Nuclear Agency, "Operation Upshot-Knothole 1953," Technical Report, January 1982, 14, 216, http://www.dtra.mil/Portals/61/Documents/1953%20-%20DNA%206014F%20-%20Operation%20UPSHOT-KNOTHOLE%20-%20

Shot%20BADGER.pdf (consulted July 1, 2015); Carr, "Rationalizing the Cold War Home Front," 13–14; Duncan, *Miles from Nowhere*, 239; Roberts and Olson, *John Wayne*, 412.

54. Duncan, *Miles from Nowhere*, 241.

55. Carr, "Rationalizing the Cold War Home Front," 14; Chester Mc-Queary, "Meeting Dirty Harry in 1953," *Common Dreams*, May 26, 2003, http://web.archive.org/web/20130618094720/http://www.commondreams.org/views03/0526-05.htm (consulted July 1, 2015); Levy, *John Wayne*, 254; Roberts and Olson, *John Wayne*, 412.

56. McGilligan, *Clint*, 206, 207; Schickel, *Clint Eastwood*, 260, 266–67, 268, 271; Ken Plume, interview with John Milius, 2001, 8, http://uk.ign.com/articles/2003/05/07/an-interview-with-john-milius?page=8 (consulted October 21, 2013); Siegel, *A Siegel Film*, 361–67. Adding to the links between Wayne and Eastwood, Rita M. and Harry Julian Fink scripted a 1971 Wayne vehicle, *Big Jake* (Sherman, 1971), in which Wayne retools Ethan Edwards's "that'll be the day" line and illustrates the superiority of his killing and tracking instincts over the technologically superior Texas Rangers, much like Walt Coogan and later Harry Callahan. Wills, *John Wayne*, 289, 291.

Chapter 2. The Roots of *Dirty Harry*

Epigraph: Eastwood quoted in R. Thompson and Hunter, "Eastwood Direction," 43.

1. Richard Nixon, "Address to the Nation on the War in Vietnam," November 3, 1969, *The American Presidency Project*, http://www.presidency.ucsb.edu/ws/?pid=2303 (consulted July 11, 2014).

2. Reagan quoted in Jeffery Kahn, "Ronald Reagan Launched Political Career Using the Berkeley Campus as a Target," *UC Berkeley News*, June 8, 2004, http://www.berkeley.edu/news/media/releases/2004/06/08_reagan.shtml (consulted July 29, 2013).

3. Cook, "Ballistic Balletics," 132–33. "The Motion Picture Production Code of 1930 (Hays Code)," http://www.artsreformation.com/a001/hays-code.html (consulted August 8, 2012).

4. Cook, "Ballistic Balletics," 133–36, quotation on 136.

5. Harris, *Pictures at a Revolution*, 175, 263–65; P. Monaco, *The Sixties*, 57–59, 61.

6. Prince, "The Hemorrhaging of American Cinema," 132.

7. P. Monaco, *The Sixties*, 59; Harris, *Pictures at a Revolution*, 99. Unless otherwise noted, all quotations derive from the film under discussion.

8. Valenti quoted in Harris, *Pictures at a Revolution*, 184.

9. Prince, "The Hemorrhaging of American Cinema," 133.

10. Ibid., 134.

11. Crowther, "*Bonnie and Clyde* Arrives," 177.

12. Prince, "The Hemorrhaging of American Cinema," 135–38, 143, quotation on 139–40.

13. Cook, "Ballistic Balletics," 142–43.

14. Prince, Introduction, 15–17; Cook, "Ballistic Balletics," 145–47.

15. Peckinpah quoted in Weddle, "*If They Move*," 334. Incidentally, Peckinpah worked on numerous films that were directed by Don Siegel, which had a formative influence on his directorial career, including *Riot in Cell Block 11* and *Invasion of the Body Snatchers*. Prince, Introduction, 4–5.

16. As Peckinpah commented, "the Western is a universal frame within which it is possible to comment on today." See also comments by Phil Feldman (producer of *The Wild Bunch*) and William Holden (who starred in the film as Pike Bishop) at a press screening for the film in June 1969. "Press Violent about Film's Violence, Prod. Sam Peckinpah Following 'Bunch,'" *Variety* July 2, 1969, in Prince, *Sam Peckinpah's* The Wild Bunch, 210–11, quotation on 212.

17. Peckinpah quoted in Chong, "From 'Blood Auteurism' to the Violence of Pornography," 263.

18. K. Thompson and Bordwell, *Film History*, 233.

19. *Dirty Harry* theatrical trailer in *Dirty Harry* Special Edition DVD. Peter Biskind states that an unused tagline contained similar words: "Dirty Harry and the homicidal maniac. Harry's the one with the badge." Biskind, "Any Which Way He Can," 201.

20. Quart and Auster, *American Film and Society,* 25.

21. Spicer, *Film Noir*, 5–7, 11–13, 16–19; Quart and Auster, *American Film and Society,* 25.

22. Abbott, *The Street Was Mine*, 2; K. Thompson and Bordwell, *Film History*, 234.

23. Chandler quoted in Slotkin, *Gunfighter Nation*, 218; Spicer, *Film Noir*, 66–67.

24. Spicer, *Film Noir*, 60–61, 69–70.

25. FBI crime statistics indicate that the national crime rate (per 100,000 population) rose from 158.1 in 1961 to 363.5 in 1970. During this period, robbery increased threefold, aggravated assault and rape doubled, and murder increased by nearly 65 percent. U.S. Department of Justice, *Uniform Crime Reporting Statistics*, http://www.ucrdatatool.gov/Search/Crime/State/RunCrimeStatebyState. cfm (consulted July 11, 2014). Data were not available for the period before 1960.

26. L. C., "'Detective' as Cynical as Its Hero," *Washington Post*, June 27, 1968, 51; Vincent Canby, "'The Detective' Opens," *New York Times*, May 29, 1968, 20. See also Leitch, *Crime Films*, 231.

27. "Three with Frank Sinatra," *New York Times*, May 24, 2005, E3.

28. Romao, "Guns and Gas," 134, 137.

29. Isserman and Kazin, *America Divided*, 202, 208–9, 210.

30. Talbot, *Season of the Witch*, 97.

31. Evans, *The Education of Ronald Reagan*, 3–4, 167–68.

32. Ronald Reagan, "A Time for Choosing," speech, October 27, 1964, text at http://www.reaganfoundation.org/tgcdetail.aspx?p=TG0923RRS&h1=0&h2=0 &sw=&lm=reagan&args_a=cms&args_b=1&argsb=N&tx=1736 (consulted May 17, 2013). Note Schoenwald, *A Time for Choosing*, 195–96, for the genesis of The Speech.

33. Ronald Reagan, 1964 Republican campaign advertisement at Museum of the Moving Image, *The Living Room Candidate: Presidential Campaign Commercials, 1952–2012*, http://www.livingroomcandidate.org/commercials/1964 (consulted July 11, 2014).

34. Schoenwald, *A Time for Choosing*, 190.

35. Bell, *California Crucible*, 184.

36. Ibid., 190–91.

37. Ibid., 193, 235; *The Governor's Gallery*, http://governors.library.ca.gov/list. html (consulted November 1, 2012); California Taxpayers Association, *Cal-Tax News*, October 1963, quoted in Bell, *California Crucible*, 192.

38. Isserman and Kazin, *America Divided*, 224–25; Rarick, *California Rising*, 344; note also Russell Kirk, "New Direction in the U.S.: Right?" *New York Times Magazine*, August 7, 1966, 20, 23, 26, 28. The 1966 Reagan campaign essentially ignored California's African American community, since, as campaign manager William Roberts noted, "There were no votes there to speak of." William E. Roberts, "Professional Campaign Management and the Candidate, 1960–1966," oral history conducted in 1979 by Sarah Sharp, in *Issues and Innovations in the 1966 Republican Gubernatorial Campaign* (Regional Oral History Office, The Bancroft Library, University of California, Berkeley, 1980), 21.

39. Bell, *California Crucible*, 236 (Coate quotation), 239; Flamm, *Law and Order*, 70.

40. Schoenwald, *A Time for Choosing*, 141, 214; Kirk, "New Direction in the U.S."; Wills, *Reagan's America*, 291.

41. Putnam, "Governor Reagan," 26–29; Schrag, *California*, 98–99; Crawford, *Thunder on the Right*, 120–21.

42. Austin, *Up against the Wall*, xiii–xvi; Vincent, *Party Music*, 71. Reagan quoted in "Armed Negroes Protest Gun Bill: 30 Black Panthers Invade Sacramento Legislature," *New York Times*, May 3, 1967, 23.

43. Isserman and Kazin, *America Divided*, 174–76; Kahn, "Ronald Reagan Launched Political Career Using the Berkeley Campus as a Target"; DeGroot,

"Ronald Reagan and Student Unrest," 107; Ronald Reagan, "On Becoming Governor," oral history conducted in 1979 by Sarah Sharp, in *Governor Reagan and His Cabinet: An Introduction* (Regional Oral History Office, The Bancroft Library, University of California, Berkeley, 1986), 20–21; Fred Dutton, Reagan's attorney William Smith, and Reagan campaign manager Stuart K. Spencer agree. Frederick Dutton, *Democratic Campaigns and Controversies, 1954–1966,* oral history conducted by Amelia R. Fry, 1977–78 (Regional Oral History Office, The Bancroft Library, University of California, Berkeley, 1981), 167; William French Smith, *Evolution of the Kitchen Cabinet, 1965–1973,* oral history conducted in 1988 by Gabrielle Morris (Regional Oral History Office, The Bancroft Library, University of California, Berkeley, 1989), 7, 46; Spencer, "Developing a Campaign Management Organization," oral history conducted in 1979 by Gabrielle Morris, in *Issues and Innovations in the 1966 Republican Gubernatorial Campaign* (Regional Oral History Office, The Bancroft Library, University of California, Berkeley, 1980), 31.

44. DeGroot, "Ronald Reagan and Student Unrest," 109, 111, 112 (quotation).

45. Wallace Turner, "Gov. Reagan Proposes Cutback in U. of California Appropriation," *New York Times,* January 7, 1967, 14; Wallace Turner, "Kerr Says He Will Not Quit as U. of California Head," *New York Times,* January 8, 1967, 36; Gladwin Hill, "Reagan's Budget Rankles Regents," *New York Times,* January 10, 1967, 24; Rosenfeld, *Subversives,* 372.

46. Seymour Korman, "U. of California President Out," *Chicago Tribune,* January 21, 1976, 1, 2; "President Kerr of U. Cal. Fired," *Boston Globe,* January 21, 1967, 1, 5; Lawrence E. Davies, "Kerr Ousted as President by California U. Regents," *New York Times,* January 21, 1967, 1, 28; "Kerr Fired by Regents at Berkeley," *Washington Post,* January 21, 1967, A1, A4; Carolyn Anspacher, "Kerr Called Victim of Right and Left," *Boston Globe,* January 24, 1967, 1, 2; Sara Davidson, "The Politics of Kerr's Ouster," *Boston Globe,* January 27, 1967, 2; Rosenfeld, *Subversives,* 370–71, 376.

47. Reeves, "'Obey the Rules or Get Out,'" 277, 294, 297, 298; Rosenfeld, *Subversives,* 430. The *Berkeley Barb* thought that Reagan was merely demonstrating the protesting students' own gestures for the benefit of others present in the hall. G. K., "Regent Reagan Egged On," *Berkeley Barb,* January 24–30, 1969, 6.

48. The other elected officials were the incumbent liberal Bernice Hubbard May, who had been sponsored by the Berkeley Democratic Caucus, and two Republicans, Joseph Bort and John DeBonis. Bell, *California Crucible,* 230–31; "Berkeley City Council Race, April 4, 1967," http://www.ourcampaigns.com/RaceDetail.html?RaceID=546532 (consulted November 20, 2012); Rorabaugh, *Berkeley at War,* 110–12.

49. Pearlman, *The Sky's the Limit,* 494.

50. Lawrence E. Davies, "Shotguns and Tear Gas Disperse Rioters Near the

Berkeley Campus," *New York Times,* May 16, 1969, 1, 50; Steven V. Roberts, "The War between Reagan and Berkeley," *New York Times,* May 25, 1969, E13; Rarick, *California Rising,* 344; Pearlman, *The Sky's the Limit,* 495. The "noisy, dissident" jibe was first aired in the 1966 campaign and was clearly a favorite of Reagan's. Reeves, "'Obey the Rules or Get Out,'" 286.

51. Ronald Reagan speech announcing candidacy for governor of California, January 4, 1966, quoted in Rosenfeld, *Subversives,* 302.

52. Reagan quoted in DeGroot, *The Sixties Unplugged,* 376.

53. Reagan quoted in Rosenfeld, *Subversives,* 468.

54. Reagan quoted in ibid., 469.

55. Schrag, *California,* 97; Schoenwald, *A Time for Choosing,* 218; DeGroot, "Ronald Reagan and Student Unrest," 114 (quotation from *San Francisco Chronicle,* December 3, 1966), 122, 125, 128.

56. Reagan cited in DeGroot, "Ronald Reagan and Student Unrest," 115, 120–21; Rosenfeld, *Subversives,* 323–24.

57. *San Diego Union* November 27, 1967, quoted in DeGroot, "Ronald Reagan and Student Unrest," 120.

58. George Christopher, oral history conducted by Sarah Sharp and Miriam Stein, 1977, 1978, in *San Francisco Republicans* (Regional Oral History Office, The Bancroft Library, University of California, Berkeley, 1980), 42–43; Harry T. Everingham, "America Can Use the Good Common Sense of Ronald Reagan," flyer, 1966, at *The Sixties: Primary Documents and Personal Narratives, 1960–1974,* http://asp6new.alexanderstreet.com/sixt (consulted July 1, 2015); Dutton, *Democratic Campaigns and Controversies,* 146.

59. Reeves, "'Obey the Rules or Get Out,'" 278.

60. Ibid., 281.

61. Dochuk, *From Bible Belt to Sun Belt,* xii (quotation), xiii, 122. Evangelicals were similarly dismayed by campus unrest, including Bob Wells, who linked Vietnam War teach-ins with the "Spirit of Antichrist." Ibid., 298.

62. Flamm, *Law and Order,* 83–84; DeConde, *Gun Violence in America,* 178; Louis Dombrowski, "Urge 'Revolution' in Approach to Crime in US," *Chicago Tribune,* February 19, 1967, 28; Fred Graham, "Crime Panel Asks Sweeping Reform in 18-Month Study," *New York Times,* February 19, 1967, 1; Slotkin, *Gunfighter Nation,* 555.

63. *National Review,* June 18, 1968, quoted in Flamm, *Law and Order,* 152.

64. Isserman and Kazin, *America Divided,* 239–41; H. S. Thompson, "Chicago—Summer of '68," 113–18; Farber, *Chicago '68,* 167–68; T. H. Anderson, *The Movement and the Sixties,* 219; testimony of Abbie Hoffman, December 23 and 29, 1969, "The Chicago Seven Trial: Excerpts from the Trial Transcript," http://law2.

umkc.edu/faculty/projects/ftrials/Chicago7/Hoffman.html (consulted August 29, 2012).

65. Quoted in "Daley City under Siege," *Time*, August 30, 1968, 19.

66. Schoenwald, *A Time for Choosing*, 251; Flamm, *Law and Order*, 155, 157; Isserman and Kazin, *America Divided*, 241–42 (Daley quotation on 242).

67. Schoenwald, *A Time for Choosing*, 251.

68. Flamm, *Law and Order*, 2.

69. Isserman and Kazin, *America Divided*, 213–28, 244–48, 269–86; Kirk, "New Direction in the U.S.," 23.

70. This policy was suggested by Daniel Patrick Moynihan. Adam Clymer, "Former Senator Daniel Patrick Moynihan Dead at 76," *New York Times*, March 26, 2003, http://www.nytimes.com/2003/03/26/obituaries/26CND-MOYNIHAN.html (consulted July 6, 2010).

71. Furr to Ervin, June 18, 1968, quoted in Simon Hall, *American Patriotism, American Protest*, 3.

72. 1968 campaign ads "The First Civil Right," "Convention," "Failure," and "Crime" (quotation from "Failure") at Museum of the Moving Image, *Living*, http://www.livingroomcandidate.org/commercials/1968 (consulted August 29, 2012).

73. "Woman" script in McGinniss, *The Selling of the President*, 233–34. The ad may be viewed at http://www.youtube.com/watch?v=fahhDIm8Hys (consulted August 29, 2012). Its message is startlingly similar to remarks made by Barry Goldwater in the midst of his 1964 presidential campaign. Flamm, *Law and Order*, 36, 41–42.

74. "Excerpts from the Address by Nixon on Crime and Violence," *New York Times*, September 30, 1968, 41.

75. Isserman and Kazin, *America Divided*, 245, 278; D. T. Carter, *The Politics of Rage*, 367.

76. National Commission on the Causes and Prevention of Violence, *Violence in America*, quoted in Slotkin, *Gunfighter Nation*, 555.

77. DeGroot, *The Sixties Unplugged*, 382–83; Jim Klurfeld, "Laborers Smash Anti-War Rally," *Newsday*, May 9, 1970, 6; Homer Bigart, "War Foes Here Attacked by Construction Workers," *New York Times*, May 9, 1970, 1; Jim Herron Zamora, "Plaque Honors Slain Police Officer," *San Francisco Chronicle*, February 17, 2007, http://www.sfgate.com/crime/article/Plaque-honors-slain-police-officer-Eight-others-2617109.php (consulted August 29, 2012); Peter Jamison, "Time Bomb," *SF Weekly*, September 16, 2009, http://www.sfweekly.com/2009-09-16/news/time-bomb (consulted August 29, 2012); Robert D. McFadden, "More Body Parts Discovered in Debris of Blast on 11th Street," *New York Times*, March 16,

1970, 49; Mel Gussow, "The House on West 11th Street," *New York Times,* March 5, 2000, CY1; DeGroot, *The Sixties Unplugged,* 431–35.

78. Agnew quoted in Schoenwald, *A Time for Choosing,* 254.

79. John Milius audio commentary on *Magnum Force* Special Edition.

80. Martin Rubin highlights the contrast between the presentation of San Francisco in *Bullitt* and *Dirty Harry* but does not examine this in depth. Rubin, *Thrillers,* 140, 142. For the notion that popular films refract contemporary issues, see Spittles, *John Ford,* 9–11.

81. Hoberman, *The Dream Life,* 326. *Magnum Force* solidifies the vigilante link: Callahan's superior officer—a member of a vigilante "death squad" embedded in the police force—notes at one point that "[a] hundred years ago in this city people did the same thing. History justified the vigilantes."

82. Ethington, *The Public City,* 86–111 (quotation on 87).

83. Brown, "Violence," 393–94, 395–96 (quotation on 393); Gallagher, *John Ford,* 94, 144, 173–74, 179, 226, 336–37, 479–80. Callahan's vigilantism might usefully be contrasted with the indictment of such actions in the 1943 Western *The Ox-Bow Incident* (Wellman, 1943).

84. Peters, "The Beat Generation," 206–9; Matusow, *The Unraveling of America,* 275. Note also Gould, *Can't Buy Me Love,* 347, which argues that San Francisco became the counterculture's world capital on August 29, 1966, when the Beatles ended their final full concert at Candlestick Park.

85. Savio quoted in Matusow, *The Unraveling of America,* 317.

86. Sara Davidson, "San Francisco Becoming a Mecca for Non Student Sub-Culture," *Boston Globe,* February 5, 1967, 8–9. Note also Hunter S. Thompson, "The 'Hashbury' Is the Capital of the Hippies," *New York Times Magazine,* May 14, 1967, 29, 120–24.

87. Matusow, *The Unraveling of America,* 275 (first and third quotations); Rick Griffin, *Pow-Wow: A Gathering of the Tribes for a Human Be-In* poster c. 1966/1967 in Ward, *The 1960s,* 100 (second quotation).

88. Matusow, *The Unraveling of America,* 299–302; Talbot, *Season of the Witch,* 22–23.

89. H. S. Thompson, "The 'Hashbury' Is the Capital," 121; T. H. Anderson, *The Movement and the Sixties,* 175–76; Talbot, *Season of the Witch,* 44–45, 129–30, 159–60.

90. Quoted in Isserman and Kazin, *America Divided,* 210.

91. Cahill quoted in Talbot, *Season of the Witch,* 35.

92. Booth cited in Michael Sragow, "'Gimme Shelter': The True Story," *Salon,* August 10, 2000, http://www.salon.com/2000/08/10/gimme_shelter_2 (consulted July 11, 2014).

93. Stanley Goldstein, "Candidates for the National Film Registry: The Wild One and Gimme Shelter," November 10, 1998, *National Film Preservation Board,* https://web.archive.org/web/20130626214102/http://www.loc.gov/film/goldstein.html (consulted July 14, 2014).

94. Michael Sragow, "'Gimme Shelter': The True Story," *Salon,* August 10, 2000 at http://www.salon.com/2000/08/10/gimme_shelter_2 (consulted July 11, 2014); Goldstein, "Candidates for the National Film Registry; "The Rolling Stones Disaster at Altamont: Let It Bleed," *Rolling Stone,* January 21, 1970, 1–10, http://www.rollingstone.com/music/news/the rolling-stones-disaster-at-altamont-let-it-bleed-19700121 (consulted July 14, 2014); Booth, *True Adventures,* 354, 356, 358–59, 363–66. Two other audience members were killed while sitting at a nearby campsite when a car ran them over, and a fourth drowned in an irrigation canal near the track. Ibid., 9.

95. "The Rolling Stones Disaster at Altamont: Let It Bleed," *Rolling Stone,* January 21, 1970, 2, 3, http://www.rollingstone.com/music/news/the-rolling-stones-disaster-at-altamont-let-it-bleed-19700121 (consulted July 14, 2014).

96. Baker, *Masculinity in Fiction and Film,* 89; P. T. Miller, *The Postwar Struggle for Civil Rights,* 9, 62, 94; Sides, *Erotic City,* 84, 96, 100–102, 107–11, 131–37.

97. Bell, *California Crucible,* 197, 199 (quotation); Society for Individual Rights, "Statement of Policy," December 1964, in Ridinger, *Speaking for Our Lives,* 115–16. Note that the Bay Area housed nearly 250,000 African Americans by 1960. Bell, *California Crucible,* 212.

98. Bell, *California Crucible,* 221; Kevin Starr, "Art Agnos and the Paradoxes of Power," *San Francisco Magazine,* January/February 1988, 157; "John Shelley," *Biographical Dictionary of the United States Congress,* http://bioguide.congress.gov/scripts/biodisplay.pl?index=S000327 (consulted April 20, 2010). San Francisco largely falls within the boundaries of the Eighth Congressional District of California, which consistently returned Democratic representatives to Congress between 1952 and the making of *Dirty Harry.* It should be noted, however, that *Dirty Harry* emphasizes the political agency of the mayor, making him a pivotal character in the city, so the congressional returns should not be considered as important to the film's politics as the mayoral elections. Office of the Clerk of the U.S. House of Representatives, congressional election data, http://clerk.house.gov/member_info/electionInfo (consulted April 20, 2010).

99. Walker, "California Rages," 70.

100. Bell, *California Crucible,* 201–2.

101. Talbot, *Season of the Witch,* 150–51, 153–54, 163.

102. Irvin Molotsky, "Joseph Alioto, 81, Dies: Antitrust Lawyer Was San Francisco's Mayor in Boom Years," *New York Times,* January 30, 1998, http://www.nytimes.com/1998/01/30/us/joseph-alioto-81-dies-antitrust-lawyer-was-

san-francisco-s-mayor-in-boom-years.html?pagewanted=1 (consulted April 20, 2010). See also "Alioto's Odyssey," *Time,* November 13, 1972, http://www.time.com/time/magazine/article/0,9171,910444,00.html (consulted April 20, 2010).

103. C. Hartman, *The Transformation of San Francisco,* 16, 19, 26–27, 28; P. T. Miller, *The Postwar Struggle for Civil Rights,* 3, 113–16, 120–21, 123–24; Baker, *Masculinity in Fiction and Film,* 90; Sides, *Erotic City,* 4; Rosen, "Joseph L. Alioto's 1967 Mayoral Campaign"; Michael Harris, "Candidates Give Views on Taxes, Race, Transport," *San Francisco Chronicle,* October 20, 1967; Walker, "An Appetite for the City," 5–7, 11, 12. Note the CGI-enabled time-lapse shot of the construction of the Transamerica Pyramid used to signify the passage of time during the early 1970s in *Zodiac* (Fincher, 2007).

104. Mollenkopf, "Post-War Politics," 249 (first quotation), 256–57 (second quotation).

105. Frey and Speare, *Regional and Metropolitan Growth and Decline,* 261; Fossey, "School Desegregation Is Over," 20–21; Walker, "An Appetite for the City," 9–10, 11.

106. Graysmith, *Zodiac,* 179.

107. Ibid., 104, 105, 109, 111–12, 140, 148–49, 173, 184, 268, 287; David M. Halbfinger, "Lights, Bogeyman, Action," *New York Times,* February 18, 2007 (quotation), http://www.nytimes.com/2007/02/18/movies/18halb.html (consulted August 1, 2011). See also Taubin, "Interview: David Fincher," 27. Hoberman, *The Dream Life,* 328, suggests that Scorpio also referenced the kidnapping and live burial of Barbara Jane Mackle, and Charles Joseph Whitman's murder spree in Austin, Texas, on August 1, 1966, which resulted in Whitman's being dubbed the "Madman in the Tower." Incidentally, the actor who played Scorpio, Andy Robinson, later claimed that an early draft of the *Dirty Harry* script imagined Scorpio as "a balding guy in a t-shirt with a paunch," which brings to mind John Carroll Lynch's performance as Arthur Leigh Allen, the prime suspect in the Zodiac case, in Fincher's *Zodiac,* which was based on the real events. Robinson quoted in *Dirty Harry: The Original* (2001 documentary) in *Dirty Harry* Special Edition DVD.

108. "Zodiac" to *Vallejo Times-Herald,* July 31, 1969, http://www.zodiackiller.com/VTHCipher.html (consulted July 4, 2010). According to the film critic Roger Ebert, the similarities extend to Callahan himself, who was apparently based on the lead investigator of the Zodiac case, David Toschi. There is an almost complete lack of evidence for Ebert's claim. Roger Ebert, "Zodiac," August 23, 2007, http://www.rogerebert.com/reviews/zodiac-2007 (consulted July 1, 2015). Howard Hughes repeats this claim: Hughes, *Aim for the Heart,* 52. John Milius suggests otherwise: interview on *Dirty Harry* Special Edition.

It is possible that Ebert et al. mistook Callahan for Frank Bullitt, since Robert Graysmith notes that Steve McQueen met with Toschi and adopted Toschi's highly unusual method of holstering his gun as the eponymous lead in *Bullitt*. Graysmith, *Zodiac*, 96.

109. Graysmith, *Zodiac*, 180.

110. See letters from the Zodiac Killer to the *San Francisco Chronicle*, October 13, 1969, http://www.zodiackiller.com/StineLetter.html (consulted July 4, 2010), and June 26, 1970, http://www.zodiackiller.com/ZButtonLetter.html (consulted July 4, 2010).

111. Siegel, *A Siegel Film*, 373.

112. Siegel, 1974 comment quoted in P. Smith, *Clint Eastwood*, 96.

113. Siegel, *A Siegel Film*, 372–73.

114. Ibid., 366.

Chapter 3. *Dirty Harry*: San Francisco in the Nixon Era

Epigraphs: Eastwood quoted in McGilligan, "Clint Eastwood," 32; Siegel in Siegel, *A Siegel Film*, 373.

1. Philip Hager of the *Los Angeles Times* reported that Bill McCarthy of the SFPD would be present on film shoots during this period to supervise and offer technical assistance. Should a film not present the SFPD in an acceptable light, McCarthy was free to offer suggestions. The fact that no objections were leveled at *Dirty Harry*, coupled with the city's continued cooperation with the series, suggests that the film met with McCarthy's approval. Philip Hager, "Background for Films? Often It's San Francisco," *Los Angeles Times*, December 9, 1973, box 3, folder 36, Alioto Papers; "San Francisco Facilities to Be Used in Warner Bros. Photoplay 'Dirty Harry'—3/24/71," box 3, folder 36, Alioto Papers.

2. The Holiday Inn is now the Hilton–San Francisco hotel. Information from "555 California Street Facts and History," https://web.archive.org/web/20101007213202/http://555cal.com/about/facts-and-history (consulted July 6, 2010); "History of Hilton–San Francisco, California," http://www.sanfranciscohiltonhotel.com/history-of-hotel.aspx (consulted July 6, 2010). *Dirty Harry*'s implicit link between the skyscrapers and a world of danger and death is amplified in *The Towering Inferno* (Guillermin, 1974), which also used the Bank of America Center as a key location, albeit in a context where the skyscraper itself is a symbol of hubris rather than an enabling factor.

3. Scorpio returns this fearful compliment in advance of the final scene, uttering the word as he spots Callahan monitoring his stolen school bus from a nearby railroad bridge. Wanat, "Irony as Absolution," 89–91, hints at the film's equation of height with mastery. Please note that all unreferenced quotes are from the film itself.

4. "San Francisco City Facilities to Be Used in Warner Bros. Photoplay 'Dirty Harry.'"—3/24/71," Alioto papers, box 3 folder 37: Film-making, Committee on, 1971–74.

5. See, e.g., campaign ads "Moral Responsibility" and "Morality" at Museum of the Moving Image, *The Living Room Candidate: Presidential Campaign Commercials, 1952–2012*, http://www.livingroomcandidate.org/commercials/1964 (consulted May 20, 2013).

6. Eastwood quoted in *Dirty Harry: The Original* (2001 documentary) in *Dirty Harry* Special Edition DVD.

7. Slotkin, *Gunfighter Nation*, 498.

8. D. T. Carter, *The Politics of Rage*, 367.

9. Siegel, *A Siegel Film*, 369–70. Earlier comments, however, suggested that Siegel understood Callahan to be a racist. P. Smith, *Clint Eastwood*, 96, quoting Stuart Kaminsky's 1974 biography of Siegel.

10. Siegel, *A Siegel Film*, 370; "San Francisco: Potrero Hill," http://www.sfgate.com/neighborhoods/sf/potrerohill (consulted August 7, 2010).

11. There are subtle echoes here of Malcolm X's house Negro–field Negro analogy. Of course, *Dirty Harry*'s position was diametrically opposed to that of Malcolm X. See, e.g., Malcolm X, "I'm a Field Negro," in *By Any Means Necessary*, 183; Malcolm X, "Message to the Grass Roots," in *Malcolm X Speaks,* 10–12.

12. D. T. Carter, *The Politics of Rage*, 425; Isserman and Kazin, *America Divided*, 227; McGilligan, *Clint*, 213.

13. McGilligan, *Clint*, 207.

14. Self, *American Babylon*, 264 (Brown quotation); Rarick, *California Rising*, 362–63; Brilliant, *The Color of America Has Changed*, 191, 195–98, 220, 222, 228. The U.S. Supreme Court upheld the California Supreme Court's verdict in 1967, and the Fair Housing Act in 1968 further enshrined fair housing in American law.

15. P. T. Miller, *The Postwar Struggle for Civil Rights*, 91–97, 136; Talbot, *Season of the Witch*, 217. The situation in Oakland was roughly similar during the late 1960s. Rhomburg, *No There There*, 150. Police departments were exempted from Title VI of the 1964 Civil Rights Act, which proposed to withdraw federal funds from government agencies that were found to discriminate on the basis of race, color, or national origin. Flamm, *Law and Order*, 136.

16. P. T. Miller, *The Postwar Struggle for Civil Rights*, 91–97; Sol Stern, "The Call of the Black Panthers," *New York Times Magazine*, August 6, 1967, 62.

17. "1966 Hunters Point Uprising and Other Tales of 'San Francisco's Last Black Neighborhood,'" *San Francisco Bay View*, September 24, 2009, http://sfbayview.com/2009/1966-hunters-point-uprising-and-other-tales-of-san-francis

cos-last-black-neighborhood (consulted July 16, 2012); Rarick, *California Rising*, 358–59.

18. D. T. Carter, *George Wallace, Richard Nixon, and the Transformation of American Politics*, 15; Dionne, *Why Americans Hate Politics*, 39, 62, 179.

19. "San Francisco City Facilities to Be Used in Warner Bros. Photoplay 'Dirty Harry.'"—3/24/71," Alioto papers, box 3 folder 37: Film-making, Committee on, 1971–74.Locations are also identified at http://www.filminamerica.com/Movies/ DirtyHarry (consulted July 2, 2010).

20. Talbot, *Season of the Witch*, 234. In addition, more than one hundred men were sentenced to between fifteen years and life for "sodomy and oral copulation" in 1971 alone. Ibid.

21. Bolton, "Sacred or Profane?" 552 (quotation), 557.

22. Plaza cited in McGilligan, *Clint*, 206.

23. Thomson, "Cop on a Hot *Tightrope*," 87.

24. Matt Wanat argues that the camera is "indifferent" to Scorpio's pain, although if Siegel were truly indifferent, the torture scene would surely have either remained shot in close-up or the retreating camera would not have become covered by the fog. Wanat, "Irony as Absolution," 94.

25. C. Hartman, *The Transformation of San Francisco*, 51–80.

26. Mollenkopf, "Post-War Politics," 251.

27. AELE brochure (1976) quoted in Crawford, *Thunder on the Right*, 109.

28. Unnamed Chicago ACLU spokesman quoted in ibid.

29. *Escobedo v. Illinois*, 378 U.S. 478 (1964), http://caselaw.lp.findlaw.com/ scripts/getcase.pl?navby=CASE&court=US&vol=378&page=478; *Miranda v. Arizona*, 384 U.S. 436 (1966),http://caselaw.lp.findlaw.com/scripts/getcase. pl?court=US&vol=384&invol=436 (consulted April 20, 2010); Richard Nixon, "Toward Freedom from Fear," May 1968 position paper, cited in White, *Miranda's Waning Protections*, 57. According to Patrick McGilligan, Eastwood made donations to Nixon's 1968 campaign. McGilligan, *Clint*, 213.

30. Note, e.g., T. H. Anderson, *The Movement and the Sixties*, 89, 133.

31. Brilliant, *The Color of America Has Changed*, 220–22.

32. Flamm, *Law and Order*, 124.

33. In Wallace's rhetoric, "pointy-headed" was a term of abuse for overeducated intellectuals or bureaucrats who "couldn't park their bicycles straight." See, e.g., L. Carter, "George C. Wallace," 436; editorial, *Life*, May 26, 1972, 36; Chafe, *The Unfinished Journey*, 377.

34. McGilligan, *Clint*, 207.

35. Shadoian, *"Dirty Harry,"* 172.

36. For contemporary references to counterculture/New Left as nihilists, see Walter Trohan, "New Left," *Chicago Tribune*, July 9, 1967, H20–22, 25, 30, 33–35,

45, 47–49, 51; James Hitchcock, "Comes the Cultural Revolution," *New York Times,* July 27, 1969, SM4–5, 40, 50–51; and Staughton Lynd, "A Radical Speaks in Defense of SNCC," *New York Times Magazine,* September 10, 1967, 50, 148–53.

37. Callahan's apartment makes its first appearance in *Magnum Force* (Post, 1973).

38. Mask, "Movies and the Exploitation of Excess," 69.

39. Biskind, *Seeing Is Believing,* 47.

40. Judy Fayard, "Who Can Stand 32,580 Seconds of Clint Eastwood?" *Life,* July 23, 1971, 48.

41. Henry, "Interview with Clint Eastwood," 111–12.

42. Of course, the appearance of four sequels suggests that Callahan was able to overcome his animosity toward the police force and reclaim his badge.

43. Lalo Schifrin comments in *The Craft of Dirty Harry* (2008) documentary in *The Dead Pool* Special Edition DVD (Warner Bros. DVD, 2008).

44. Eastwood quoted in Dirty Harry: *The Original.*

45. Eastwood quoted in *Long Shadow of* Dirty Harry documentary in *Dirty Harry* Special Edition.

46. Eastwood quoted in Kapsis and Coblentz, Introduction, xi; Eastwood's "callous" comment is in McGilligan, "Clint Eastwood," 29, 33. In this sense, we might interpret Callahan as a founder member of the new populist right that emerged during this period in American history. Sandbrook, *Mad as Hell,* 58, 82, 117, 132–33, 186–87, 271, 286, 289–90, 330, 336–37.

47. Schickel, *Clint Eastwood,* 265, e.g.

48. Note that Antonio Gramsci and Stuart Hall suggest that "common sense" is itself a key battleground of ideas in the struggle for hegemony. While it is often presented as (or assumed to be) natural and fixed, it is actually highly contingent and related to hegemonic forces. Gramsci, *Selections from the Prison Notebooks,* 323, 324–26, 328, 419, 423; Stuart Hall, "Gramsci's Relevance," 431; Stuart Hall, "Culture, the Media and the 'Ideological Effect,'" 325.

49. Rubin, *Thrillers,* 142.

50. Wanat, "Irony as Absolution," 89–91.

51. Jim Harwood, "Frisco Cops Reflecting Screen Image, or Are Films Mirroring Real-Life Men in Blue?" *Variety,* January 10, 1974, box 3, folder 36, Alioto Papers.

52. That the first was a film star prone to conflating the movies with reality and the latter frequently emphasized his (nonexistent) cowboy credentials adds further layers to this suggestion. Jones and Wills, *The American West,* 87–88, 100–113.

Chapter 4. *Dirty Harry*'s Sequels and the Backlash

Epigraphs: McGilligan, "Clint Eastwood," 33; Hentoff, "Flight of Fancy," 154.

1. Berliner, "The Pleasures of Disappointment."

2. Jess-Cooke, *Film Sequels*, 9, 19 (quotation).

3. Jess-Cooke and Verevis, *Second Takes*, 5. See also Ryan and Kellner, *Camera Politica*, 76, 77. Ryan and Kellner refer here to genre films, but their comments are equally applicable to sequels.

4. Allison, "Courting the Critics/Assuring the Audiences," 18–28.

5. Jess-Cooke, *Film Sequels*, 6.

6. John Milius audio commentary on *Magnum Force* Special Edition DVD. James Franco agrees, stating that "these were not expensive movies." Franco audio commentary on *The Enforcer* Special Edition DVD (Warner Bros. DVD, 2008).

7. Kapsis and Coblentz, Introduction, xii.

8. Eliot, *American Rebel*, 172, 206; Schickel, *Clint Eastwood*, 340. Note Post's frustration at Eastwood's interference cited in ibid., 302–3; McGilligan, *Clint*, 234–35, 236.

9. Milius audio commentary, *Magnum Force*.

10. All unreferenced quotations derive from the particular film being discussed.

11. Ryan and Kellner, *Camera Politica*, 81; Corkin, *Starring New York*, 125–27.

12. Patterson, "Every Which Way But Lucid," 97; Biskind, "Any Which Way He Can," 201; P. Smith, *Clint Eastwood*, 101–7. The film's director, Ted Post, stated that Callahan was pitted on the side of democracy against fascism in a "provocative, intelligent, controversial picture," which somewhat overstates the film's importance. Post quoted in Kaminsky, *Clint Eastwood*, 131.

13. Schickel, *Clint Eastwood*, 299; John F. Milius profile at https://web.archive.org/web/20090105233628/http://www.nrawinningteam.com/milius.html (consulted August 28, 2012).

14. Milius commentary; Ross, *Hollywood Left and Right*, 374. Milius later directed films that further expounded on conservative themes. *Conan the Barbarian* (1982) presented a decidedly Nietzschean view of humanity and the role of the *Übermensch*, and *Red Dawn* (1984) remains one of the staunchest anticommunist films of the 1980s. Roger Ebert expressed concern about *Conan's* unsettling racial undertones. David Denby thought that Milius "worships force" but did not have the skills to be a "good fascist filmmaker" (suggesting that he was merely a bad fascist filmmaker). Michael Cimino, who rewrote the *Magnum Force* script, later directed *The Deer Hunter* (1978), a film with racist and Nietzschean undertones. Roger Ebert, "Conan the Barbarian," *Chicago Sun-Times*, January 1, 1982, http://www.rogerebert.com/reviews/conan-the-barbarian-1982 (consulted July 1, 2015); David Denby, "Sweat and Strain," *New York*, May 24,

1982, 70; Mark Kermode, "Oh Deer, Oh Deer, Oh Deer," https://web.archive.org/web/20120618014443/http://www.film4.com/features/article/oh-deer-oh-deer-oh-deer (consulted January 20, 2012).

15. Milius commentary; Schickel, *Clint Eastwood*, 299–300; P. Smith, *Clint Eastwood*, 106.

16. Judith Crist, "Pure Honey," *New York*, December 31, 1973, 76. All box-office figures from http://www.the-numbers.com/movies/series/DirtyHarry.php (consulted July 10, 2012).

17. Kael, *Reeling*, 252.

18. Talbot, *Season of the Witch*, 193–200; Franco commentary, *The Enforcer*. Presumably, the scriptwriters felt that the so-called Zebra killings in the city during 1973 and 1974 were somewhat reminiscent of Scorpio and consequently unworthy of Callahan's attention. Yet the fact that these murders had a distinct racial edge, since they were linked to a Nation of Islam mosque in the Fillmore, would have placed them firmly within Callahan's purview. The reappearance, however, of the Zodiac Killer in January 1974 added a further reminder of Callahan's most famous case. Somewhat ironically, three San Francisco women wrote to the head of the Motion Picture Association of America to suggest that violent movies set in their city—such as the two previous *Dirty Harry* movies—were responsible for turning it into a "crime mecca." Talbot, *Season of the Witch*, 204–23 (quotation on215).

19. Mennel, *Cities and Cinema*, 49.

20. Vincent Canby, review of *Sudden Impact*, *New York Times*, December 9, 1983, http://movies.nytimes.com/movie/review?res=9404EFD61F39F93AA35751C1A965948260 (consulted July 16, 2012).

21. Allison, "Courting the Critics/Assuring the Audiences," 25.

22. Eastwood quoted in Pavlović, "Clint Eastwood Interviewed by Milan Pavlović," 146.

23. Eastwood quoted in Verniere, "Clint Eastwood Stepping Out," 209.

24. Brilliant, *The Color of America Has Changed*, passim, esp. 6, highlights the diversity of the state's minority experiences.

25. Milius commentary.

26. P. Smith, *Clint Eastwood*, 125.

27. In 1980, California's Asian and Asian American population totaled 1.2 million, 5.3 percent of the state's total. Kotkin and Grabowicz, *California, Inc.*, 207.

28. Milius commentary.

29. Ibid.

30. D. T. Carter, *The Politics of Rage*, 367.

31. Westbrook, "Feminism and the Limits of Genre," 24–48.

32. Milius commentary.

33. Richard Schickel, audio commentary on *Sudden Impact* Special Edition DVD. No corroboration of this claim could be found in the major newspapers of the time.

34. Midge is a designer of bras, or "doohickey[s]," as Scottie calls them. "Revolutionary uplift," Midge tells him. "No shoulder straps, no back straps, but does everything a brassiere should do. It works on the principle of the cantilever bridge. . . . An aircraft engineer down the peninsula designed it. He worked it out in his spare time."

35. Jeffords, *Hard Bodies*, 10.

36. Kael, *Deeper into Movies*, 385–88.

37. McGilligan, *Clint*, 266–67 (quotation on 267); Kael quoted in Schickel, *Clint Eastwood*, 336.

38. Dochuk, *From Bible Belt to Sun Belt*, 379–80; Pauline Kael, review of *The Enforcer*, quoted in Allison, "Courting the Critics/Assuring the Audiences," 22.

39. David Talbot reports that undercover San Francisco police wielded .357 Magnums in the 1970s in homage to Callahan. Talbot, *Season of the Witch*, 219.

40. Tetzlaff, "'Too Much Red Meat!'" 273–78.

41. Abbott, *The Street Was Mine*, 2.

42. Haut, *Pulp Culture*, 73.

43. Abbott, *The Street Was Mine*, 89.

44. William F. Buckley, "Our Mission Statement," *National Review,* November 19, 1955, http://www.nationalreview.com/article/223549/our-mission-statement-william-f-buckley-jr (consulted July 1, 2015).

45. Wanat, "Irony as Absolution," 95.

46. Mickey Spillane, *One Lonely Night,* quoted in Haut, *Pulp Culture*, 96.

47. Patterson, "Every Which Way But Lucid," 103.

48. Eliot, *American Rebel*, 202.

49. Schaller, *Right Turn*, 50.

50. Troy, *Morning in America*, 100.

51. Ibid., 88.

52. Davis quoted in "Edward M. Davis, 89, Ex-Police Chief, Dies," *New York Times,* April 26, 2006, http://www.nytimes.com/2006/04/26/us/26davis.html?partner=rssnyt&emc=rss&pagewanted=print (consulted November 1, 2012).

53. Davis quoted in Crawford, *Thunder on the Right*, 104.

54. Philip Hager, "Background for Films? Often It's San Francisco," *Los Angeles Times*, December 9, 1973, box 3, folder 36, Alioto Papers; Milius commentary; Fargo commentary, *The Enforcer*; Schickel commentary, *Sudden Impact*; Jack Green and David Valdes audio commentary on *The Dead Pool* Special Edition DVD.

55. Kevin Starr, "Art Agnos and the Paradoxes of Power," *San Francisco Magazine,* January/February 1988, 157.

56. San Francisco placed ninth in a 2005 study of the most liberal cities in the United States conducted by the Bay Area Center for Voting Research, with Berkeley and Oakland placing third and fifth, respectively. Bay Area Center for Voting Research, "The Most Conservative and Liberal Cities in the United States," http://alt.coxnewsweb.com/statesman/metro/081205libs.pdf, 10 (consulted March 29, 2012). The city has not elected a Republican mayor since George Christopher in 1964, and the Eighth Congressional District, which includes all of the city except its southwest corner, has returned Democrats to the House with significant majorities since 1953. Curiously, it seems as though the city authorities had no problem with the series' presentation of local politics. The Alioto Papers contain no objections from he San Francisco Film Office to the movies' scripts, and James Franco commented that the city was extremely cooperative during the shoot of *The Enforcer.* Box 3, folders 36 and 37, Alioto Papers; Franco commentary.

57. Kotkin and Grabowicz, *California, Inc.,* 94–95.

58. Ibid.

59. Reagan quoted in Rarick, *California Rising,* 344.

60. Clint Eastwood, comments in *A Moral Right: The Politics of Dirty Harry* (2008) documentary on *Magnum Force* Special Edition DVD. According to David Valdes, the criticism of bureaucracy lies behind the support for the *Dirty Harry* films among American police officers: "They're so confined and constrained by our judicial system that Dirty Harry represents the maverick, the guy they would like to be but can't be because of the rules." Valdes commentary, *The Dead Pool.*

61. Eastwood quoted in Henry, "Interview with Clint Eastwood," 111.

62. Schrag, *California,* 101, 106, 107, 130; Sandbrook, *Mad as Hell,* 285, discusses the impact of Proposition 13 on public services in California.

63. Kotkin and Grabowicz, *California, Inc.,* 90, 256, 257; Putnam, "Governor Reagan," 31; Huey, *Negotiating Demands,* 89.

64. Knapp quoted in Kotkin and Grabowicz, *California, Inc.,* 47. Knapp, along with two other Wespercorp officers, was later charged with filing false financial reports that inflated the company's financial condition in 1983, a case that was settled in court without Knapp submitting a plea. "Wespercorp Is Charged," *New York Times,* May 19, 1987, http://www.nytimes.com/1987/05/19/business/wespercorp-is-charged.html (consulted July 19, 2012).

65. Andy Soltis, "Steve's Bam Slam," *New York Post,* October 22, 2011, http://www.nypost.com/p/news/national/steve_bam_slam_lAtEFW3iqsCQESMjs2N PfI (consulted July 23, 2012).

66. Quoted in Kotkin and Grabowicz, *California, Inc.,* 49.

67. Kotkin and Grabowicz, *California, Inc.*, 47.

68. Ibid., 90.

69. Eastwood quoted in Eliot, *American Rebel*, 89. That Malpaso was a skeleton operation echoed the observation of campaign manager William Roberts of Reagan's organization when they first met in 1965: "Reagan was literally a one-man band when we met him." William E. Roberts, "Professional Campaign Management and the Candidate, 1960–1966," oral history conducted in 1979 by Sarah Sharp, in *Issues and Innovations in the 1966 Republican Gubernatorial Campaign* (Regional Oral History Office, The Bancroft Library, University of California, Berkeley, 1980), 14.

70. Grant quoted in Dochuk, *From Bible Belt to Sun Belt*, 387.

71. Simon Hall, *American Patriotism, American Protest*, 96, 97–98, 107.

72. Jarvis quoted in Crawford, *Thunder on the Right*, 101.

73. Jarvis quoted in Sandbrook, *Mad as Hell*, 280; William French Smith, *Evolution of the Kitchen Cabinet, 1965–1973*, oral history conducted in 1988 by Gabrielle Morris (Regional Oral History Office, The Bancroft Library, University of California, Berkeley, 1989), 55–56.

74. Dochuk, *From Bible Belt to Sun Belt*, 377.

75. Simon Hall, *American Patriotism, American Protest*, 111–12.

76. Edsall and Edsall, *Chain Reaction*, 131.

77. Sandbrook, *Mad as Hell*, 283; Schulman, *The Seventies*, 212–14, 215.

78. Quoted in Sandbrook, *Mad as Hell*, 286.

79. Edsall and Edsall, *Chain Reaction*, 145, 152.

80. McBirnie quoted in Kotkin and Grabowicz, *California, Inc.*, 55.

81. Edsall and Edsall, *Chain Reaction*, 145.

82. Three in *Dirty Harry*, ten in *Magnum Force*, five in *The Enforcer*, twelve in *Sudden Impact*, and ten in *The Dead Pool*.

83. Talbot, *Season of the Witch*, 259–60.

84. Gramsci, *Selections from the Prison Notebooks*, 323, 324–26, 328, 419, 423.

85. Grindon, "Mocking Success," 122–23.

86. Varon, *Bringing the War Home*, 342n217.

87. Eastwood quoted in McGilligan, "Clint Eastwood," 32.

Chapter 5. Callahan's Legacy

Epigraph: "Clint Eastwood RNC Speech (COMPLETE): Actor Assails Obama through Empty Chair," https://www.youtube.com/watch?v=933hKyKNPFQ (consulted July 1, 2015).

1. Paul Miller, "Eastwood Says His Convention Appearance Was 'Mission Accomplished,'" *Carmel Pine Cone*, September 7, 2012, http://www.pineconearchive.com/120907-1.html; Lisa de Moraes, "Republicans win the Election among Last

Week's TV Viewers," *Washington Post*, September 5, 2012, http://www.wash ingtonpost.com/blogs/tv-column/post/what-was-the-second-most-watched-tv-program-last-week-clint-eastwood-and-the-chair-on-fox-news-chan nel/2012/09/05/f99addf6-f7a2-11e1-8398-0327ab83ab91_blog.html (consulted July 21, 2014), estimates that thirty million Americans watched the broadcast or news items that included coverage of the speech.

2. "Transcript: Clint Eastwood's Convention Remarks," August 30, 2012, *NPR*, http://www.npr.org/2012/08/30/160358091/transcript-clint-eastwoods-convention-remarks (consulted July 22, 2014).

3. Michael Barbaro and Michael D. Shear, "Before Eastwood's Talk with a Chair, Clearance from the Top," *New York Times*, August 31, 2012, http://www. nytimes.com/2012/09/01/us/politics/romney-aides-scratch-their-heads-over-eastwoods-speech.html?_r=0 (consulted March 20, 2014).

4. Ibid.

5. Quoted in Paul Miller, "Eastwood Says His Convention Appearance Was 'Mission Accomplished,'" *Carmel Pine Cone*, September 7, 2012, http://www.pine-conearchive.com/120907-1.html.

6. Michael Barbaro and Michael D. Shear, "Before Eastwood's Talk with a Chair, Clearance From the Top," *New York Times*, August 31, 2012, http://www. nytimes.com/2012/09/01/us/politics/romney-aides-scratch-their-heads-over-eastwoods-speech.html?_r=0 (consulted March 20, 2014).

7. "The Road to Jeb Bush," *The Daily Show*, August 31, 2012, http://thedaily show.cc.com/videos/yj67do/rnc-2012---the-road-to-jeb-bush-2016---a-fistful-of-awesome (consulted June 9, 2014); Aaron Couch, "Jon Stewart Gives Hilarious Take on Clint Eastwood's RNC Speech," *Hollywood Reporter*, September 2, 2012, http://www.hollywoodreporter.com/live-feed/jon-stewart-daily-show-clint-eastwood-speech-republican-367443 (consulted June 9, 2014).

8. Brent Lang, "Stephen Colbert Interviews Clint Eastwood's Chair," *The Wrap*, September 2, 2012, http://www.thewrap.com/tv/column-post/stephen-colbert-interviews-clint-eastwoods-chair-54436 (consulted June 9, 2014).

9. Barack Obama, "This Seat's Taken," August 30, 2012, http://twitter.com/ BarackObama/status/241392153148915712/photo/1 (consulted June 9, 2014).

10. Eastwood quoted in Paul Miller, "Eastwood Says His Convention Appear-ance Was 'Mission Accomplished,'" *Carmel Pine Cone*, September 7, 2012, http:// www.pineconearchive.com/120907-1.html.

11. "Clinton Delivers Impassioned Plea for Obama Second Term," *New York Times*, September 6, 2012, http://www.nytimes.com/2012/09/06/us/politics /clinton-delivers-stirring-plea-for-obama-second-term.html?_ r=1&pagewanted=all (consulted September 7, 2012).

12. Richard Harrington, "The Good, the Bad, and the Be-Bop: Director Clint

Eastwood, Bringing Charlie Parker to the Screen," *Washington Post,* October 17, 1988, B2; "Eastwood Takes Reins in Carmel," *Chicago Tribune,* April 16, 1986, 14.

13. "Eastwood Bows Out as Mayor," *Washington Post,* April 6, 1988, B4; "Eastwood Pays Price and Makes Carmel Sunny," *Chicago Tribune,* December 19, 1986, 4; "Eastwood Keeps a Promise," *New York Times,* October 12, 1986, A35; Mark A. Stein, "Ice Cream Is In Again under Eastwood Rule," *Los Angeles Times,* October 1, 1986, A3; Mark A. Stein, "Mayor Eastwood Solves Another Thorny Issue," *Los Angeles Times,* December 19, 1986, 26, 36 (quotation).

14. "Eastwood Bows Out as Mayor," B4.

15. William Rice, "In Like Clint," *Chicago Tribune,* March 18, 1987, A26.

16. Phyllis Meras, "Carmel Wrestles with an Image," *Chicago Tribune,* November 23, 1986, J5.

17. Robert Lindsey, "Eastwood Marks Landslide Victory," *New York Times,* April 10, 1986, A20.

18. Eastwood quoted in "Chatter," *People,* September 6, 1976, in McGilligan, *Clint,* 374.

19. Lloyd Grove, "Unmaking His Day," *Washington Post,* April 10, 1986, C9.

20. Mark A. Stein, "Eastwood Asks Carmel to Make His Day, Elect Him as Mayor," *Los Angeles Times,* January 312, 1986, 3.

21. John Hubner, "Hizzoner Dirty Harry? Election Victory Would Surely Make His Day," *Chicago Tribune,* April 1, 1986, D1.

22. Ruth Marcus, "For Eastwood, It's Ballots, Not Bullets," *Washington Post,* April 1, 1986, A3.

23. Hubner, "Hizzoner Dirty Harry?" D2.

24. *Doonesbury,* March 5, 1986, *GoComics,* http://www.gocomics.com/doonesbury/1986/03/05 (consulted July 24, 2013).

25. *Doonesbury,* March 8, 1986, *GoComics,* http://www.gocomics.com/doonesbury/1986/03/08 (consulted July 24, 2013). Eastwood concluded that the strips were "funny" and "cute." "Doonesbury Jibes at Him Are 'Cute' Says Eastwood," *Baltimore Sun,* March 6, 1986, 2B.

26. Quoted in Marcus, "For Eastwood, It's Ballots, Not Bullets," A3.

27. Ibid.; Eliot, *American Rebel,* 226.

28. Quoted in Mark Stein, "Campaigning with Clint," *Los Angeles Times,* March 30, 1986, U16.

29. "Eastwood Bows Out as Mayor," B4.

30. "Clint Eastwood Fires Away in His New Role," *Chicago Tribune,* June 5, 1986, 15. The *Washington Post* took a similarly jovial tone, noting that, in firing the planners, Eastwood put his "foes out of commission." The *New York Times,* by contrast, resisted any humor, reporting instead that Eastwood had merely "Oust[ed] 'Unfriendly' Planners." "New Mayor Eastwood Fires Away, Putting

Foes Out of Commission," *Washington Post,* June 5, 1986, A8; "Mayor Eastwood Ousts 'Unfriendly' Planners," *New York Times,* June 5, 1986, A16.

31. Grove, "Unmaking His Day," C9.

32. "Reagan Welcomes Eastwood to Ranks," *Chicago Tribune,* April 10, 1986, 16.

33. Ibid.

34. Eastwood quoted in Hubner, "Hizzoner Dirty Harry?" D2. See also Schickel, *Clint Eastwood,* 412–13.

35. Michael W. Miller, "Quiet Little Carmel Is Suddenly Having a Very Noisy Race," *Wall Street Journal,* March 19, 1986, 1.

36. Mark A. Stein, "Eastwood Wins Easy Victory in Carmel Vote," *Los Angeles Times,* April 9, 1986, 1.

37. Ibid., 21; Rice, "In Like Clint," A26; Hubner, "Hizzoner Dirty Harry?" D2. P. Smith, *Clint Eastwood,* 249, also notes the revenge motif.

38. Aljean Harmetz, "Clint Eastwood's Riff on Charlie 'Bird' Parker," *New York Times,* January 17, 1988, H24.

39. "Eastwood Bows Out as Mayor," B4. Richard Schickel argues that boredom at the mundanity of municipal politics was behind Eastwood's decision. Schickel, *Clint Eastwood,* 419.

40. Robert Lindsey, "Eastwood's Law and (Mostly) Order," *New York Times,* September 1, 1987, A10.

41. David Evans, "If Tower Tumbles, How about Trump or 'Dirty Harry'?" *Chicago Tribune,* February 17, 1989, 23.

42. Natalie Angier letter, *New York Times,* August 28, 1988, E22.

43. For Eastwood and aging, see Gates, "A Good Vintage or Damaged Goods?"; Metz, "The Old Man and the C"; Rinne, "The End of History and America First," 131 (quotation).

44. All unreferenced quotations are from the particular film under discussion.

45. Quoted in Grindon, "Mocking Success," 119.

46. The execrable *City Heat* (Benjamin, 1984) remains notable only for its promotional poster in which Eastwood, in homage to Callahan, wields a far larger pistol than his partner, Burt Reynolds.

47. Hughes, *Aim for the Heart,* 70.

48. Schickel, *Clint Eastwood,* 388–89. The original script was apparently inspired by a San Francisco–based serial rapist. Ibid., 390.

49. Thomson, "Cop on a Hot *Tightrope,*" 85–86; Henry, "Interview with Clint Eastwood," 109.

50. Cornell, *Clint Eastwood and Issues of American Masculinity,* 44.

51. McGilligan, *Clint,* 365–66.

52. Beard, "Lies of Our Fathers, 227–29; P. Smith, *Clint Eastwood,* 187.

53. Quotation is from *Sudden Impact* (Eastwood, 1983).

54. "Review: 'The Rookie,'" *Variety*, December 31, 1989, http://variety.com/1989/film/reviews/the-rookie-1200428184 (consulted May 16, 2014).

55. McGilligan, *Clint*, 460.

56. P. Smith, *Clint Eastwood*, 259.

57. Rinne, "The End of History and America First," 142.

58. Klypchak, "'All on Accounta Pullin' a Trigger,'" 160. Richard Hutson argues that even Eastwood's John Wilson in *White Hunter Black Heart* (Eastwood, 1990) shares major characteristics with Callahan (namely, an individual in perpetual combat with his superiors). Hutson, "'You Can't Hunt Alone,'" 125.

59. Rinne, "The End of History and America First," 139.

60. Note, e.g., Manohla Dargis, "Hope for a Racist, and Maybe a Country," *New York Times*, December 11, 2008, http://movies.nytimes.com/2008/12/12/movies/12tori.html?_r=0 (consulted July 26, 2013).

61. Gourlie and Engel, "*Gran Torino*," 269.

62. Vaux, *Ethical Vision of Clint Eastwood*, 33, 167.

63. Reagan quoted in Brandt, *Ronald Reagan and the House Democrats*, 141.

64. Ronald Reagan, "Looking Back, Looking Ahead," speech, February 3, 1994, in Reagan, *Greatest Speeches*, 284.

65. Eastwood quoted in Cahill, "Clint Eastwood," 127.

66. For Reagan as outsider note, e.g., Norman (Skip) Watts, oral history conducted in 1983 by Gabrielle Morris, in *Republican Campaigns and Party Issues, 1964–1976* (Regional Oral History Office, The Bancroft Library, University of California, Berkeley, 1986), 50–53.

67. Doherty, "Presidential Rhetoric," 420–21.

68. Druckman and Holmes, "Does Presidential Rhetoric Matter?" 755. See also Zarefsky, "Presidential Rhetoric and the Power of Definition," 611.

69. Schoenwald, *A Time for Choosing*, 219.

70. Stuart K. Spencer, "Developing a Campaign Management Organization," oral history conducted in 1979 by Gabrielle Morris, in *Issues and Innovations in the 1966 Republican Gubernatorial Campaign* (Regional Oral History Office, The Bancroft Library, University of California, Berkeley, 1980), 27.

71. Cowie, *Stayin' Alive*, 16.

72. Note, e.g., "One of my favorite quotations about age comes from Thomas Jefferson. He said that we should never judge a President by his age, only by his work. And ever since he told me that—[laughter]—I've stopped worrying. And just to show you how youthful I am, I intend to campaign in all 13 States." Ronald Reagan, "Remarks at a White House Briefing for the National Alliance of Senior Citizens," February 29, 1984, in *The Public Papers of President Ronald W.*

Reagan [hereafter *PPRR*], Ronald Reagan Presidential Library, http://www.rea gan.utexas.edu/archives/speeches/1984/22984b.htm (consulted July 22, 2013).

73. Fahrenkopf quoted in von Bothmer, *Framing the Sixties*, 31.

74. Kapsis and Coblentz, Introduction, xi.

75. Quoted in Levy, *John Wayne*, 281.

76. Ronald Reagan, "Inaugural Address as Governor," Sacramento, January 6, 1967, *PPRR*, http://www.reagan.utexas.edu/archives/speeches/govspeech /01051967a.htm (consulted July 10, 2013).

77. See *The Long Shadow of* Dirty Harry documentary in *Dirty Harry* Special Edition DVD.

78. Ronald Reagan, "Remarks at the Annual Meeting of the International Association of Chiefs of Police in New Orleans, Louisiana," September 28, 1981, *PPRR*, http://www.reagan.utexas.edu/archives/speeches/1981/92881a.htm (consulted on July 11 2013).

79. Ibid.

80. Ibid.

81. Ibid.

82. Ibid. This was a favorite anecdote of Reagan's and was repeated a number of times during his presidency. Reagan, "Remarks at a White House Briefing for the National Alliance of Senior Citizens," February 29, 1984, *PPRR*, http:// www.reagan.utexas.edu/archives/speeches/1984/22984b.htm (consulted July 12, 2013).

83. Reagan, "Remarks at the Annual Meeting of the International Association of Chiefs of Police in New Orleans, Louisiana," September 28, 1981, *PPRR*, http://www.reagan.utexas.edu/archives/speeches/1981/92881a.htm (consulted on July 11 2013).

84. Ibid. Emphasis added.

85. Ronald Reagan, "Radio Address to the Nation on Proposed Crime Legislation," February 18, 1984, *PPRR*, http://www.reagan.utexas.edu/archives/ speeches/1984/21884a.htm (consulted July 12, 2013). See also Ronald Reagan, "Remarks on Signing the Missing Children Act and the Victim and Witness Protection Act of 1982," October 12, 1982, *PPRR*, http://www.reagan.utexas.edu/ archives/speeches/1982/101282c.htm (consulted July 12, 2013).

86. Ronald Reagan, "Remarks at the Annual Conference of the National Sheriff's Association in Hartford, Connecticut," June 20, 1984, *PPRR*, http://www.rea gan.utexas.edu/archives/speeches/1984/62084c.htm (consulted July 12, 2013). See also Ronald Reagan, "Remarks on the Supreme Court Nomination of Robert H. Bork to Law Enforcement Officials in Los Angeles, California," August 28, 1987, *PPRR*, http://www.reagan.utexas.edu/archives/speeches/1987/082887a. htm (consulted July 12, 2013).

87. Ronald Reagan, "Radio Address to the Nation on Crime and Criminal Justice Reform," September 11, 1982, *PPRR*, http://www.reagan.utexas.edu/archives/speeches/1982/91182a.htm (consulted July 12, 2013). See also Ronald Reagan, "Remarks Announcing Federal Initiatives against Drug Trafficking and Organized Crime," October 14, 1982, *PPRR*, http://www.reagan.utexas.edu/archives/speeches/1982/101482c.htm (consulted July 12, 2013); Ronald Reagan, "Message to the Congress Transmitting Proposed Criminal Justice Reform Legislation," September 13, 1982, *PPRR*, http://www.reagan.utexas.edu/archives/speeches/1982/91382c.htm (consulted July 12, 2013); Ronald Reagan, "Remarks at a White House Briefing for the National Alliance of Senior Citizens," February 29, 1984, *PPRR*, at http://www.reagan.utexas.edu/archives/speeches/1984/22984b.htm (consulted July 12, 2013). In April 1982, Reagan proclaimed Crime Victims Week with a promise to establish a presidential task force empowered to recommend legislative and executive action to support victims and protect them from evildoers. Ronald Reagan, "Proclamation 4929—Crime Victims Week," April 14, 1982, *PPRR*, http://www.reagan.utexas.edu/archives/speeches/1982/41482e.htm (consulted July 12, 2013). See also Ronald Reagan, "Proclamation 5638—Victims of Crime Week, 1987," April 24, 1987, *PPRR*, http://www.reagan.utexas.edu/archives/speeches/1987/042487a.htm (consulted July 12, 2013); Ronald Reagan, "1988 Legislative and Administrative Message: A Union of Individuals," January 25, 1988, *PPRR*, http://www.reagan.utexas.edu/archives/speeches/1988/012588e.htm (consulted July 12, 2013).

88. Ronald Reagan, "Remarks on the Supreme Court Nomination of Robert H. Bork to Law Enforcement Officials in Los Angeles, California," August 28, 1987, *PPRR*, http://www.reagan.utexas.edu/archives/speeches/1987/082887a.htm (consulted July 12, 2013).

89. Reagan quoted in Bernard Weinraub, "Reagan, Lobbying for Bork, Calls Judge Tough on Crime," *New York Times*, August 29, 1987, 6.

90. Ronald Reagan, "Remarks at a White House Briefing on Proposed Criminal Justice Reform Legislation," October 16, 1987, *PPRR*, http://www.reagan.utexas.edu/archives/speeches/1987/101687f.htm (consulted July 12, 2013).

91. Kenneth B. Noble, "New Views Emerge of Bork's Role in Watergate," *New York Times*, July 26, 1987, 23. See especially comments from William L. Taylor.

92. Joseph Tybor, "In the Shadow of Bork, Kennedy Thrives Despite Sketchy Testimony," *Chicago Tribune*, December 20, 1987, C4.

93. Kennedy quoted in Lou Cannon and Edward Walsh, "Reagan Nominates Appeals Judge Bork to Supreme Court," *New York Times*, July 2, 1987, A17.

94. Quoted in "Kennedy Blasts Bork's Record on Liberal Issues," *Chicago Tribune*, September 12, 1987, 3. Reagan made more statements defending Bork's nomination than the total number of statements made by all his predecessors in

favor of their nominees. Stras and Scott, "Navigating the New Politics of Judicial Appointments," 1904.

95. Von Bothmer, *Framing the Sixties*, 40.

96. Ronald Reagan, "Remarks at the Annual Conference of the National Sheriff's Association in Hartford, Connecticut," June 20, 1984, *PPRR*, http://www.reagan.utexas.edu/archives/speeches/1984/62084c.htm (consulted July 12, 2013).

97. Ronald Reagan, "Remarks at the Annual Meeting of the International Association of Chiefs of Police in New Orleans, Louisiana," September 28, 1981, *PPRR*, http://www.reagan.utexas.edu/archives/speeches/1981/92881a.htm (consulted on July 11 2013).

98. Ibid. See also Ronald Reagan, "Remarks Announcing Federal Initiatives against Drug Trafficking and Organized Crime," October 14, 1982, *PPRR*, http://www.reagan.utexas.edu/archives/speeches/1982/101482c.htm (consulted July 12, 2013); Ronald Reagan, "Remarks at the Annual Conference of the National Sheriff's Association in Hartford, Connecticut," June 20, 1984, *PPRR*, http://www.reagan.utexas.edu/archives/speeches/1984/62084c.htm (consulted July 12, 2013); Ronald Reagan, "Remarks at a White House Ceremony Observing Crime Victims Week," April 18, 1983, *PPRR*, http://www.reagan.utexas.edu/archives/speeches/1983/41883d.htm (consulted July 12, 2013); Ronald Reagan, "Remarks at the Annual Convention of the American Legion in Salt Lake City, Utah," September 4, 1984, *PPRR*, http://www.reagan.utexas.edu/archives/speeches/1984/90484a.htm (consulted July 12, 2013); Ronald Reagan, "Remarks at a White House Briefing on Proposed Criminal Justice Reform Legislation, October 16, 1987, *PPRR*, http://www.reagan.utexas.edu/archives/speeches/1987/101687f.htm (consulted July 12, 2013).

99. Ronald Reagan, "Remarks on Signing the Victims of Crime Week Proclamation," April 19, 1985, *PPRR*, http://www.reagan.utexas.edu/archives/speeches/1985/41985c.htm (consulted July 12, 2013).

100. Ronald Reagan, "Remarks at the Annual Convention of the Lions Club International in Dallas, Texas," June 21, 1985, *PPRR*, http://www.reagan.utexas.edu/archives/speeches/1985/62185a.htm (consulted July 17, 2014).

101. Von Bothmer, *Framing the Sixties*, 58.

102. Ronald Reagan, "Radio Address to the Nation on Administration Policies," August 25, 1984, *PPRR*, http://www.reagan.utexas.edu/archives/speeches/1984/82584b.htm (consulted July 12, 2013). See also Ronald Reagan, "Remarks at the Annual Convention of the American Legion in Salt Lake City, Utah," September 4, 1984, *PPRR*, http://www.reagan.utexas.edu/archives/speeches/1984/90484a.htm (consulted July 12, 2013).

103. Ronald Reagan, "Remarks at the Annual Members Banquet of the

National Rifle Association in Phoenix, Arizona," May 6, 1983, *PPRR*, http://www.reagan.utexas.edu/archives/speeches/1983/50683c.htm (consulted July 12, 2013).

104. Ronald Reagan, "Proclamation 5845—National Neighborhood Crime Watch Day, 1988," August 9, 1988, *PPRR*, http://www.reagan.utexas.edu/archives/speeches/1988/080988e.htm (consulted July 12, 2013).

105. Ronald Reagan, "Remarks at the Annual Meeting of the International Association of Chiefs of Police in New Orleans, Louisiana," September 28, 1981, *PPRR*, http://www.reagan.utexas.edu/archives/speeches/1981/92881a.htm (consulted on July 11 2013). See also Ronald Reagan, "Remarks at the Annual Members Banquet of the National Rifle Association in Phoenix, Arizona," May 6, 1983, *PPRR*, http://www.reagan.utexas.edu/archives/speeches/1983/50683c.htm (consulted July 12, 2013).

106. Ronald Reagan, "Radio Address to the Nation on Crime and Criminal Justice Reform," September 11, 1982, *PPRR*, http://www.reagan.utexas.edu/archives/speeches/1982/91182a.htm (consulted July 12, 2013).

107. Ronald Reagan, "Radio Address to the Nation on Proposed Crime Legislation," February 18, 1984, *PPRR*, http://www.reagan.utexas.edu/archives/speeches/1984/21884a.htm (consulted July 12, 2013).

108. Ronald Reagan, "Remarks on Signing the Victims of Crime Week Proclamation," April 19, 1985, *PPRR*, http://www.reagan.utexas.edu/archives/speeches/1985/41985c.htm (consulted July 12, 2013).

109. Ronald Reagan, "Radio Address to the Nation on Law Enforcement and Crime," July 7, 1984, *PPRR*, http://www.reagan.utexas.edu/archives/speeches/1984/70784a.htm (consulted July 12, 2013). See also Ronald Reagan, "Remarks at the Annual Conference of the National Sheriff's Association in Hartford, Connecticut," June 20, 1984, *PPRR*, http://www.reagan.utexas.edu/archives/speeches/1984/62084c.htm (consulted July 12, 2013); Ronald Reagan, "Remarks at a White House Briefing for the National Alliance of Senior Citizens," February 29, 1984, *PPRR*, http://www.reagan.utexas.edu/archives/speeches/1984/22984b.htm (consulted July 12, 2013).

110. Ronald Reagan, "Remarks at the Annual Convention of the Texas State Bar Association in San Antonio," July 6, 1984 *PPRR*, http://www.reagan.utexas.edu/archives/speeches/1984/70684a.htm (consulted July 12, 2013).

111. Jerry Parr and Ronald Reagan, comments, "Remembering the Assassination Attempt on Ronald Reagan," *Larry King Live*, March 30, 2001, transcript at http://transcripts.cnn.com/TRANSCRIPTS/0103/30/lkl.00.html (consulted September 9, 2013); Reagan, *An American Life*, 260; Francis X. Clines, "Radio Buffs Tune in on Air Force One," *New York Times*, June 10, 1982, B16.

112. "Reagan Officials on the March 30, 1981 Assassination Attempt," *Miller*

Center, http://millercenter.org/oralhistory/news/reagan-assassination-attempt (consulted September 9, 2013); "Interview with Lyn Nofziger," *Miller Center*, at http://millercenter.org/president/reagan/oralhistory/lyn-nofziger (consulted September 9, 2013).

113. Reagan, *An American Life*, 260.

114. "Interview with Lyn Nofziger."

115. "Reagan Given Ovation on Returning to Offices," *New York Times*, April 25, 1981, 7; Max Friedersdorf comments at "Reagan Officials on the March 30, 1981 Assassination Attempt," *Miller Center*, http://millercenter.org/oralhistory/news/reagan-assassination-attempt (consulted September 9, 2013); "Interview with Caspar Weinberger," *Miller Center*, at http://millercenter.org/president/reagan/oralhistory/caspar-weinberger (consulted September 9, 2013).

116. Bates, *The Reagan Rhetoric*, 7.

117. Reagan quoted in ibid., 73.

118. "George Bush: Fighting the Wimp Factor," *Newsweek*, October 19, 1987, cover story.

119. George Bush, "Address Accepting the Presidential Nomination at the Republican National Convention in New Orleans," August 18, 1988, online by Peters and Woolley, *The American Presidency Project* [hereafter *APP*], http://www.presidency.ucsb.edu/ws/?pid=25955 (consulted May 6, 2014). The 2008 PBS documentary on Bush's presidency identified this as a line from an unnamed Clint Eastwood movie. *George H. W. Bush*, transcript at *American Experience*, http://www.pbs.org/wgbh/americanexperience/features/transcript/bush-transcript (consulted May 6, 2014).

120. George Bush, "Address Accepting the Presidential Nomination at the Republican National Convention in New Orleans," August 18, 1988," *APP*, http://www.presidency.ucsb.edu/ws/?pid=25955 (consulted May 6, 2014).

121. Bush campaign ads "The Risk" and "Revolving Door" and the National Security PAC ad "Willie Horton" are available at Museum of the Moving Image, *The Living Room Candidate: Presidential Campaign Commercials, 1952–2012*, http://www.livingroomcandidate.org/commercials/1988 (consulted May 14, 2014); Richard Cohen, "William Horton's Furlough," *Washington Post*, July 8, 1988, A23.

122. Ehrman, *The Eighties*, 165.

123. David Hoffman, "Bush Attacks Dukakis as a Tax-Raising Liberal," *Washington Post*, June 10, 1988, A1.

124. David Hoffman and Ann Devroy, "Bush: No Regrets on Campaign's Tone," *New York Times*, November 1, 1988, A1. A *New York Times*/CBS poll revealed that 27 percent of Americans considered Dukakis a liberal in May 1988, indicating both that the word had become an epithet and the public's indifference to the

accusation early in the campaign. Roger Stone, "Burying Bush Already? That's Silly," *New York Times,* May 26, 1988, A35.

125. Bush quoted in Troy, *Morning in America*, 305.

126. Tulis, "Revising the Rhetorical Presidency," 6.

127. George Bush, "Address Accepting the Presidential Nomination at the Republican National Convention in New Orleans," August 18, 1988, *APP,* http://www.presidency.ucsb.edu/ws/?pid=25955; George Bush, "Remarks at the Dedication Ceremony for the Police Memorial in Portland, Oregon," May 20, 1990, *APP,* http://www.presidency.ucsb.edu/wo/?pid=18502. For the *Waltons* quip see George Bush, "Remarks at the Annual Convention of the National Religious Broadcasters," January 27, 1992, *APP,* http://www.presidency.ucsb.edu/ws/?pid=20540 (consulted May 7, 2014).

128. George Bush, "Remarks at an Antidrug Rally in Santa Ana, California," March 2, 1990, *APP,* http://www.presidency.ucsb.edu/ws/?pid=18211 (consulted May 7, 2014).

129. George Bush, "Remarks at a Fundraising Breakfast for Gubernatorial Candidate Pete Wilson in Irvine, California," October 26, 1990, *APP,* http://www.presidency.ucsb.edu/ws/?pid=18963 (consulted May 7, 2014).

130. George Bush, "Remarks at an Antidrug Rally in Philadelphia, Pennsylvania," July 24, 1990, *APP,* http://www.presidency.ucsb.edu/ws/?pid=18704 (consulted May 7, 2014).

131. George Bush, "Remarks at an Antidrug Rally in Billings, Montana," July 20, 1990, *APP,* http://www.presidency.ucsb.edu/ws/?pid=18693 (consulted May 7, 2014).

132. George Bush, "Remarks at the Acres Homes War on Drugs Rally in Houston, Texas," December 7, 1989, *APP,* http://www.presidency.ucsb.edu/ws/?pid=17917 (consulted May 7, 2014).

133. George Bush, "Remarks to Law Enforcement Officers in Orange County, California," April 25, 1989, *APP,* http://www.presidency.ucsb.edu/ws/?pid=16965 (consulted May 6, 2014).

134. George Bush, "Proclamation 5953—Crime Victims Week, 1989," April 12, 1989, *APP,* http://www.presidency.ucsb.edu/ws/?pid=23516 (consulted May 6, 2014); Presidential Candidates Debates, "Presidential Debate at the University of California in Los Angeles," October 13, 1988, *APP,* http://www.presidency.ucsb.edu/ws/?pid=29412 (consulted May 6, 2014).

135. George Bush, "Remarks to the Law Enforcement Community in Wilmington, Delaware," March 22, 1989, *APP,* http://www.presidency.ucsb.edu/ws/?pid=16826 (consulted May 6, 2014).

136. George Bush, "Remarks at the Annual Republican Congressional

Fundraising Dinner," June 14, 1989, *APP*, http://www.presidency.ucsb.edu/ws/?pid=17152 (consulted May 7, 2014).

137. George Bush, "Remarks to the Law Enforcement Community in Kansas City, Missouri," January 23, 1990, *APP*, http://www.presidency.ucsb.edu/ws/?pid=18055 (consulted May 7, 2014).

138. George Bush, "The President's News Conference on the Persian Gulf Conflict," March 1, 1991, *APP*, http://www.presidency.ucsb.edu/ws/?pid=19352 (consulted May 7, 2014).

139. George Bush, "Remarks and a Question-and-Answer Session with Reporters in Kennebunkport, Maine, Following a Meeting with Prime Minister Brian Mulroney of Canada," August 27, 1990, *APP*, http://www.presidency.ucsb.edu/ws/?pid=18787 (consulted May 8, 2014).

140. George Bush, "Remarks and an Exchange with Reporters on the Iraqi Invasion of Kuwait," August 5, 1990, *APP*, http://www.presidency.ucsb.edu/ws/?pid=18741 (consulted May 8, 2014).

141. George Bush, "Remarks at a Republican Party Fundraising Luncheon in Denver, Colorado," September 18, 1990, *APP*, http://www.presidency.ucsb.edu/ws/?pid=18837 (consulted May 8, 2014). See also George Bush, "Remarks and a Question-and-Answer Session with Reporters in Aspen, Colorado, Following a Meeting with Prime Minister Margaret Thatcher of the United Kingdom," August 2, 1990, *APP*, http://www.presidency.ucsb.edu/ws/?pid=18727 (consulted May 8, 2014); George Bush, "The President's News Conference," August 8, 1990, *APP*, http://www.presidency.ucsb.edu/ws/?pid=18751 (consulted May 8, 2014); George Bush, "Remarks and a Question-and-Answer Session with Reporters in Kennebunkport, Maine, Following a Meeting with Prime Minister Brian Mulroney of Canada," August 27, 1990, *APP*, http://www.presidency.ucsb.edu/ws/?pid=18787 (consulted May 8, 2014); George Bush, "Remarks at a Fundraising Barbecue for Representative Bill Grant in Tallahassee, Florida," September 6, 1990, *APP*, http://www.presidency.ucsb.edu/ws/?pid=18800 (consulted May 8, 2014); George Bush, "Remarks to Participants in the International Appellate Judges Conference," September 14, 1990, *APP*, http://www.presidency.ucsb.edu/ws/?pid=18828 (consulted May 8, 2014).

142. George Bush, "Remarks to Officers and Troops at Hickam Air Force Base in Pearl Harbor, Hawaii," October 28, 1990, *APP*, http://www.presidency.ucsb.edu/ws/?pid=18972 (consulted May 8, 2014).

143. Renshon, "Presidential Address," 588.

144. Lemann quoted in von Bothmer, *Framing the Sixties*, 196.

145. George W. Bush, "Address Accepting the Presidential Nomination at the Republican National Convention in Philadelphia," August 3, 2000, *APP*, http://www.presidency.ucsb.edu/ws/?pid=25954 (consulted May 15, 2014).

146. George W. Bush, "Remarks to Employees in the Pentagon and an Ex-change with Reporters in Arlington, Virginia," September 17, 2001, *APP*, http://www.presidency.ucsb.edu/ws/?pid=65079 (consulted May 8, 2014).

147. Prasad et al., "The Undeserving Rich," 237–38, 243–46.

148. Johnson, "Defending Ways of Life," 225.

149. Quoted in Woodward, *Bush at War*, 15. An indication of Bush's instinctive response in positions of stress occurred during a December 1999 Republican debate. When asked which political philosopher or thinker he most identified with, Bush answered, "Christ." According to his memoirs, "The words tumbled out of my mouth . . . I had just blurted out what was in my heart." Bush, *Decision Points*, 71.

150. Quoted in Renshon, "Presidential Address," 591. See also Bush, *Decision Points*, 127, 128. Woodward reports Bush stating that he knew prior to September 2001 that Osama bin Laden and al-Qaeda were major threats to the United States, "but I didn't feel that sense of urgency [to pursue them] and my blood was not nearly as boiling." Afterward, he was prepared to pay "whatever it takes" to eliminate them. Quoted in Woodward, *Bush at War*, 39, 41.

151. Quoted in Woodward, *Bush at War*, 16.

152. Bush, *Decision Points*, 140. When asked by Dick Cheney to authorize the shooting down of any commercial aircraft that had been hijacked, his answer was instant: "You bet." Quoted in Woodward, *Bush at War*, 18. In his first National Security Council briefing after the event, Bush "impulsively" and without appreciating the security issue insisted that all commercial flights would be restored within one day. Ibid., 27.

153. Quoted in Woodward, *Bush at War*, 41.

154. Quoted in ibid., 45. "Our responsibility to history is already clear," Bush argued the following day: to "rid the world of evil." Ibid., 67.

155. George W. Bush, "Address to a Joint Session of Congress and the American People," September 20, 2011, http://georgewbush-whitehouse.archives.gov/news/releases/2001/09/20010920-8.html (consulted August 7, 2013).

156. Quoted in Woodward, *Bush at War*, 17, 18.

157. George W. Bush, "Remarks to Police Department Command and Control Center Personnel in New York City," February 6, 2002, *APP*, http://www.presidency.ucsb.edu/ws/?pid=63023 (consulted May 8, 2014).

158. George W. Bush, "Address to a Joint Session of Congress and the American People," September 20, 2011, http://georgewbush-whitehouse.archives.gov/news/releases/2001/09/20010920-8.html (consulted August 7, 2013). Woodward suggests that Bush first articulated this sentiment on September 11. Woodward, *Bush at War*, 33.

159. George W. Bush, "9/11 Address to the Nation," September 11, 2001,

http://www.americanrhetoric.com/speeches/gwbush911addresstothenation.htm (consulted August 7, 2013).

160. George W. Bush, "Remarks at a Republican Party of Florida Reception in St. Petersburg," March 8, 2002, *APP*, http://www.presidency.ucsb.edu/ws/?pid=64044 (consulted May 8, 2014).

161. Renshon, "Presidential Address," 588.

162. Quoted in Woodward, *Bush at War*, 281.

163. George W. Bush, "Remarks in a Meeting with the National Security Team and an Exchange with Reporters at Camp David, Maryland," September 15, 2001, *APP*, http://www.presidency.ucsb.edu/ws/?pid=63199 (consulted May 8, 2014).

164. George W. Bush, "Remarks on Signing the Department of Defense and Emergency Supplemental Appropriations for Recovery from and Response to Terrorist Attacks on the United States Act, 2002, in Arlington, Virginia," January 10, 2002, *APP*, http://www.presidency.ucsb.edu/ws/?pid=73223 (consulted May 8, 2014).

165. George W. Bush, "Remarks to the Community in Atlanta, Georgia," January 31, 2002, *APP*, http://www.presidency.ucsb.edu/ws/?pid=63663 (consulted May 8, 2014).

166. George W. Bush, "The President's News Conference," July 8, 2002, *APP*, http://www.presidency.ucsb.edu/ws/?pid=64951 (consulted May 8, 2014).

167. Quoted in Woodward, *Bush at War*, 145. Bush repeated this in September 2011. Ibid., 168.

168. Ibid., 256.

169. Ibid., 26. Emphasis added. Bush suggests that he felt much the same way about his advisers: they were there to think for him. Ibid., 74.

170. Ibid., 342.

171. Quoted in ibid., 256.

172. Quoted in ibid., 259.

173. Quoted in Renshon, "Presidential Address," 608.

174. Rhodes, "The Good, the Bad, and the Righteous," 124–28; Kellner, "9/11, Spectacles of Terror, and Media Manipulation," 45; Woodward, *Bush at War*, 133.

175. George W. Bush, "9/11 Address to the Nation," September 11, 2001, http://www.americanrhetoric.com/speeches/gwbush911addresstothenation.htm (consulted August 7, 2013).

176. Bush cited in Renshon, "Presidential Address," 605. See also George W. Bush, Inaugural Address, January 20, 2005: "We are led, by events and common sense, to one conclusion: The survival of liberty in our land increasingly depends on the success of liberty in other lands" (http://www.gpo.gov/fdsys/pkg/PPP-2005-book1/html/PPP-2005-book1-doc-pg66.htm; consulted April 29, 2014).

177. Quoted in Woodward, *Bush at War*, 146.

178. Quoted in ibid., 342.

179. Quoted in Renshon, "Presidential Address," 605; emphasis is Renshon's.

180. Kellner, "9/11, Spectacles of Terror, and Media Manipulation," 54.

181. Kellner, "Bushspeak and the Politics of Lying," 640.

182. John M. Broder, "Delay Could Allow Recall Fever Time to Cool," *New York Times*, September 16, 2003, A21.

183. Jennifer Nelson, "Why Davis Is Being Recalled," *San Francisco Chronicle*, August 11, 2003, http://www.sfgate.com/default/article/Why-Davis-is-being-recalled-2596958.php (consulted August 5, 2013); Stone and Datta, "Rationalizing the California Recall," 19–21; Bowler and Cain, "Introduction—Recalling the Recall," 7.

184. Maureen Dowd, "Brawny or Scrawny?" *New York Times*, August 10, 2003, WK11.

185. Quoted in John M. Broder, "Schwarzenegger Calls Budget Opponents 'Girlie Men,'" *New York Times*, July 19, 2004, A11.

186. John M. Broder, "After a Hard Month, a Budget Agreement in California," *New York Times*, July 28, 2004, A10; Messner, "The Masculinity of the Governator," 469.

187. John Tierney and Sheryl Gay Stolberg, "Political Points: Terminator Talks Tough," *New York Times*, September 1, 2004, P4.

188. Mark Leibovich, "Who Can Possibly Govern California?" *New York Times*, July 5, 2009, SM33.

189. Michael Lewis, "California and Bust," *Vanity Fair*, November 2011, http://www.vanityfair.com/business/features/2011/11/michael-lewis-201111#gotopage1 (consulted August 5, 2013).

190. "National Briefing: West," *New York Times*, September 30, 2005, A18; Jennifer Steinhauer, "For Governors in G.O.P. Slots, a Liberal Turn," *New York Times*, September 20, 2006, A1, A23; Jesse McKinley, "California Court Upholds State's Ban on Same-Sex Marriage," *New York Times*, October 6, 2006, A16; David M. Herszenhorn, "A Republican Supporter," *New York Times*, October 7, 2009, A16; Erik Eckholm, "Sharp Reversal for California Over Welfare," *New York Times*, October 7, 2009, A1; Jennifer Steinhauer, "California's Fiscal Health Continues to Deteriorate, Despite Many Deep Cuts," *New York Times*, November 1, 2009, 30.

191. Wayne LaPierre statement at NRA Press Conference, December 21, 2012, transcript, 5, at http://www.nytimes.com/interactive/2012/12/21/us/nra-news-conference-transcript.html (consulted August 7, 2013).

Chapter 6. "Dirty" Harry Callahan in American Popular Culture

Epigraph: Miller quoted in Daniel Robert Epstein, "Frank Miller, Creator of Sin City," *Suicide Girls*, August 3, 2005, https://web.archive.org/web/2013062

0015201/http://suicidegirls.com/interviews/Frank+Miller+Creator+of+Sin+City (consulted October 31, 2011).

1. Images of Hollywood Boulevard at http://www.shutterstock.com/pic-107604095/stock-photo-los-angeles-june-handprint-of-clint-eastwood-in-hollywood-boulevard-on-june-in-los.html (consulted July 21, 2014); http://www.srcalifornia.com/triennial/sights2.htm (consulted July 21, 2014).

2. Vincent Canby, "Will Duke Wayne Survive 'McQ'?" *New York Times*, March 10, 1974, section 2, 5.

3. Gene Siskel, "'McQ': Citified Duke," *Chicago Tribune*, February 13, 1974, B5.

4. Wills, *John Wayne*, 284.

5. P. Smith, *Clint Eastwood*, 185.

6. Cohen, "Cowboys Die Hard," 73.

7. David Denby, review of *Black Rain*, New York, October 2, 1989, 66; David Denby, review of *Cobra*, New York, June 9, 1986, 130.

8. All unreferenced quotations are from the particular production under discussion.

9. Jeffords, *Hard Bodies*, 25.

10. Nash quoted in McCracken, *Pulp*, 10.

11. "An Interview with Ric Meyers," November 2001, *the-dirtiest.com,* http://web.archive.org/web/20120824013444/http://www.the-dirtiest.com/ric.htm (consulted October 1, 2013).

12. Bloom, *Cult Fiction*, 152.

13. Ibid., 16. See also 153.

14. "An Interview with Ric Meyers," November 2001, *the-dirtiest.com,* http://web.archive.org/web/20120824013444/http://www.the-dirtiest.com/ric.htm (consulted October 1, 2013).

15. Note, e.g., that Frank DiGeorgio reappears despite having been killed in *The Enforcer*. D. Hartman, *Duel for Cannons*, 33; D. Hartman, *Death on the Docks*; D. Hartman, *Hatchet Men*, 87; D. Hartman, *Death in the Air*, 151.

16. D. Hartman, *Death on the Docks*; D. Hartman, *The Mexico Kill*.

17. D. Hartman, *Family Skeletons*.

18. D. Hartman, *City of Blood*; D. Hartman, *Hatchet Men*; D. Hartman, *Massacre at Russian River*; D. Hartman, *The Blood of Strangers*.

19. D. Hartman, *Duel for Cannons*, 62, 167–73.

20. See http://thealamo.org (consulted October 7, 2013).

21. D. Hartman, *Duel for Cannons*, 72–73, 160.

22. Ibid., 58.

23. D. Hartman, *Family Skeletons*, 19, 75, 96, 126.

24. Ibid., 155.

25. D. Hartman, *Hatchet Men*; D. Hartman, *City of Blood*; D. Hartman, *The Blood of Strangers*; D. Hartman, *Death in the Air*; D. Hartman, *Dealer of Death*.

26. D. Hartman, *Death on the Docks*; D. Hartman, *Massacre at Russian River*; D. Hartman, *Mexico Kill*, 12, 31–32; see also D. Hartman, *Family Skeletons*, 39.

27. D. Hartman, *Death in the Air*; "An Interview with Ric Meyers," November 2001, *the-dirtiest.com*, http://web.archive.org/web/20120824013444/http://www.the-dirtiest.com/ric.htm (consulted October 1, 2013).

28. For example, D. Hartman, *Family Skeletons*, 155; D. Hartman, *Death in the Air*, 23; D. Hartman, *Dealer of Death*, 119.

29. D. Hartman, *The Blood of Strangers*.

30. Ric Meyers states that the books were published simply to generate profits. "An Interview with Ric Meyers," November 2001, *the-dirtiest.com*, http://web.archive.org/web/20120824013444/http://www.the-dirtiest.com/ric.htm (consulted October 1, 2013).

31. All quotes are from *The Simpsons*, episode 88 (Anderson, 1993), "Bart's Inner Child."

32. *The Simpsons*, episode 101 (Lynch, 1994), "The Boy Who Knew Too Much."

33. *Sledge Hammer*, "The Spa Who Loved Me." This was the concluding episode to the first season, written when the show's creator thought that there was no chance that the show would be recommissioned. The second season was hastily written as an "Early Years" prequel that supposedly took place five years prior to the city's destruction. *Sledge Hammer! Go Ahead, Make Me Laugh* (2004) documentary on *Sledge Hammer! Season One* DVD (Anchor Bay DVD, 2004). The documentary's subtitle is a knowing nod to Callahan.

34. Dusty Saunders, "Cosby Show to Face Real 'Sledge Hammer!'" *Chicago Tribune*, July 16, 1987, D5; Spencer quoted in *Go Ahead, Make Me Laugh* documentary.

35. Spencer quoted in Saunders, "Cosby Show to Face Real 'Sledge Hammer!'"

36. Spencer comments in *Go Ahead, Make Me Laugh* documentary.

37. Ibid.

38. Saunders, "Cosby Show to Face Real 'Sledge Hammer!'" Saunders was presumably fed this line, which featured in the *Sledge Hammer* pilot episode, "Under the Gun." Terry Clifford also noted the links between Hammer and Callahan. Terry Clifford, "Satire with the Subtlety of a Sledgehammer," *Chicago Tribune*, January 18, 1987, I3.

39. John J. O'Connor, "2 New Series, 'Matlock' and 'Sledge Hammer!'" *New York Times*, September 23, 1986, C18.

40. Bradford Evans, "Talking with Alan Spencer about 'Bullet in the Face,' Andy Kaufman, 'Sledge Hammer,' and Life as a Hollywood Script Doctor," *Split*

Sider, August 15, 2012, http://splitsider.com/2012/08/talking-with-alan-spen cer-about-bullet-in-the-face-andy-kaufman-sledge-hammer-and-life-as-a-holly wood-script-doctor (consulted May 24, 2013).

41. *Sledge Hammer,* "Under the Gun" (Coolidge, 1986).

42. *Sledge Hammer,* "They Shoot Hammers Don't They?" (Wechter, 1986).

43. *Sledge Hammer,* "Brother Can You Spare a Crime?" (Braverman, 1987).

44. *Sledge Hammer,* "Wild About Hammer" (Walcow, 1987).

45. *Sledge Hammer,* "Dori Day Afternoon" (Sheldon, 1986).

46. *Sledge Hammer,* "To Live and Die on TV" (Attias, 1986); *Sledge Hammer,* "State of Sledge" (Attias, 1987); *Sledge Hammer,* "Witless" (Cooper, 1986); *Sledge Hammer,* "They Shoot Hammers Don't They?"

47. *Sledge Hammer,* "Sledgepoo" (Schlamme, 1987); *Sledge Hammer,* "Magnum Farce" (Braverman, 1986).

48. *Sledge Hammer,* "They Call Me Mister Trunk" (Robbie, 1987).

49. *Sledge Hammer,* "Haven't Gun Will Travel" (Wechter, 1987).

50. Ibid.

51. *Sledge Hammer,* "The Color of Hammer" (Bilson, 1987).

52. *Sledge Hammer,* "Brother Can You Spare a Crime?"

53. *Sledge Hammer,* "Under the Gun"; *Sledge Hammer,* "Dori Day Afternoon."

54. *Sledge Hammer,* "To Sledge with Love" (Wechter, 1986) (quotation); *Sledge Hammer,* "Play It Again Sledge" (Bixby, 1987).

55. *Sledge Hammer,* "Suppose They Gave a War and Sledge Came?" (Martin, 1988).

56. *Sledge Hammer,* "Wild about Hammer."

57. *Sledge Hammer,* "Over My Dead Bodyguard" (Dubin, 1986).

58. *Sledge Hammer,* "Under the Gun"; *Sledge Hammer,* "Hammer Gets Nailed" (Braverman, 1986); *Sledge Hammer,* "Brother Can You Spare a Crime?"

59. *Sledge Hammer,* "They Shoot Hammers Don't They?"

60. *Sledge Hammer,* "Hammeroid" (Walkow, 1987). Spoofs were regularly featured in *Sledge Hammer,* including *DOA* in "Miss of the Spiderwoman" (Braverman, 1986); *Assault on Precinct 13* in "State of Sledge"; *The Color of Money* in "The Color of Hammer"; *Shampoo* in "Sledgepoo"; *Jagged Edge* in "Jagged Sledge" (Badiyi, 1987); and *Vertigo* in "Vertical" (Badiyi, 1987).

61. *Sledge Hammer,* "Comrade Hammer" (Bilson, 1987).

62. *Sledge Hammer,* "Hammer Gets Nailed."

63. *Sledge Hammer,* "State of Sledge."

64. *Sledge Hammer,* "Magnum Farce." See also *Sledge Hammer,* "Here's to You Mrs Hammer" (Bixby, 1988).

65. *Sledge Hammer,* "Under the Gun."

66. Ibid.

67. *Sledge Hammer*, "They Shoot Hammers Don't They?"

68. *Sledge Hammer*, "To Sledge with Love"; *Sledge Hammer*, "If I Had a Little Hammer" (Manner, 1986).

69. *Sledge Hammer*, "To Sledge with Love."

70. *Sledge Hammer*, "It Happened What Night" (Bixby, 1988).

71. *Sledge Hammer*, "Under the Gun."

72. *Sledge Hammer*, "Dori Day Afternoon."

73. *Sledge Hammer*, "They Shoot Hammers Don't They?" features an appearance by the actor Jack Thibeau, who also appeared in *Sudden Impact*.

74. *Sledge Hammer*, "Magnum Farce."

75. Ibid.

76. *Sledge Hammer*, "Hammer Gets Nailed"; see also *Sledge Hammer*, "State of Sledge."

77. The show's cancellation was in large part due to poor audience figures, which were a result of the show being broadcast against the most popular show on American television during its second season. As Spencer later pointed out, *The Cosby Show* destroyed everything in its path. Spencer cited in *Go Ahead, Make Me Laugh* documentary. See also Saunders, "Cosby Show to Face Real 'Sledge Hammer!'"

78. "Dirty Harry FAQ/Walkthrough," http://www.gamefaqs.com/nes/587230-dirty-harry/faqs/18257 (consulted July 26, 2012); "Dirty Harry NES Instruction Manual," https://web.archive.org/web/20120207002242/http://www.the-dirti est.com/manual.htm (consulted July 26, 2012); "Harry Callahan as You've Never Seen Him Before!" https://web.archive.org/web/20120207001845/http://www.the-dirtiest.com/nes.htm (consulted July 26, 2012); "Dirty Harry (NES) Ending," http://www.youtube.com/watch?v=o3VD-uyCIjQ&feature=related (consulted July 26, 2012). The passwords for the game reference other Eastwood movies: "Clyde" (his orangutan in the *Every Which Way* movies); "Misty" (*Play Misty for Me*); "Bird" (Eastwood's Charlie Parker biopic); "Gunny" (the character he played in *Heartbreak Ridge*). *GameFAQs* at http://www.gamefaqs.com/nes/587230-dirty-harry/cheats (consulted July 26, 2012).

79. Jones and Wills, *The American West*, 265–66. Jones and Wills are discussing the representation of the nineteenth-century American West in video games, but these observations equally apply to the video-game representation of Harry Callahan.

80. Allison, "Courting the Critics/Assuring the Audiences," 27.

81. "Dirty Harry, Clint Eastwood Making Next-Gen Consoles' Day," February 24, 2005, http://www.gamespot.com/articles/dirty-harry-clint-eastwood-mak ing-next-gen-consoles-day/1100-6119150 (consulted July 26, 2012).

82. "E3 2006: Dirty Harry Demo Impressions," May 10, 2006, at http://uk.xbox360.ign.com/articles/707/707407p1.html (consulted July 26, 2012).

83. Patrick Garratt, "Dirty Harry Rumours Start Feeling Lucky, Punk," June 16, 2004, http://www.eurogamer.net/articles/news_160604_dirtyharry (consulted June 12, 2013).

84. "E3 2006: Dirty Harry Demo Impressions," May 10, 2006, http://uk.xbox360.ign.com/articles/707/707407p1.html (consulted July 26, 2012).

85. "Dirty Harry Trailer Xbox360," http://www.youtube.com/watch?v=ZICPDBJW228&feature=related (consulted July 26, 2012).

86. "Collective Staff Cuts Follow Dirty Harry 'Transitioning,'" March 1, 2007, http://www.gamespot.com/articles/collective-staff-cuts-follow-dirty-harry-transitioning/1100-6166620 (consulted July 26, 2012).

87. Jess-Cooke, Film Sequels, 10, 68. See also 75.

88. Ibid., 75.

89. McGilligan, Clint, 272.

90. Brooker, Using the Force, xvi; see also 88.

91. Ibid., 133, 134.

92. Ibid., 150–51, 170.

93. Post by rr-electricangel on April 14, 2012, Clint Eastwood Forums, http://www.clinteastwood.org/forums/index.php?topic=9258.0 (consulted June 12, 2013).

94. Ibid.

95. Posts by Whistledixie, June 29, 2012, January 31, 2013, Clint Eastwood Forums, http://www.clinteastwood.org/forums/index.php?topic=9320.0 (consulted June 14, 2013).

96. Post by Whistledixie, February 6, 2013, Clint Eastwood Forums, http://www.clinteastwood.org/forums/index.php?topic=9320.20 (consulted June 14, 2013).

97. Miller quoted in Daniel Robert Epstein, "Frank Miller, Creator of Sin City," Suicide Girls, August 3, 2005, http://suicidegirls.com/interviews/Frank+Miller+Creator+of+Sin+City (consulted October 31, 2011); emphasis added.

98. Miller interview with Kim Thompson, June 1985, in George, The Comics Journal Library, Volume Two, 35.

99. Joe Strike, "Frank Miller's 'Dark Knight' Brought Batman Back to Life," New York Daily News, July 15, 2008, http://www.nydailynews.com/entertainment/tv-movies/frank-miller-dark-knight-brought-batman-back-life-article-1.351685 (consulted June 11, 2013).

100. Finigan, "'To the Stables, Robin!'" paragraphs 12, 13.

101. Miller quoted in Elvis Mitchell interview with Frank Miller on *The Treatment*, KCRW Santa Monica, March 30, 2005, http://www.kcrw.com/etc/programs/tt/tt050330frank_miller (consulted June 3 2013).

102. Miller interview with Gary Groth, in George, *The Comics Journal Library, Volume Two*, 100; Miller interview with Kim Thompson, 1985, in George, *The Comics Journal Library, Volume Two*, 38.

103. Miller interview with Kim Thompson, 1985, in George, *The Comics Journal Library, Volume Two*, 40.

104. Ibid., 33.

105. Miller interview with Christopher Brayshaw, 1998, in George, *The Comics Journal Library, Volume Two*, 82–83; Miller interview with Gary Groth, 1998, ibid., 101.

106. Arnott, *"Blam!"* 381.

107. Miller quoted in Elvis Mitchell interview with Frank Miller on *The Treatment*, KCRW Santa Monica, March 30, 2005, http://www.kcrw.com/etc/programs/tt/tt050330frank_miller (consulted June 3 2013). Miller read and was heavily influenced by Ayn Rand when he was a young man; the Roark family name could also be a reference to Howard Roark, the architect protagonist of Rand's *The Fountainhead*. Miller interview with Dwight Decker, 1981, in George, *The Comics Journal Library, Volume Two*, 28.

108. Miller interview with Christopher Brayshaw, 1998, in George, *The Comics Journal Library, Volume Two*, 71.

109. Text box indicating Hartigan's thoughts, F. Miller, *That Yellow Bastard*, 15.

110. F. Miller, *That Yellow Bastard*, 15.

111. Ibid., 17.

112. Ibid., 20–21, 24–27, 30–31, 36–37, 40–42.

113. Ibid., 56–59.

114. Ibid., 60–67.

115. Finigan, "'To the Stables, Robin!'" paragraph 23.

116. Note Finigan, "'To the Stables, Robin!'" paragraph 29, which asserts that a similar relationship characterizes much of Miller's other work.

117. F. Miller, *That Yellow Bastard*, 68–71, 75–79 (quotation on 76).

118. Ibid., 186.

119. Ibid., 217.

120. Cowie, *Stayin' Alive*, 7, 125–66 (quotation on 127).

121. Ibid., 16 (quotations), 130.

122. Biskind, "Any Which Way He Can," 195.

Bibliography

Abbott, Megan A. *The Street Was Mine: White Masculinity in Hardboiled Fiction and Film Noir*. New York: Palgrave, 2002.

Allison, Deborah. "Courting the Critics/Assuring the Audiences: The Modulation of Dirty Harry in a Changing Cultural Climate." *Film International* 5, no. 5 (September 2007): 17–29.

The American Presidency Project. http://www.presidency.ucsb.edu.

Anderson, Steve F. *Technologies of History: Visual Media and the Eccentricity of the Past*. Hanover: Dartmouth College Press, 2011.

Anderson, Terry H. *The Movement and the Sixties: Protest in America from Greensboro to Wounded Knee*. New York: Oxford University Press, 1995.

Arnott, Luke. "*Blam!* The Literal Architecture of *Sin City*." *International Journal of Comic Art* 10, no. 2 (2008): 380–401.

Austin, Curtis J. *Up Against the Wall: Violence in the Making and Unmaking of the Black Panther Party*. Fayetteville: University of Arkansas Press, 2006.

Baker, Brian. *Masculinity in Fiction and Film: Representing Men in Popular Genres, 1945–2000*. London: Continuum, 2006.

Bates, Toby Glenn. *The Reagan Rhetoric: History and Memory in 1980s America*. DeKalb: Northern Illinois University Press, 2011.

Baudrillard, Jean. *America*. London: Verso, 1998.

Beard, William. "Lies of Our Fathers: Mythology and Artifice in Eastwood's Cinema." In Engel, *New Essays on Clint Eastwood*, 224–48.

Bell, Jonathan. *California Crucible: The Forging of Modern American Liberalism*. Philadelphia: University of Pennsylvania Press, 2012.

Berliner, Todd. "The Pleasures of Disappointment: Sequels and *The Godfather, Part II*." *Journal of Film and Video* 53, no. 2/3 (Summer 2001): 107–23.

Biskind, Peter. "Any Which Way He Can." In Kapsis and Coblentz, *Clint Eastwood*, 193–206.

———. *Seeing Is Believing: Or How Hollywood Taught us to Stop Worrying and Love the 50s*. 2nd ed. London: Bloomsbury, 2000.

Bloom, Clive. *Cult Fiction: Popular Reading and Pulp Theory*. Basingstoke: Macmillan, 1996.

Bolton, Marie. "Sacred or Profane? The Cross at Mount Davidson Park, San Francisco." *Pacific Historical Review* 67, no. 4 (November 1998): 543–71.

Booth, Stanley. *The True Adventures of the Rolling Stones*. Chicago: A Capella, 2000.

Bowler, Shaun, and Bruce Cain. "Introduction—Recalling the Recall: Reflections on California's Recent Political Adventure." *Political Science and Politics* 37, no. 1 (January 2004): 7–10.

Brandt, Karl Gerard. *Ronald Reagan and the House Democrats: Gridlock, Partisanship and the Fiscal Crisis*. Columbia: University of Missouri Press, 2009.

Brilliant, Mark. *The Color of America Has Changed: How Racial Diversity Shaped Civil Rights Reform in California, 1941–1978*. New York: Oxford University Press, 2010.

Brinkley, Douglas, ed. *Fear and Loathing in America: Hunter S. Thompson: The Brutal Odyssey of an Outlaw Journalist, 1968–1976*. London: Bloomsbury, 2000.

Brooker, Will. *Using the Force: Creativity, Community and Star Wars Fans*. New York: Continuum, 2002.

Brown, Richard Maxwell. "Violence." In *The Oxford History of the American West*, ed. Clyde A. Milner II, Carol A. O'Connor, and Martha A. Sandweiss, 393–426. New York: Oxford University Press, 1994.

Bush, George W. *Decision Points*. New York: Random House, 2010.

Byers, Thomas B. "History Re-Membered: *Forrest Gump*, Postfeminist Masculinity, and the Burial of the Counterculture." *Modern Fiction Studies* 42, no. 2 (1996): 419–44.

Cahill, Tim. "Clint Eastwood: The *Rolling Stone* Interview." In Kapsis and Coblentz, *Clint Eastwood*, 117–29.

Carr, Leisl A. "Rationalizing the Cold War Home Front." *IEEE Technology and Society Magazine* 27, no. 3 (Fall 2008): 13–18.

Carter, Dan T. *George Wallace, Richard Nixon, and the Transformation of American Politics*. Waco, Tex.: Baylor University Press, 1992.

———. *The Politics of Rage: George Wallace, the Origins of the New Conservatism, and the Transformation of American Politics*. New York: Simon and Schuster, 1995.

Carter, Luther J. "George C. Wallace: He's Not Just Whistling Dixie." *Science*, October 25, 1968, 436–40.

Chafe, William H. *The Unfinished Journey: America since World War II.* 4th ed. New York: Oxford University Press, 1999.

Chong, Sylvia. "From 'Blood Auteurism' to the Violence of Pornography: Sam Peckinpah and Oliver Stone." In *New Hollywood Violence,* ed. Steven Jay Schneider, 249–68. Manchester: Manchester University Press, 2004.

Cohen, Paul. "Cowboys Die Hard: Real Men and Businessmen in the Reagan-Era Blockbuster." *Film and History: An Interdisciplinary Journal of Film and Television Studies* 41, no. 1 (Spring 2011): 71–81.

Connelly, Mark. "*Gallipoli* (1981): A Poignant Search for National Identity." In *The New Film History: Sources, Methods, Approaches,* ed. James Chapman, Mark Glancy, and Sue Harper, 41–54. Basingstoke: Palgrave, 2007.

Cook, David A. "Ballistic Balletics: Styles of Violent Representation in *The Wild Bunch* and After." In Prince, *Sam Peckinpah's* The Wild Bunch, 130–54.

Corkin, Stanley. *Starring New York: Filming the Grime and Glamour of the Long 1970s.* Oxford University Press, 2011.

Cornell, Drucilla. *Clint Eastwood and Issues of American Masculinity.* New York: Fordham University Press, 2009.

Cowie, Jefferson. *Stayin' Alive: The 1970s and the Last Days of the Working Class.* New York: New Press, 2010.

Crawford, Alan. *Thunder on the Right: The "New Right" and the Politics of Resentment.* New York: Pantheon, 1980.

Crowther, Bosley. "*Bonnie and Clyde* Arrives." In *Arthur Penn's* Bonnie and Clyde, ed. Lester D. Friedman, 177–78. Cambridge, UK: Cambridge University Press, 2000.

DeConde, Alexander. *Gun Violence in America: The Struggle for Control.* Lebanon, N.H.: Northeastern University Press, 2003.

DeGroot, Gerard J. "Ronald Reagan and Student Unrest in California, 1966–1970." *Pacific Historical Review* 65, no. 1 (February 1996): 107–29.

———. *The Sixties Unplugged: A Kaleidoscopic History of a Disorderly Decade.* London: MacMillan, 2008.

Dionne, E. J., Jr. *Why Americans Hate Politics.* New York: Simon and Schuster, 1991.

Dochuk, Darren. *From Bible Belt to Sun Belt: Plain-Folk Religion, Grassroots Politics, and the Rise of Evangelical Conservatism.* New York: Norton, 2011.

Doherty, David. "Presidential Rhetoric, Candidate Evaluations, and Party Identification: Can Parties 'Own' Values?" *Political Research Quarterly* 61, no. 3 (September 2008): 419–33.

Druckman, James N., and Justin W. Holmes. "Does Presidential Rhetoric Matter? Priming and Presidential Approval." *Presidential Studies Quarterly* 34, no. 4 (December 2004): 755–78.

Duncan, Dayton. *Miles from Nowhere: Tales from America's Contemporary Frontier*. Lincoln: University of Nebraska Press, 1993.

Edsall, Thomas Byrne, and Mary D. Edsall. *Chain Reaction: The Impact of Race, Rights, and Taxes on American Politics*. New York: Norton, 1991.

Ehrman, John. *The Eighties: America in the Age of Reagan*. New Haven: Yale University Press, 2005.

Eliot, Marc. *American Rebel: The Life of Clint Eastwood*. New York: Three Rivers Press, 2009.

Engel, Leonard, ed. *Clint Eastwood, Actor and Director: New Perspectives*. Salt Lake City: University of Utah Press, 2007.

———, ed. *New Essays on Clint Eastwood*. Salt Lake City: University of Utah Press, 2012.

Ethington, Philip J. *The Public City: The Political Construction of Urban Life in San Francisco, 1850–1900*. Berkeley: University of California Press, 1994.

Evans, Thomas W. *The Education of Ronald Reagan: The General Electric Years and the Untold Story of His Conversion to Conservatism*. New York: Columbia University Press, 2006.

Farber, David. *Chicago '68*. Chicago: University of Chicago Press, 1988.

Finigan, Theo. "'To the Stables, Robin!': Regenerating the Frontier in Frank Miller's *Batman: The Dark Knight Returns*." *ImageTexT: Interdisciplinary Comics Studies* 5, no. 1 (2010). Consulted June 3, 2013. http://www.english.ufl.edu/imagetext/archives/v5_1/finigan.

Flamm, Michael W. *Law and Order: Street Crime, Civil Unrest, and the Crisis of Liberalism in the 1960s*. New York: Columbia University Press, 2005.

Fossey, Richard. "School Desegregation Is Over in the Inner Cities: What Do We Do Now?" In *Reinterpreting Urban School Reform: Have Urban Schools Failed, or Has the Reform Movement Failed Urban Schools?* ed. Louis F. Mirón and Edward P. St. John, 15–32. Albany: State University of New York Press, 2003.

Frey, William H., and Alden Speare, Jr. *Regional and Metropolitan Growth and Decline in the United States*. New York: Russell Sage Foundation, 1988.

Gallagher, Tag. *John Ford: The Man and His Films*. Berkeley: University of California Press, 1986.

Gates, Philippa. "A Good Vintage or Damaged Goods? Clint Eastwood and Aging in Hollywood Film." In Engel, *New Essays on Clint Eastwood*, 168–89.

George, Milo, ed. *The Comics Journal Library, Volume Two: Frank Miller*. Seattle: Fantagraphics Books, 2003.

Gould, Jonathan. *Can't Buy Me Love: The Beatles, Britain and America*. New York: Random House, 2007.

Gourlie, John M., and Leonard Engel. "*Gran Torino*: Showdown in Detroit, Shrimp Cowboys, and a New Mythology." In Engel, *New Essays on Clint Eastwood*, 266–75.

Gramsci, Antonio. *Selections from the Prison Notebooks of Antonio Gramsci*. Ed. and trans. Quintin Hoare and Geoffrey Nowell Smith. London: Lawrence and Wishart, 1971.

Grant, Barry Keith. *Invasion of the Body Snatchers*. London: Palgrave, 2010.

———. "John Ford and James Fenimore Cooper: Two Rode Together." In *John Ford Made Westerns: Filming the Legend in the Sound Era*, ed. Gaylyn Studlar and Matthew Bernstein, 193–219. Bloomington: Indiana University Press, 2001.

Graysmith, Robert. *Zodiac: The Shocking True Story of America's Most Elusive Serial Killer*. 1976. London: Titan Books, 2007.

Grindon, Leger. "Mocking Success in *Every Which Way But Loose* (1978)." In Engel, *Clint Eastwood, Actor and Director*, 119–28.

Hall, Simon. *American Patriotism, American Protest: Social Movements since the Sixties*. Philadelphia: University of Pennsylvania Press, 2011.

Hall, Stuart. "Culture, the Media and the 'Ideological Effect.'" In *Mass Communication and Society*, ed. James Curran, Michael Gurevitch, and Janet Woollacott, 315–48. London: Sage, 1979.

———. "Encoding/Decoding." In *Culture, Media, Language: Working Papers in Cultural Studies*, ed. Stuart Hall, Dorothy Hobson, Andrew Lowe, and Paul Willis, 128–38. London: Hutchinson, 1980.

———. "Gramsci's Relevance for the Study of Race and Ethnicity." In *Stuart Hall: Critical Dialogues in Cultural Studies*, ed. David Morley and Kuan-Hsing Chen, 411–41. London: Routledge, 1996.

Harris, Mark. *Pictures at a Revolution: Five Movies and the Birth of the New Hollywood*. New York: Penguin, 2008.

Hartman, Chester. *The Transformation of San Francisco*. Totowa, N.J.: Rowman and Allanheld, 1984.

Hartman, Dane. *The Blood of Strangers*. New York: Warner Books, 1982.

———. *City of Blood*. Sevenoaks: New English Library, 1982.

———. *Dealer of Death*. New York: Warner Books, 1983.

———. *Death in the Air*. New York: Warner Books, 1983.

———. *Death on the Docks*. Sevenoaks: New English Library, 1982.

———. *Duel for Cannons*. Sevenoaks: New English Library, 1982.

———. *Family Skeletons*. Sevenoaks: New English Library, 1982.

———. *Hatchet Men*. New York: Warner Books, 1982.

———. *Massacre at Russian River*. New York: Warner Books, 1982.

———. *The Mexico Kill*. Sevenoaks: New English Library, 1982.

Haut, Woody. *Pulp Culture: Hardboiled Fiction and the Cold War*. London: Serpent's Tail, 1995.

Henry, Michael. "Interview with Clint Eastwood." In Kapsis and Coblentz, *Clint Eastwood*, 96–116.

Hentoff, Nat. "Flight of Fancy." In Kapsis and Coblentz, *Clint Eastwood*, 153–59.

Hoberman, J. *The Dream Life: Movies, Media, and the Mythology of the Sixties*. New York: New Press, 2003.

Huey, Laura. *Negotiating Demands: The Politics of Skid Row Policing in Edinburgh, San Francisco, and Vancouver*. Toronto: University of Toronto Press, 2007.

Hughes, Howard. *Aim for the Heart: The Films of Clint Eastwood*. London: I.B. Taurus, 2009.

Hutson, Richard. "'You Can't Hunt Alone': *White Hunter, Black Heart*." In Engel, *New Essays on Clint Eastwood*, 121–29.

Isserman, Maurice, and Michael Kazin. *America Divided: The Civil War of the 1960s*. 2nd ed. New York: Oxford University Press, 2004.

Jeffords, Susan. *Hard Bodies: Hollywood Masculinity in the Reagan Era*. New Brunswick, N.J.: Rutgers University Press, 1994.

Jess-Cooke, Carolyn. *Film Sequels: Theory and Practice from Hollywood to Bollywood*. Edinburgh: Edinburgh University Press, 2009.

Jess-Cooke, Carolyn, and Constantine Verevis. *Second Takes: Critical Approaches to the Film Sequel*. Albany: State University of New York Press, 2010.

Johnson, Richard. "Defending Ways of Life: The (Anti-) Terrorist Rhetorics of Bush and Blair." *Theory, Culture and Society* 19, no. 4 (August 2002): 211–31.

Jones, Karen R., and John Wills. *The American West: Competing Visions*. Edinburgh: Edinburgh University Press, 2009.

Kael, Pauline. *Deeper into Movies: The Essential Kael Collection: From '69 to '72*. London: Calder and Boyars, 1975.

———. *Reeling: Film Writings, 1972–1975*. London: Marion Boyars, 1977.

Kaminsky, Stuart M. *Clint Eastwood*. New York: Signet, 1974.

Kapsis, Robert E., and Kathie Coblentz, eds. *Clint Eastwood: Interviews*. Jackson: University Press of Mississippi, 1999.

———. Introduction. In Kapsis and Coblentz, *Clint Eastwood*, vii–xx.

Kellner, Douglas. "9/11, Spectacles of Terror, and Media Manipulation: A Critique of Jihadist and Bush Media Politics." *Critical Discourse Studies* 1, no. 1 (2004): 41–64.

———. "Bushspeak and the Politics of Lying: Presidential Rhetoric in the 'War on Terror.'" *Presidential Studies Quarterly* 37, no. 4 (December 2007): 622–45.

Klypchak, Brad. "'All on Accounta Pullin' a Trigger': Violence, the Media, and the Historical Contextualization of Clint Eastwood's *Unforgiven*." In Engel, *Clint Eastwood, Actor and Director*, 157–71.

Kotkin, Joel, and Paul Grabowicz. *California, Inc.* New York: Rawson, Wade, 1982.

Leitch, Thomas. *Crime Films*. New York: Cambridge University Press, 2002.

Levy, Emanuel. *John Wayne: Prophet of the American Way of Life*. Metuchen, N.J.: Scarecrow Press, 1988.

Malcolm X *By Any Means Necessary: Speeches, Interviews and a Letter by Malcolm X*. Ed. George Breitman. New York: Pathfinder Press, 1970.

———. *Malcolm X Speaks: Selected Speeches and Statements*. Ed. George Breitman. New York: Grove Press, 1965.

Mask, Mia. "Movies and the Exploitation of Excess." In *American Cinema of the 1970s: Themes and Variations*, ed. Lester D. Friedman, 48–70. New Brunswick, N.J.: Rutgers University Press, 2007.

Matusow, Allen J. *The Unraveling of America: A History of Liberalism in the 1960s*. New York: Harper and Row, 1984.

McArthur, Colin. "Chinese Boxes and Russian Dolls: Tracking the Elusive Cinematic City." In *The Cinematic City*, ed. David B. Clarke, 19–45. London: Routledge, 1997.

McCracken, Scott. *Pulp: Reading Popular Fiction*. Manchester: Manchester University Press, 1998.

McGhee, Richard D. "John Wayne: Hero with a Thousand Faces." *Literature/ Film Quarterly* 16, no. 1 (1988): 10–21.

McGilligan, Patrick. "Clint Eastwood." In Kapsis and Coblentz, *Clint Eastwood*, 21–41.

———. *Clint: The Life and Legend*. London: HarperCollins, 1999.

McGinniss, Joe. *The Selling of the President*. Harmondsworth: Penguin, 1970.

Mennel, Barbara. *Cities and Cinema*. London: Routledge, 2008.

Messner, Michael A. "The Masculinity of the Governator: Muscle and Compassion in American Politics." *Gender and Society* 21, no. 4 (August 2007): 461–80.

Metz, Walter. "The Old Man and the C: Masculinity and Age in the Films of Clint Eastwood." In Engel, *Clint Eastwood, Actor and Director*, 204–17.

Miller, Frank. *That Yellow Bastard: A Sin City Yarn*. Milwaukie, OR: Dark Horse Comics, 1997.

Miller, Paul T. *The Postwar Struggle for Civil Rights: African Americans in San Francisco, 1945–1975*. Abingdon: Routledge, 2010.

Mollenkopf, John H. "The Post-War Politics of Urban Development." *Politics and Society* 5, no. 3 (September 1975): 247–95.

Monaco, James. *How to Read a Film: The Art, Technology, Language, History, and Theory of Film and Media*. Rev. ed. New York: Oxford University Press, 1981.

Monaco, Paul. *The Sixties, 1960–1969*. Berkeley: University of California Press, 2003.

Patterson, Eric. "Every Which Way But Lucid: The Critique of Authority in Clint Eastwood's Police Movies." *Journal of Popular Film and Television* 10, no. 3 (1982): 92–104.

Pavlović, Milan. "Clint Eastwood Interviewed by Milan Pavlović." In Kapsis and Coblentz, *Clint Eastwood*, 137–52.

Pearlman, Lise. *The Sky's the Limit: People v. Newton, The Real Trial of the 20th Century?* Berkeley: Regent Press, 2012.

Peters, Nancy J. "The Beat Generation and San Francisco's Culture of Dissent." In *Reclaiming San Francisco: History, Politics, Culture*, ed. James Brook, Chris Carlsson, and Nancy J. Peters, 199–215. San Francisco: City Lights Books, 1998.

Prasad, Monica, Andrew J. Perrin, Kieran Bezila, Steve G. Hoffman, Kate Kindleberger, Kim Manturuk, Ashleigh Smith Powers, and Andrew R. Payton. "The Undeserving Rich: 'Moral Values' and the White Working Class." *Sociological Forum* 24, no. 2 (June 2009): 225–53.

Prince, Stephen. "The Hemorrhaging of American Cinema: *Bonnie and Clyde*'s Legacy of Cinematic Violence." In *Arthur Penn's* Bonnie and Clyde, ed. Lester D. Friedman, 127–47. Cambridge: Cambridge University Press, 2000.

———. "Introduction: Sam Peckinpah, Savage Poet of American Cinema." In Prince, *Sam Peckinpah's* The Wild Bunch, 1–36.

———, ed. *Sam Peckinpah's* The Wild Bunch. Cambridge: Cambridge University Press, 1999.

The Public Papers of President Ronald W. Reagan. Ronald Reagan Presidential Library.http://www.reagan.utexas.edu.

Putnam, Jackson K. "Governor Reagan: A Reappraisal." *California History* 83, no. 4 (2006): 24–45.

Quart, Leonard, and Albert Auster. *American Film and Society since 1945*. 2nd ed. Westport, Conn.: Praeger, 1991.

Rarick, Ethan. *California Rising: The Life and Times of Pat Brown*. Berkeley: University of California Press, 2005.

Reagan, Ronald. *An American Life*. New York: Pocket Books, 1990.

———. *The Greatest Speeches of Ronald Reagan*. 2nd ed. West Palm Beach, Fla.: NewsMax, 2001.

Reeves, Michelle. "'Obey the Rules or Get Out': Ronald Reagan's 1966 Gubernatorial Campaign and the 'Trouble in Berkeley.'" *Southern California Quarterly* 92 (Fall 2010): 275–305.

Renshon, Stanley A. "Presidential Address: George W. Bush's Cowboy Politics: An Inquiry." *Political Psychology* 26, no. 4 (August 2005): 585–614.

Rhodes, Edward. "The Good, the Bad, and the Righteous: Understanding the Bush Vision of a New NATO Partnership." *Millennium—Journal of International Studies* 33 no. 1 (January 2004): 123–43.

Rhomburg, Chris. *No There There: Race, Class, and Political Community in Oakland.* Berkeley: University of California Press, 2004.

Ridinger, Robert B., ed. *Speaking for Our Lives: Historic Speeches and Rhetoric for Gay and Lesbian Rights (1892–2000).* Binghamtom, N.Y.: Harrington Park Press, 2004.

Rinne, Craig. "The End of History and America First: How the 1990s Revitalized Clint Eastwood." In Engel, *New Essays on Clint Eastwood*, 130–47.

Roberts, Randy, and James S. Olson. *John Wayne: American.* New York: Free Press, 1995.

Romao, Tico. "Guns and Gas: Investigating the 1970s Car Chase Film." In *Action and Adventure Cinema*, ed. Yvonne Tasker, 130–52. London: Routledge, 2004.

Rorabaugh, W. J. *Berkeley at War: The 1960s.* New York: Oxford University Press, 1989.

Rosen, John J. "Joseph L. Alioto's 1967 Mayoral Campaign: Democratic Party Liberalism in Transition." unpublished paper at http://bss.sfsu.edu/issel/Alioto%201967%20election.htm#_edn70.

Rosenfeld, Seth. *Subversives: The FBI's War on Student Radicals and Reagan's Rise to Power.* New York: Farrar, Straus and Giroux, 2012.

Ross, Steven J. *Hollywood Left and Right: How Movie Stars Shaped American Politics.* Oxford: Oxford University Press, 2011.

Rubin, Martin. *Thrillers.* Cambridge: Cambridge University Press, 1999.

Ryan, Michael, and Douglas Kellner. *Camera Politica: The Politics and Ideology of Contemporary Hollywood Film.* Bloomington: Indiana University Press, 1988.

Sandbrook, Dominic. *Mad as Hell: The Crisis of the 1970s and the Rise of the Populist Right.* New York: Knopf, 2011.

Sarris, Andrew. Foreword to *John Wayne: Prophet of the American Way of Life*, by Emanuel Levy, ix–xiv. Metuchen, N.J.: Scarecrow Press, 1988.

Schaller, Michael. *Right Turn: American Life in the Reagan-Bush Era, 1980–1992.* Oxford: Oxford University Press, 2007.

Schickel, Richard. *Clint Eastwood.* London: Arrow, 1996.

Schoenwald, Jonathan M. *A Time for Choosing: The Rise of Modern American Conservatism*. New York: Oxford University Press, 2001.

Schrag, Peter. *California: America's High-Stakes Experiment*. Berkeley: University of California Press, 2006.

Schulman, Bruce J. *The Seventies: The Great Shift in American Culture, Society, and Politics*. New York: Free Press, 2001.

Self, Robert O. *American Babylon: Race and the Struggle for Postwar Oakland*. Princeton: Princeton University Press, 2003.

Shadoian, Jack. "*Dirty Harry*: A Defense." *Western Humanities Review* 28, no. 2 (1974): 166–79.

Sides, Josh. *Erotic City: Sexual Revolutions and the Making of Modern San Francisco*. Oxford: Oxford University Press, 2009.

Siegel, Don. *A Siegel Film: An Autobiography*. London: Faber and Faber, 1993.

The Sixties: Primary Documents and Personal Narratives, 1960–1974. http://asp6new.alexanderstreet.com/sixt.

Slotkin, Richard. *Gunfighter Nation: The Myth of the Frontier in Twentieth-Century America*. Norman: University of Oklahoma Press, 1992.

Smith, Evan. "History and the Notion of Authenticity in *Control* and *24 Hour Party People*." *Contemporary British History* 27, no. 4 (2013): 466–89.

Smith, Paul. *Clint Eastwood: A Cultural Production*. London: UCL Press, 1993.

Spicer, Andrew. *Film Noir*. London: Pearson, 2002.

Spittles, Brian. *John Ford*. Harlow: Longman, 2002.

Stone, Walter J., and Monti Narayan Datta. "Rationalizing the California Recall." *Political Science and Politics* 37, no. 1 (January 2004): 19–21.

Stras, David R., and Ryan W. Scott. "Navigating the New Politics of Judicial Appointments." *Northwestern University Law Review* 102, no. 4 (Fall 2008): 1869–1917.

Talbot, David. *Season of the Witch: Enchantment, Terror, and Deliverance in the City of Love*. New York: Free Press, 2012.

Taubin, Amy. "Interview: David Fincher." *Sight and Sound* 17, no. 5 (2007).

Tetzlaff, David. "'Too Much Red Meat!'" In *New Hollywood Violence*, ed. Steven Jay Schneider, 269–85. Manchester: Manchester University Press, 2004.

Thompson, Hunter S. "Chicago—Summer of '68." In Brinkley, *Fear and Loathing in America*, 113–18.

Thompson, Kristin, and David Bordwell. *Film History: An Introduction*. 2nd ed. New York: McGraw Hill, 2003.

Thompson, Richard, and Tim Hunter. "Eastwood Direction." In Kapsis and Coblentz, *Clint Eastwood*, 42–61.

Thomson, David. "Cop on a Hot *Tightrope*." In Kapsis and Coblentz, *Clint Eastwood*, 81–95.

Toplin, Robert Brent. *History by Hollywood: The Use and Abuse of the American Past*. Urbana: University of Illinois Press, 1996.

Traficante, Christopher. "From Victim to Vigilante: Anomie and Misanthropy in *Gran Torino*." *Screen Education* 66 (Winter 2012): 111–16.

Troy, Gil. *Morning in America: How Ronald Reagan Invented the 1980s*. Princeton: Princeton University Press, 2005.

Tulis, Jeffrey K. "Revising the Rhetorical Presidency." In *Beyond the Rhetorical Presidency*, ed. Martin J. Medhurst, 1–14. College Station: Texas A&M University Press, 1996.

Varon, Jeremy. *Bringing the War Home: The Weather Underground, the Red Army Faction, and Revolutionary Violence in the Sixties and Seventies*. Berkeley: University of California Press, 2004.

Vaux, Sara Anson. *The Ethical Vision of Clint Eastwood*. Grand Rapids, Mich.: Eerdmans, 2012.

Verniere, James. "Clint Eastwood Stepping Out." In Kapsis and Coblentz, *Clint Eastwood*, 207–14.

Vincent, Rickey. *Party Music: The Inside Story of the Black Panthers' Band and How Black Power Transformed Soul Music*. Chicago: Lawrence Hill, 2013.

von Bothmer, Bernard. *Framing the Sixties: The Use and Abuse of a Decade from Ronald Reagan to George W. Bush*. Amherst: University of Massachusetts Press, 2010.

Walker, Richard A. "An Appetite for the City." In *Reclaiming San Francisco: History, Politics, Culture*, ed. James Brook, Chris Carlsson, and Nancy J. Peters, 1–19. San Francisco: City Lights Books, 1998.

———. "California Rages against the Dying of the Light." *New Left Review* I, no. 209 (January–February 1995): 42–74.

Wanat, Matt. "Irony as Absolution." In Engel, *Clint Eastwood, Actor and Director*, 77–98.

Wang, Jennifer Hyland. "'A Struggle of Contending Stories': Race, Gender, and Political Memory in 'Forrest Gump.'" *Cinema Journal* 39, no. 3 (Spring 2000): 92–115.

Ward, Brian, ed. *The 1960s: A Documentary Reader*. Chichester: Wiley-Blackwell, 2010.

Weddle, David. *"If They Move . . . Kill 'Em!" The Life and Times of Sam Peckinpah*. New York: Grove, 1994.

Westbrook, Brett. "Feminism and the Limits of Genre in *Fistful of Dollars and The Outlaw Josey Wales*." In Engel, *Clint Eastwood, Actor and Director*, 24–48.

———. "Thoroughly Modern Eastwood: Male/Female Power Relations in *The Beguiled* and *Play Misty for Me*." In Engel, *New Essays on Clint Eastwood*, 36–52.

White, Welsh S. Miranda's *Waning Protections: Police Interrogation Practices after Dickerson*. Ann Arbor: University of Michigan Press, 2001.

Wills, Garry. *John Wayne: The Politics of Celebrity*. London: Faber and Faber, 1997.

———. *Reagan's America: Innocents at Home*. London: Heinemann, 1988.

Woodward, Bob. *Bush at War*. London: Simon and Schuster, 2003.

Zarefsky, David. "Presidential Rhetoric and the Power of Definition." *Presidential Studies Quarterly* 34, no. 3 (September 2004): 607–19.

Index

JOE STREET is senior lecturer in American history at Northumbria University, Newcastle. His previous works include *The Culture War in the Civil Rights Movement*.

Lightning Source UK Ltd.
Milton Keynes UK
UKHW011028050720
365992UK00009B/252